THE
EVERYTHING
PARENT'S GUIDE TO
COMMON CORE SCIENCE:
GRADES 6–8

Dear Reader,

As an educator and a mom, I understand how things can change as your child leaves elementary school and enters middle school. The connections you once had with your child's elementary teachers and your child's learning seem to evaporate before your eyes. You try to stay involved and to keep close ties, but it becomes more and more difficult as you give your child opportunities to develop independence. While it's beneficial to give your child room to grow and to become less dependent on you, it's still important to have a grasp of the expectations at school.

Science seems to be a subject area that students, and parents alike, either enjoy or not. But really, when you think about it, science is a fantastic opportunity to be curious and figure out why things happen and how things work. I hope this book gives you the information you need to understand the Common Core science standards, the concepts being taught in your child's science class, and the expectations that come with the Next Generation Science Standards. I hope you are able to share, not only in your child's learning, but in the memory-making moments you have with each other.

Laurie Bloomfield, MAT

Welcome to the EVERYTHING® Series!

These handy, accessible books give you all you need to tackle a difficult project, gain a new hobby, comprehend a fascinating topic, prepare for an exam, or even brush up on something you learned back in school but have since forgotten.

You can choose to read an Everything® book from cover to cover or just pick out the information you want from our four useful boxes: e-questions, e-facts, e-alerts, and e-ssentials. We give you everything you need to know on the subject, but throw in a lot of fun stuff along the way, too.

We now have more than 400 Everything® books in print, spanning such wide-ranging categories as weddings, pregnancy, cooking, music instruction, foreign language, crafts, pets, New Age, and so much more. When you're done reading them all, you can finally say you know Everything®!

PUBLISHER Karen Cooper

MANAGING EDITOR, EVERYTHING® SERIES Lisa Laing

COPY CHIEF Casey Ebert

ACQUISITIONS EDITOR Hillary Thompson

SENIOR DEVELOPMENT EDITOR Brett Palana-Shanahan

EVERYTHING® SERIES COVER DESIGNER Erin Alexander

THE
EVERYTHING®

PARENT'S GUIDE TO
Common Core Science:
Grades 6–8

Understand the new science standards to
help your child learn and succeed

Laurie Bloomfield, MAT

Aadamsmedia
Avon, Massachusetts

I would like to dedicate this book to my aunt, Dianne Sheppard, a smart, strong, and supportive woman who has always given me the unconditional love and encouragement I needed to grow as a mom, teacher, and writer.

An Everything® Series Book.
Everything® and everything.com® are registered trademarks of F+W Media, Inc.

Published by
Adams Media, a division of F+W Media, Inc.
57 Littlefield Street, Avon, MA 02322. U.S.A.
www.adamsmedia.com

ISBN 10: 1-4405-9272-1
ISBN 13: 978-1-4405-9272-0
eISBN 10: 1-4405-9273-X
eISBN 13: 978-1-4405-9273-7

Printed in the United States of America.

10 9 8 7 6 5 4 3 2 1

CURR
LB
1585.3
.B54
2015

This book is available at quantity discounts for bulk purchases.
For information, please call 1-800-289-0963.

Contents

Introduction **10**

1 **What Are the Common Core Standards? / 13**

What Are Academic Standards? **14**

What Are the Common Core English Language Arts Standards? **14**

What Are the Common Core Mathematics Standards? **15**

Key Shifts for English Language Arts **16**

Key Shifts for Mathematics **18**

Why Focus on Math and English Language Arts? **19**

2 **What Are the Next Generation Science Standards? / 20**

Why Were the Next Generation Science Standards Developed? **21**

Previous Science Benchmark Standards **21**

The Next Generation Science Standards Dimensions **23**

Key Shifts in the Next Generation Science Standards **24**

3 **How Can You Help Your Child Be Successful? / 26**

Understanding Science **27**

Developing Good Study Habits **27**

Interactive Science Notebook **29**

Note-Taking Strategies **32**

Strategies for Responding to Questions **33**

Illustrations and Models **34**

The Metric System **35**

4 **Writing Science and Technical Subjects / 38**

Encourage Writing Skills **39**

Text Types and Purposes **39**

Research to Build and Present Knowledge **43**

Range of Writing **46**

5 **Reading in Science / 47**

Develop a Love of Reading **48**

Tips for Reading Through Science Textbooks **48**

Key Ideas and Details **50**

Craft and Structure **52**

Integration of Knowledge and Ideas **54**

6 **The Three Dimensions of Science / 56**

What Are the Scientific and Engineering Practices? **57**

What Are Crosscutting Concepts? **63**

What Are the Disciplinary Core Ideas? **67**

7 Matter and Its Interactions / 68

What Should My Child Already Understand? **69**

Disciplinary Core Ideas **69**

Key Matter Terms **71**

Key Matter Concepts **72**

Key Atomic Terms **75**

Key Atomic Concepts **76**

Key Chemical Reaction Terms **80**

Key Chemical Reaction Concepts **81**

Science and Engineering Practices **85**

Next Generation Science Standards Performance Expectations **86**

Matter Experiment **90**

Let's Review—Checklist **91**

8 Motion and Stability— Forces and Interactions / 93

What Should My Child Already Understand? **94**

Disciplinary Core Ideas **94**

Key Force and Motion Terms **96**

Key Force and Motion Concepts **97**

Science and Engineering Practices **101**

Next Generation Science Standards Performance Expectations **102**

Forces and Motion Experiment **108**

Let's Review—Checklist **109**

9 Energy / 111

What Should My Child Already Understand? **112**

Disciplinary Core Ideas **113**

Key Energy Terms **114**

Key Energy Concepts **115**

Science and Engineering Practices **118**

Next Generation Science Standards Performance Expectations **119**

Energy Experiment **123**

Let's Review—Checklist **124**

10 Waves and Their Applications / 126

What Should My Child Already Understand? **127**

Disciplinary Core Ideas **127**

Key Wave Terms **129**

Key Wave Concepts **130**

Science and Engineering Practices **133**

Next Generation Science Standards Performance Expectations **134**

Waves Experiment **138**

Let's Review—Checklist **138**

11 From Molecules to Organisms— Structures and Processes / 140

What Should My Child Already Understand? **141**

Disciplinary Core Ideas **141**

Key Molecule Terms **143**

Key Molecule Concepts 146

Science and Engineering Practices 152

Next Generation Science Standards
Performance Expectations 153

Organism Experiment 160

Let's Review—Checklist 161

**12 Ecosystems—Interactions,
Energy, and Dynamics / 162**

What Should My Child Already
Understand? 163

Disciplinary Core Ideas 163

Key Ecosystem Terms 166

Key Ecosystem Concepts 167

Science and Engineering Practices 172

Next Generation Science Standards
Performance Expectations 172

Ecosystem Experiment 177

Let's Review—Checklist 178

**13 Heredity—Inheritance and
Variation of Traits / 180**

What Should My Child Already
Understand? 181

Disciplinary Core Ideas 181

Key Heredity Terms 183

Key Heredity Concepts 184

Science and Engineering Practices 189

Next Generation Science Standards
Performance Expectations 190

Heredity Experiment 192

Let's Review—Checklist 193

**14 Biological Evolution—Unity and
Diversity / 195**

What Should My Child Already
Understand? 196

Disciplinary Core Ideas 196

Key Evolution Terms 198

Key Evolution Concepts 199

Science and Engineering Practices 201

Next Generation Science Standards
Performance Expectations 202

Evolution Experiment 207

Let's Review—Checklist 208

**15 Earth's Place in the
Universe / 210**

What Should My Child Already
Understand? 211

Disciplinary Core Ideas 211

Key Earth's Place Terms 214

Key Earth's Place Concepts 215

Science and Engineering Practices 218

Next Generation Science Standards
Performance Expectations 219

Soil Experiment 224

Let's Review—Checklist 225

16 **Earth's Systems / 226**

What Should My Child Already Understand? **227**

Disciplinary Core Ideas **227**

Key Earth's Systems Terms **229**

Key Earth's Systems Concepts **231**

Science and Engineering Practices **236**

Next Generation Science Standards Performance Expectations **237**

Earth's Systems Experiment **244**

Let's Review—Checklist **245**

17 **Earth and Human Activity / 246**

What Should My Child Already Understand? **247**

Disciplinary Core Ideas **247**

Key Earth and Human Activity Terms **249**

Key Earth and Human Activity Concepts **250**

Science and Engineering Practices **254**

Next Generation Science Standards Performance Expectations **255**

Earth and Human Activity Experiment **260**

Let's Review—Checklist **261**

18 **Engineering Design / 263**

What Should My Child Already Understand? **264**

Disciplinary Core Ideas **264**

Key Engineering Design Terms **266**

Key Engineering Design Concepts **267**

Science and Engineering Practices **271**

Next Generation Science Standards Performance Expectations **271**

Engineering Design Experiment **275**

Let's Review—Checklist **276**

19 **Science Fair Projects / 278**

Helping Your Child Choose a Project **279**

Designing Experiments and Recording Results **280**

Science Fair Project Stages **284**

Science Project Safety Tips **285**

Science Fair Project Reports **286**

Appendix A: Resources / 289

Appendix B: Bibliography / 291

Index / 293

Acknowledgments

I would like to thank both of my children, Annie and Andrew, for all of their love and support in making this project possible. As an engineering student, Andrew has been able to contribute an abundance of ideas to this book. Our lively discussions about science and engineering have made this experience especially memorable. Annie has been particularly helpful and encouraging at home, taking care of things as I worked through the writing process. I don't know how I would have gotten along without her.

Introduction

SO YOU REALIZE YOU aren't sure about what's going on in your child's science class and you want to change things. Wonderful! In days past, science was about learning new vocabulary and following procedures. If you are someone who loves language, you probably enjoyed the terminology and the lab reports. If you are someone who loves doing calculations, you probably liked using the formulas. Today's science classes offer a new perspective on science and make engineering an equally important aspect of the program.

While science still includes learning new phrases and experimentation, students are now provided a more realistic approach to scientific inquiry and engineering design. Today's students are sitting and watching less, and doing and communicating more. They are applying the theories they are learning and finding out for themselves why things happen the way they do. This new approach enables students to learn by doing as opposed to learning by watching.

The Common Core State Standards provide a foundation for literacy in science. The content and practices that are taught in middle school science classes come from the Next Generation Science Standards (NGSS). These standards provide rigorous content through a coherent system of performance expectations. Students are building their understanding and abilities on the concepts they learned in elementary school. The concepts are revisited but the details and practices are more complex. The standards place equal importance on science and engineering, making the system relevant to today's technologically adept young people. With most states across the country using these standards, students are more likely to gain the science understanding and abilities they need to be successful after high school, regardless of where they grow up and go to school.

This book offers help to parents who want to better understand what concepts their child is learning in middle school science and the practices they are required to demonstrate. It will help you become better acquainted with the middle school science curriculum and give you an opportunity to share in your child's science learning at home.

There is much to discover in middle school science, and it can't be done overnight. Take your time with this book. Use the digital resources that are included to work through simulations of the concepts being presented. Watch the Bozeman videos to gain an in-depth view of the science program. Make a goal of learning all the science terminology before you attack the concepts. This will make reading the content, watching the videos, and using the simulations much easier. Keep in mind that this book provides a foundation to the middle school science program. It does not offer all of the concepts that are taught.

Most importantly, share this book with your child. Sit down and read it together. Access the online resources side by side. Ask each other questions. Give each other answers. Talk about problems and consider different solutions. Enjoy the learning experience and enjoy your time together. These are times to treasure.

Note: All experiments in this book should be performed with adult supervision and using caution.

CHAPTER 1

What Are the Common Core Standards?

The Common Core standards are a systematic series of academic standards in English language arts and mathematics. The learning objectives define the understanding and performance expectations of each student at specific grade levels. These standards were developed to make sure that all graduating high school students have the necessary abilities and proficiencies to achieve success in postsecondary studies, employment, and life, regardless of where they grow up and where they go to school. This chapter will give you some insight into the Common Core standards and establish how these standards were designed to improve education in our country.

What Are Academic Standards?

Academic standards are the learning objectives and performance expectations of students at specific grade levels. In other words, they spell out in detail the tasks every student should be able to accomplish by the end of each grade. These benchmarks enable teachers to make sure that their students have the skills necessary to achieve success while also helping parents understand what is being expected of their children.

The Common Core was developed by education leaders in forty-eight states. The standards that are outlined in the Common Core establish the necessary English language arts and mathematics skills that students need. The standards have been accepted and are currently being applied in forty-three states.

Building on the best of existing state standards, the Common Core State Standards provide clear and consistent learning goals to help prepare students for college, employment, and life. The standards clearly describe what students are expected to learn at each grade level, so that every parent and teacher can understand and support their learning.

Why Are These Standards Important?

Quality benchmarks that are uniform throughout the country give all students, educators, and parents a coherent outline of the academic expectations that students will need in order to do well in college, in their careers, and in life. These standards foster fairness by making sure that students are able to work both independently and cooperatively and that they are able to compete with their international counterparts. While earlier standards differed among states, the Common Core establishes a set of standards that are consistent across the country.

What Are the Common Core English Language Arts Standards?

The English language arts standards concentrate on central ideas and processes beginning in the early elementary years. These standards set forth requirements for English language arts and for literacy in science, technology, and social studies. The emphasis on reading, writing, speaking, listening, viewing, and representing, across the content areas, allows students to develop the necessary skills in a variety of subject areas.

The Common Core requires students to read and comprehend literature and stories. The standards ask students to understand more complicated text and to offer background understanding and facts in social studies and science. Students are required to read and refer back to text to respond to challenging questions, developing their abilities in problem solving and critical thinking.

ALERT

English teachers will not be required to teach subjects other than their own content areas. Science will still be taught by experienced, knowledgeable science teachers who are qualified to teach the content. Science teachers will ensure that students are demonstrating writing and reading abilities through the science program.

Beginning in middle school, the literacy standards associated with English language arts enable educators of science, technology, and social studies to apply their subject area mastery in assisting students in their development of literacy and language skills in these fields of study.

What Are the Common Core Mathematics Standards?

The Common Core standards for mathematics were built out of a need to provide a more concentrated and cohesive math program. The standards have been developed out of the best math standards throughout the country.

The standards of mathematics redefine the existing broad benchmarks and make them more specific and less confusing. They concentrate on the understanding of concepts and on the continuous practice of the principles of mathematics. They also organize the objectives into a more sequential system, providing students with the necessary experiences to practice concepts until they have been mastered. The standards give students the opportunities to apply the concepts to solve both classroom and real-world problems.

The Common Core standards of mathematics require students to justify their understanding of math concepts. This enables students to prove their understanding and gives educators the opportunity to assess the level and depth of understanding each student has. By applying reasons for using math rules and demonstrating an understanding of math statements, students demonstrate how much they know and how well they can apply what they know.

FACT

The academic standards from high-performing international programs were referenced in building the Common Core standards. These standards recognize that ability and knowledge are equally important to academic success.

Key Shifts for English Language Arts

The Common Core State Standards for English language arts outline the abilities and proficiencies that students need to achieve to be college and career ready. There are several crucial shifts from the previous English language arts standards that are necessary to a successful implementation of the Common Core.

In the Common Core, students are asked to consistently practice with more complicated texts and denser subject-matter language. The standards ask students to continuously expand their elaboration of text in order to be prepared for the rigorous requirements of college and career. The standards also include advancements in reading comprehension so that as students move through the grade levels, they gain a deeper understanding of texts.

A spotlight on academic vocabulary is also outlined. Students develop their vocabulary banks through a combination of reading, instruction, and discussion. They determine meaning, grasp word nuances, and widen their range of vocabulary.

English language arts learning is grounded in evidence from both informational (nonfiction) and literary texts. The Common Core affirms the importance of using text evidence to effectively analyze and defend arguments and assumptions. The standards require students to demonstrate a deep understanding of text when responding to critical questions. Whereas in the past students may have been able to use their opinions to justify a theme in a text, they must now provide concrete evidence from the text itself. Students will respond to a variety of questions requiring them to infer and analyze based on the text details.

ESSENTIAL

Recognizing that districts and educators have the expertise and experience to determine specific reading requirements, there is no set reading list outlined in the Common Core. The standards do incorporate analytical content for every student, including international stories, traditional myths, and important works of American fiction and nonfiction.

Past writing expectations focused on students' ideas and experiences and did not necessarily prepare them for writing requirements they would face in later years. The Common Core expects students to demonstrate strong informative and argumentative writing skills. This concentration on persuasive, informative, and evidence-supported writing is an important shift from current standards.

ALERT

The Common Core standards will not lower state standards so that all areas of the United States can work at the same level. The Common Core standards were developed out of the best state standards that are currently in place. These standards will help all students, regardless of where they live, to be prepared for college, careers, and life beyond high school.

Students need to be absorbed in global information in order to gain the solid understanding and vocabulary necessary for becoming proficient readers and prepared college students and employees. Nonfiction text is vital to building content understanding in students.

In middle school there is now a stronger focus on nonfiction texts. The Common Core standards for literacy in science make certain that students are able to independently develop understanding through reading and writing. Middle school students begin to read more from textbooks that are specific to science. In earlier grades students tend to read passages from textbooks or shorter books designed for their grade levels. However, the middle school textbooks provide more content that details more complicated concepts and higher-level vocabulary.

Key Shifts for Mathematics

There are several crucial shifts from the previous mathematics standards that are necessary to a successful implementation of the Common Core. The Common Core requires a strong concentration in the study of all mathematical concepts. Instead of quickly covering several topics of wide-ranging content, the standards require math educators to drastically redefine and enhance their teaching efforts and time with students. The major focus on math is to have students truly learn the material—to understand it—rather than to just regurgitate it for a test and then forget it.

ESSENTIAL

The standards provide a common layout of what all students should know before they can proceed into the next grade. What a student is learning in one state is exactly the same as what a student in a different state is learning. Theoretically, if a family were to move across the country in the middle of the school year, there should be a seamless transition for the school-aged children into their new classrooms.

In middle school, students begin by spending more time working through problems involving ratios, proportional relationships, and basic algebraic equations and expressions. By 7th grade, students are adding arithmetic of rational numbers to their problem solving, and by the end of middle school, they are practicing linear functions and algebra. This greater focus in mathematics means that instead of racing to cover topics in today's mile-wide, inch-deep curriculum, teachers use their power to narrow and deepen the way time and energy is spent in the classroom. The standards require depth instead of breadth, with students developing strong mathematical foundations with basic concepts and solid conceptual under-standing, which means they understand why and how the math works.

The standards of mathematics reflect strong connections throughout all grades. The learning of mathematical concepts is built one upon the next, from one year to the next. Concepts become more and more expansive the older and more learned the students become. The standards ask students to show a proficient understanding of important concepts and to use these concepts in different areas. The capacity to quickly and correctly make cal-culations is also necessary. It is important for students to consistently prac-tice calculation, formula, and operation applications in order to become more skillful at solving problems of increasing complexity.

Why Focus on Math and English Language Arts?

Math and ELA were chosen for developing the standards because all other subject proficiencies are built upon these central areas of learning. Students must demonstrate proficiency in literacy in a wide range of content, and therefore the English language arts standards can be implemented within social studies, history, and science. The same can also be said for the math-ematics standards, as they can be applied to science and technology.

FACT

A three-minute video outlining the Common Core standards is avail-able online at the Common Core State Standards Initiative website: *www.corestandards.org/video.*

At this time, the Council of Chief State School Officers and the National Governors Association Center for Best Practices have no plans to develop standards in other areas; however, there are organizations that are working on content area standards. The Next Generation Science Standards have been developed by Achieve with assistance from the American Association for the Advancement of Science, the National Science Teachers Association, and the National Research Council.

CHAPTER 2

What Are the Next Generation Science Standards?

The Next Generation Science Standards provide benchmarks of performance expectations that students are required to meet. These standards are organized in a cohesive system throughout grade levels, offering every student the opportunity to experience an impressive science education. Each of these standards includes content ideas, scientific and engineering practices, and crosscutting concepts. The consolidation of challenging content and practical applications provides students with real-world learning experiences. This chapter will discuss the Next Generation Science Standards so you will have a solid grasp of what your child will be expected to learn in this subject.

Why Were the Next Generation Science Standards Developed?

There have been many significant advances made in the study of science and the world of technology. These advances need to be reflected in the expected skills and understanding of students. The Next Generation Science Standards were developed to do just that. These benchmarks ensure that students throughout the country will have the skill set and proficiencies required to achieve success after high school.

ESSENTIAL

In the last fifteen years there have been no advancements in the state standards that were developed from the documents that were provided by the National Research Council and the American Association for the Advancement in Science. However, there have been many advances in the science and technology over that time. These new standards are necessary to meet today's science, engineering, and technology innovations.

The Next Generation Science Standards were established by the National Research Council, the American Association for the Advancement of Science, the National Science Teachers Association, and Achieve. In the spring of 2013, the standards were formally released. There are currently thirteen states using the standards.

FACT

Achieve is an educational reform group that is committed to helping states increase their science academic standards, thereby improving student assessment and enhancing accountability.

Previous Science Benchmark Standards

The Next Generation Science Standards are different from previous benchmarks in three significant aspects: performance, foundations, and coherence.

Performance

In previous standards, the benchmarks expressed what students were required to understand or know. The benchmarks did not state what performances were connected with that knowledge base. Application is necessary for students to prove what understanding they have. The Next Generation Science Standards clearly express the performance expectations of each standard, detailing what students need to be able to *do* to show their ability to apply scientific concepts.

Foundations

Every performance expectation included in the Next Generation Science Standards includes three essential dimensions: a science and engineering practice, a core disciplinary idea, and a crosscutting concept. These dimensions ensure that student performance is based on science and engineering applications involving science and engineering concepts.

Coherence

Every performance expectation within the Next Generation Science Standards provides associations to concepts within the Common Core English language arts and mathematics standards. This enables students to see the relevance of science through all of their subject areas.

ALERT

The Next Generation Science Standards are not curricula for teachers to teach but rather performance expectations of the concepts students should understand and practices they should apply.

The Next Generation Science Standards strive to dismiss any methods of teaching to specific test questions. The goal is to concentrate less on memorizing facts and more on applying scientific concepts. Many times students are able to respond to questions about a particular concept but are unable to apply those concepts in practical applications. The standards provide opportunities for learning new science concepts through the application of scientific principles.

The Next Generation Science Standards Dimensions

There are three dimensions of scientific thought that are incorporated into the Next Generation Science Standards: science content, science and engineering practices, and crosscutting concepts. This systematic framework provides students with the perspective they need to understand how science applies across subject areas.

ESSENTIAL

The Next Generation Science Standards reflect the experiences and practices of real-world science. The concepts covered build a coherent system from basic to deep understanding and application. The standards are aligned with the Common Core and will prepare students for studies and life beyond high school.

Science and Engineering Practices

Science and engineering practices detail the important processes that scientists and engineers use to analyze and construct models and theories about the universe, and to design and construct solutions to problems. Through practice, students will have the opportunity to participate in the learning of concepts rather than simply knowing how and why things occur.

Crosscutting Concepts

Crosscutting concepts provide a means of connecting all of the domains of science, including the physical, life, earth and space, and engineering and technology sciences. This dimension enables students to see how specific concepts and practices relate to other scientific disciplines.

Disciplinary Core Ideas

With the expanding scientific information that is available today, it is increasingly difficult to provide students with every idea associated to all science disciplines. Rather than being taught all of the facts, students will have the opportunity to learn the core concepts they need to independently gain more knowledge and understanding. A core set of science and engineering ideas has been developed and will give students the essential information they need. These core ideas are broad in importance through science disciplines, offer vital tools for analyzing more complicated concepts and becoming more adept problem solvers, connect to the life experiences and interests of students, and can be taught and learned across several grades at increasing levels of complexity. The core ideas are divided into the four domains of science: the life sciences; the physical sciences; the earth and space sciences; and engineering, technology, and applications of science.

Key Shifts in the Next Generation Science Standards

The Next Generation Science Standards offer an essential opportunity to develop the science program and increase student achievement, reflecting an innovative perspective for science education. They establish the need for a connection between science education in the classroom and science practice in the real world. The integration of the three dimensions—science and engineering practices, core ideas, and crosscutting concepts—provides students with opportunities for practical applications of real-world science principles.

FACT

The Next Generation Science Standards website offers short videos with explanations that outline the system at *http://nextgenscience .org/resources.*

These standards define the performance expectations of students and are *not* curriculum documents. The connections between the three dimensions do not define lessons or units, but rather describe the concepts and ideas that students will know and apply at each grade level. The coherence of the science concepts from kindergarten through high school is a major aspect of the Next Generation Science Standards. These basic core ideas provide students with opportunities to begin with a broad understanding of a particular concept in the early years of schooling and then move toward more complex ideas about the same topic as they progress through middle school and high school.

Depth of understanding and application of concepts are equally important in the Next Generation Science Standards. Students should demonstrate a grasp of core ideas rather than just an ability to recall and relate facts. The engagement of the student and the practical application of the science concepts are more important. The practices of scientists and engineers are incorporated into the standards. Both disciplines are equally relevant to the study of science.

The Next Generation Science Standards were developed to ready students for college, employment, and life beyond high school. The study of science is key to making sense of the world today. It is central to innovation development, job creation, and social awareness. Students need a strong understanding of scientific concepts and principles to become positive community members and achieve success in life beyond high school. These standards are aligned with the Common Core standards for English language arts and mathematics, ensuring harmonious learning progress across all content areas. All three standard systems are interrelated in significant and authentic ways, providing equitable opportunities for all students to demonstrate performance expectations within each learning standard.

CHAPTER 3

How Can You Help Your Child Be Successful?

As a parent, you strive to provide your child with all of the help possible to be successful in school. Sometimes it becomes difficult, particularly when you are unsure of the content being taught and the practices being used in the classroom. The science and technical subjects are often challenging, as they require a firm grasp of abstract topics, a knowledge of mathematics and measurement, and the ability to present research and experimental findings clearly and succinctly. The tips provided in this chapter will help you understand what is expected of your child in science and how he can be the best science student possible.

Understanding Science

In order to help your child be successful in science, it's important to have a good grasp of the subject area. Science is the study of all things in the universe. Science is the process of finding out who, what, when, where, and how all things come to be, how they are, and how they will continue to be, using data derived from our universe.

There are specific ways that scientists and engineers work through questions and problems. The scientific method and the engineering process are both important to the study of science.

The scientific method is the process by which something in the universe is investigated. This method includes asking questions, forming hypotheses, testing hypotheses, recovering data, forming conclusions, and sharing results.

The engineering process is the idea of using scientific and mathematical knowledge to create a solution to a problem. The solution must be for the betterment of scientific advancements and not be for one's own nefarious deeds.

Developing Good Study Habits

Studying is necessary to learning and is an important aspect of scientific inquiry and problem solving. By recognizing and applying the best studying habits, your child will learn more and spend less time going over the same concepts.

Finding the Best Place to Study

Make sure your child has the best possible spot at home to get to work. An optimal area would be a spot where there are few distractions. A room that is bright makes staying focused much easier. Consider these points when choosing the study spot that will work for your child: the noise level, the amount of light, the possible distractions, the availability of assistance, and the comfort level of the space. A well-organized workspace with a comfortable chair makes getting down to studying less of a chore.

Finding the Best Time to Study

Once your child has found the best place to study, work out a plan on when she will get to work. Some children prefer to get to their studies right after school. Others have athletic and club commitments that make studying after school difficult. For these children, studying after dinner is a better option. Discuss these issues with your child and set out a plan based on her personal obligations.

Setting a Study Time Limit

When studying any topic, the concepts become more difficult to work on after a period of time. It's important to schedule five-minute breaks during half-hour study periods to give your child a chance to move around or have a snack. These short activities make it possible for your child to get back to work after this bit of rest. Except for certain circumstances, middle school science studies should be limited to an hour each evening, with breaks in between.

Don't just think science, think engineering design. Today's science classes involve both science concepts and engineering designs. Your child will be asked to practice scientific applications as well as solve design problems.

Reading Science Texts

Science textbooks provide your child with a wealth of scientific information. Textbooks are written and published in such a way as to make the information easier to understand. Sit down with your child and take a look at her textbook together. Open the cover and look for the table of contents. It will list all of the units within the book. Next, turn to the first unit and you will find a list of the concepts that will be presented in that unit. Each of the following units will also provide a list of the important ideas for that section of the text. Most science texts provide an index at the back of the book. An index is different from the table of contents. The table of contents lists all of the units in the order that they appear in the book. The index is organized in alphabetical order and provides the page number for specific terms and topics.

Now that you have a good understanding of the layout of the book, it's important to be familiar with the text features on each page. Topic headings, subheadings, maps, illustrations, graphs, and captions are all forms of text features. These aspects of the text are crucial to better understanding the concepts being presented. Read through each of the sections on the page and refer to the graphs and illustrations as you read. Be sure to also read through any of the captions that are included as well. Most texts print important key words in a bold font. This makes the word stand out from the page and tells your child that it is an important term to know. If your child is unable to define the word, turn to the glossary at the back of the book. The glossary provides definitions for the key words in the book. The text on each page of the book is typically organized into paragraphs. As she finishes each page, she should go back and reread the first sentence of each paragraph. These sentences provide an idea of the topic being discussed and rereading them is a useful review.

Taking Science Notes

Note taking is essential to studying and learning new concepts. Taking effective notes requires good organizational skills. When your child is taking notes on science topics, there are a few points she should keep in mind. She should use an outline system to put the points down on paper. Her notes should be kept in a well-organized notebook. As the topic of study changes, a new section of notes should begin. The format of her writing will be based on the type of note she is taking or report she is making. While an investigation report lists facts, a hypothesis debate considers opposing conditions and supporting evidence. Regardless of the type of report, the notes should be neat and well organized.

Interactive Science Notebook

An interactive science notebook is used for organizing and managing science notes. It provides a means for processing science learning through text, illustrations, and discussions. It is a place where students can write their own notes about their hands-on learning activities. Your child will be able to make better sense of concepts by creating visual notes. He will also become better at understanding informational texts and taking notes.

This useful video offers help in setting up an interactive science notebook: *www.youtube.com/watch?v=vHbT8zFZmFo*.

Why Are Interactive Notebooks Beneficial?

Interactive science notebooks improve your child's ability to keep his notes organized, to think critically, and to express understanding in a creative format. Your child uses these notebooks to record information, study for his quizzes and tests, demonstrate his learning progress, and communicate his ideas. Interactive science notebooks help students increase their understanding and literacy proficiency by providing a means for hands-on, minds-on science and making sense of scientific investigations.

How to Make an Interactive Notebook

Your child needs a spiral notebook just for science, a pencil, an eraser, colored pencils, scissors, a glue stick, and highlighters. No markers should be used in an interactive science notebook because the ink can leak through the pages.

This notebook is divided into sections: the Input and the Output. The Input represents the concepts and information that the teacher is providing, and the Output represents your child's expression of the concepts that he is learning. The Input and the Output are placed on opposite sides: the right side and the left side of the notebook.

The right side of the notebook is for learning. On the right side of the notebook, your child puts notes and content provided by his teacher. In this area he will put handouts from class, discussion and video notes, and text assignments. His teacher guides the information that goes on the right side. This information can be evaluated and scored.

The left side of the notebook is for reflection. On the left side of the notebook, your child puts his ideas and expressions. He uses lots of color in order to better remember the concepts. He creates concept maps and illustrations; does reflective writing; answers questions; creates songs, cartoons, and poems; and records data from lab experiments. Your child processes the information on the left side. The left side helps him to make better sense of the information that is on the right side of the notebook. These activities help him to develop deeper comprehension.

QUESTION

What does reflection mean in the science class?
In order to fully understand the observations and activities in class, your child needs to reflect on class experiences by making more personal connections with the concepts that are introduced or practiced.

Setting Up an Interactive Science Notebook

Your child begins by putting his name, grade, and science period on the cover of his notebook. Then he adds a science illustration to the cover. He then opens the notebook and numbers the first fifty pages, beginning with page one on the first page of the notebook. His numbers should be printed in a small font on the top corner of each page.

On page two he prints the title "Reflections." Under the title he prints the following questions: What makes you curious? What would you like to test? What is the main idea? What are the key details? How did the activity connect to your life and the world around you? What did you have trouble understanding?

ESSENTIAL

To learn more about how an interactive science notebook works, check out this video: *www.youtube.com/watch?v=cQVvAXD0Mzs.*

Next he prints the title "Table of Contents" on the top of pages three, four, and five. He divides each page into three columns. He prints the headings "Date," "Description," and "Page Number" at the top of each column. This section is where he will note the location of all of the other entries in his notebook.

Each new unit that is presented to your child should begin with a title page in his notebook. The title page should be illustrated, labeled, and colored. The illustrations should include three or four drawings of key concepts from the unit. A caption for each picture should be included.

Ensuring Success with an Interactive Science Notebook

Your child should be sure to always take his notebook to class. He should date and label everything that he adds to his notebook. He should complete every assignment on the correct page. Whenever possible, he should use color in his notebook. Color helps him to remember concepts and to organize his ideas. If he happens to be absent from a class, he should check with his science teacher to see what concepts he might have missed. He should write all of his text in pencil. He should begin all of his drawings in pencil as well. He should not write any notes in pen or colored pencils.

ALERT

Keep in mind that each student works at a different pace. Some are able to complete all of their assignments in class; others are not. Assignments that your child does not complete in class should go home to be finished. Once the homework is complete, she should go back and read through her notes again, making sure to carefully go over the left side of the page to check her own entries.

Note-Taking Strategies

Students are required to take notes from middle school through college. There are several types of note-taking strategies that can be used for writing informational text.

Concept Maps and Venn Diagrams

A concept map is one effective strategy. The main idea that is presented is written in the center of the page. The details connected to the main idea are written in point form around the center. An illustration for each detail is drawn next to each point.

Venn diagrams include two overlapping circles. They are used to compare and contrast: to express the similarities and differences about two concepts. These diagrams require students to label the circles properly, to make point-to-point comparisons about the concept, to include at least five facts in each circle and three facts that are shared, and to provide an illustration for each topic.

Question Notes

Question notes provide a means of writing key concepts as answers. The title and text pages are written at the top of the notebook page. The page is then divided into two columns. The heading on the first column is "Question," and the heading on the second column is "Answer." The concept is written as a question in the first column. For example, when learning about matter, the question might be written as "What is matter?" Students then look for the evidence in their textbooks that supports that specific question and write it into the answer column next to the question.

Using Poetry

Poetry is a creative format for expressing scientific concepts. It can even help your child write a summary of the information that was presented in class. His poem should show his understanding of the concept presented. It should contain as few basic or common words as possible. Phrases in the poem should be carefully selected and connect to the concept.

Strategies for Responding to Questions

There are usually three or four questions within a text worksheet that your child receives from her teacher. She should read through the text then go back and re-read the text, using highlighters to highlight each of the questions included. Using a different colored highlighter for each question, she should read through the text to find the evidence that supports the first question. She should highlight those points using the same color that she used for the corresponding question. She should continue with the next questions until she has found the evidence to support all of the questions and has highlighted them accordingly.

ESSENTIAL

Talk to your child about her ideas and explanations. Encourage her to ask you questions and to solve problems. Ask her questions as well. Provide a positive role model in searching for answers and creating solutions.

Fill-in-the-blank notes are another form of response writing. These activities require students to complete a missing portion of a statement based on information that is presented in class. It is important to pay careful attention to the presentation in order to complete this type of note. (If your child is absent from science class her teacher will be able to give her these types of pages with the work completed.)

Illustrations and Models

Illustrations and drawings play a vital role in science notes. While observations can be put down in text, illustrations provide a different perspective on a particular concept. Scientific drawing enables your child to develop his thoughts and ideas. In designing a solution to a problem, he might begin with a sketch of his initial design that he could share with classmates. His drawings should be as large as possible so that the smaller details will be easily discernible. From there he could develop the illustration to include more detail. Science drawings should be as accurate as possible, clearly illustrated, neatly presented, and labeled. Labels of all of the important components should be underlined with a ruler. The illustration itself should include a title and date.

Creating Science Models

Models are an effective tool in communicating a scientific concept or discovery. A model can represent a specific object or an entire system. They are used to explain a phenomenon, theory, or law. Various materials can be used to construct models. From paper to clay to recycled materials, models display two- and three-dimensional images of scientific concepts. Your child's model should be as accurate as possible, clearly illustrated or constructed, neatly presented, and labeled.

The Metric System

The metric system is the worldwide scientific standard for measurement. Your child uses the metric system in science courses to take measurements. This system allows for measurements all within values of ten. This system allows for easy conversion between lengths, volumes, and masses.

FACT

The metric system is built on a base-ten system. Each unit within the metric system is either ten times greater or ten times less than the next unit.

Understanding Measurement

Measurement is the recorded value of something. A measurement will show how long, dense, or massive something is. Your child uses measurements in order to record the size or magnitude of something in order to compare or contrast it with something else.

Measuring Length

Length is the measurement of distance. By measuring length, you are determining distance. Your child can measure how long, tall, or far apart objects are. Length in the metric system is based on the standard unit of a meter. All other units for length are multiples or submultiples of a meter. Length is measured using a ruler, meter stick, or measuring tape.

Kilometers are used to measure the distance between one place and another. The distance from a subdivision to downtown or the distance between two cities is measured in kilometers. If your child wanted to measure the distance between one end of a football field and the other, he would use meters. There are 1,000 meters in 1 kilometer. The distance around your house or your backyard is measured in meters.

Centimeters are used for measuring smaller distances. There are 100 centimeters in 1 meter. The distance from the tip of your finger to your wrist is measured in centimeters. Your child would use millimeters to measure very small distances. There are 10 millimeters in 1 centimeter. The distance across your fingernail is measured in millimeters.

Here are some other helpful measurements:

- 1 mile = 1.61 kilometers
- 1 yard = 0.91 meters
- 1 foot = 30.48 centimeters
- 1 inch = 2.54 cm

Measuring Volume

Volume is the measurement of space that a substance occupies. By measuring volume you are determining how much space a substance occupies. Volume in the metric system is based on the standard unit of the liter. All other units for volume are multiples or submultiples of a liter. Volume is measured using a graduated cylinder. The volume of a gas tank is measured in liters. Your child would use liters to measure the amount of space a liquid occupies.

If your child wanted to measure the amount of space a small substance occupies, he would use milliliters. There are 1,000 milliliters in 1 liter. The volume of a juice box is measured in milliliters.

Here are some other conversions:

- 1 gallon = 3.78 liters
- 1 quart = .94 liters
- 1 pint = .47 liters
- 1 fluid ounce = 29.57 milliliters

Measuring Mass

Mass is the measurement of the amount of matter in an object. Mass determines the amount of matter within an object. Your child measures mass by weighing an object. By measuring mass your child is determining the amount of matter within an object. There is a difference between mass and weight. Mass in the metric system is based on the standard unit of the gram. All other units for mass are multiples or submultiples of a gram. Mass is measured using a triple beam balance.

Kilograms are large units. If you wanted to measure the mass of a large item, you would use kilograms. The mass of a person is measured in kilograms.

Grams are smaller units. There are 1,000 grams in 1 kilogram. Your child would use grams to measure the mass of a small item. The mass of a paperclip is measured in grams.

Milligrams are used for measuring the mass of very small objects. There are 1,000 milligrams in 1 gram. Your child would use milligrams to measure the mass of a very small item; for example, the mass of a pinch of salt is measured in milligrams.

Here are a few more useful conversions:

- 1 ton = 907.184 kilograms
- 1 pound = 453.592 grams
- 1 ounce = 28.349 grams

The following chart will help your child see the relationship between metric units:

Length		Mass		Volume	
Units	*Value*	*Units*	*Value*	*Units*	*Value*
kilometer (km)	1000 m	kilogram (kg)	1000 g	kiloliter (kL)	1000 L
hectometer (hm)	100 m	hectogram (hg)	100 g	hectoliter (hL)	100 L
dekameter (dam)	10 m	dekagram (dag)	10 g	dekaliter (daL)	10 L
meter (m)	1	gram (g)	1	liter (L)	1
decimeter (dm)	.1 m	decigram (dg)	.1 g	deciliter (dL)	.1 L
centimeter (cm)	.01 m	centigram (cg)	.01 g	centiliter (cL)	.01 L
millimeter (mm)	.001 m	milligram (mg)	.001 g	milliliter (mL)	.001 L

CHAPTER 4

Writing Science and Technical Subjects

The Common Core English language arts and literacy for science typify the future kindergarten through 12th grade standards that will help students achieve success beyond high school. The Common Core requires students to read and comprehend literature along with complicated nonfiction texts that include background understanding and facts in science. Students are asked challenging questions and must look over what they have read to find the answers. This accentuates analytical thinking, problem solving, and investigative abilities that are necessary for achievement in life.

Encourage Writing Skills

Starting in middle school, the literacy standards provide specialist educators with the opportunity to use subject-area mastery to help students address the language arts challenges in their fields of study. The English language arts standards call on your child to develop his abilities in writing argument, explanatory, informational, and narrative text. The more your child writes, the stronger his skills become. Give your child lots of writing materials and prompts for putting his ideas down. From stories, to songs, to giving instructions, all of these forms of writing will help your child grow as a writer.

The following sections outline the expectations for writing in history, science, and technical studies.

Text Types and Purposes

The standards grouped under the text type and purpose section detail the types of texts your child will be reading and why she will be reading them.

Writing Arguments

According to the Common Core standards, in order to write a successful argument, your child should be able to:

- **Write an argument focused on discipline-specific content.** Your child will develop and write argument reports about specific science content. Her report will include the necessary text features along with the evidence to support her argument.
- **Introduce a claim about a topic, distinguish the claim from alternate or opposing claims, and organize her reasons and evidence logically.** In order to write an argument paper, it is necessary to make a claim, or take a stand about a particular issue. This claim is then written in a clear statement. This statement sentence will be the basis for the claim.
- **Support her claim with logical reasoning and accurate data and evidence that demonstrate an understanding of the topic, and by using credible sources.** Once the claim has been stated, it will need to be researched and supported with reliable and relevant information. Those sources

need to be noted. Both the evidence information and the source of the data need to be cited.

- **Use words, phrases, and clauses to create cohesion and clarify the relationships among the claim, counterclaims, reasons, and evidence.** Specific words and phrases indicate a position in an argument report. Some phrases that show more information is being given include: *in fact*, *with respect to*, and *furthermore*. Other features that indicate a claim to a specific point include lists, providing examples, and introducing viewpoints.
- **Establish and maintain a formal style.** An argument report should begin with an introduction of the claim. It should continue through the body with evidence to support the claim, and end with a conclusion.
- **Provide a concluding statement or section that supports the argument presented.** The conclusion to an argument report should restate the claim, provide a summary of the key points, and end with a final comment on the issue.

An argument is a main point or claim that is backed up by evidence and logical reasoning. Students who are writing arguments cannot simply summarize or repeat an idea that has been expressed. It is necessary to take a stance and have proof to support it. It is also important to predict counterarguments to a claim. These counterarguments enable students to discredit oppositions to their claims. The types of evidence used to support an argument might include quotations, details, facts, and other data. The evidence that is provided should be obtained from reputable and reliable sources. Students writing science-specific arguments must critically read research texts in order to have a deep understanding of the content and message.

Writing Explanatory Texts

Explanatory writing differs from an argument paper. When students are writing arguments they must make a claim and provide evidence to support it. Explanatory writing does not involve persuasion or argument. It includes various writing opportunities, including lab reports, science journal writing, answering questions, reflections, and research papers.

According to the Common Core standards, in order to write an explanatory text, your child must:

- **Introduce a topic clearly, previewing what is to follow; organize ideas, concepts, and information into broader categories as appropriate to achieving purpose; include formatting (e.g., headings), graphics (e.g., charts, tables), and multimedia when useful to aiding comprehension.** Once your child has a topic to explain, she will begin her writing text by clearly introducing her topic in her first paragraph. She will continue on with information that explains her topic. Each paragraph that she adds to her assignment should be about one subcategory of her main topic. She will finish with a paragraph that brings all of her ideas together and retells her explanation. Graphics including images and charts can be added to her written assignment.
- **Develop the topic with relevant, well-chosen facts, definitions, concrete details, quotations, or other information and examples.** Her written explanatory assignment should contain evidence to support her explanation. It is important for her to research relevant resources including textbooks and the Internet to find the information she needs to support her explanation.
- **Use appropriate and varied transitions to create cohesion and clarify the relationships among ideas and concepts.** Transition terms are a vital component of explanatory text. These words express agreements and similarities, opposition and contradictions, cause and effect, example support and conclusions. Examples include: *first, second, third, also, similarly, on the contrary, on the other hand, while, with this in mind, unless, in other words, in particular, as a result,* and *in summary.*
- **Use precise language and domain-specific vocabulary to inform about or explain the topic.** Written text is far more effective when the vocabulary being used is precise. Generalized words make it more difficult to make sense of the text. Your child should use vocabulary that specifically pertains to her topic as much as possible.
- **Establish and maintain a formal style and objective tone.** While inferences do play a role in science, subjective opinions on topics in written text assignments tend to reduce the credibility of the writer. Your child should, as much as possible, stick to the facts when writing the content of her assignment.

- **Provide a concluding statement or section that follows from and supports the information or explanation presented.** The conclusion of her written text should restate the points she has explained throughout her assignment and bring the explanation to a well-organized end.

Explanatory texts investigate and express sophisticated concepts in a clear, concise, and precise manner. The intent of explanatory writing is to show understanding of a concept or process. Students express themselves through writing as a means of responding to a particular source, including text, graphs, charts, and multimedia. An effective response calls upon students to read intently so that they show their comprehension of a subject and find the proof from the source to back up their statements.

Writing Organization

Organization is an important aspect of scientific writing. The objective of scientific writing is to establish several ideas that have a common theme and are connected. Some of the ideas that are presented include a large amount of sophisticated words, facts, and concepts. According to the Common Core standards, your child's writing should "produce clear and coherent writing in which the development, organization, and style are appropriate to task, purpose, and audience."

An organized framework makes presenting the ideas more effective and efficient. There are several ways to organize a framework. These organizational patterns can be determined by the transitional phrases used by the writer. Recognizing and understanding organizational patterns can help your child to put all the facts together in a cohesive format. Organizational patterns include cause and effect, chronological order, classification, comparison and contrast, definition, example, generalization, listing, order of importance, process, spatial order, statements of clarification, and summaries.

The Revision Process

In order for students to effectively revise and edit their own work and the works of others, they need to fully understand the writing process. The writing process involves a series of steps that take a writing assignment from an idea to a complete final draft. The process includes brainstorming ideas, drafting, revising, proofreading, and editing for spelling and grammar.

The Common Core standards make a point of emphasizing the revision process of writing by stating that students should, "with some guidance and support from peers and adults, develop and strengthen writing as needed by planning, revising, editing, rewriting, or trying a new approach, focusing on how well purpose and audience have been addressed."

Every writing piece should have an organized structure that includes an introduction, a body, and a conclusion. The text should demonstrate coherence, transitioning logically from one idea to the next. The ideas and content should be supported with reliable evidence. Grammar, spelling, and mechanics should be clear, make sense, and be accurate. The voice, style, and word choices will vary based on the type of text that is being written.

Using Technology to Present Ideas

The Common Core State Standards state that students should "use technology, including the Internet, to produce and publish writing and present the relationships between information and ideas clearly and efficiently."

There are many ways that students can express themselves through their scientific writing. These include, but are not limited to, sharing their ideas aloud, presenting their ideas, sharing their ideas online, and producing and publishing their writing.

There are many technology platforms upon which students can create and communicate the works they have written. For instance, there are several iPad apps and computer programs that provide students with the platforms they need to present their written work. The iPad apps might include Book Creator and Explain Everything, and the computer programs might include Publisher, PowerPoint, and Prezi.

Research to Build and Present Knowledge

The standards grouped under this section detail how your child will be conducting research, and how he will be required to present his findings.

Performing Research Projects

The Common Core State Standards state that students should be able to "conduct short research projects to answer a question (including a self-generated question), drawing on several sources and generating additional related, focused questions that allow for multiple avenues of exploration."

Middle school research projects require students to follow a specific process in writing their assignments. The process includes planning, prewriting, drafting, revising, editing, and publishing.

- Planning involves choosing a topic, creating compelling questions, and developing a thesis. A thesis statement provides the purpose for writing the paper.
- Prewriting refers to researching the chosen topic, creating fact and source cards, and developing an outline. An outline maps out the plan for the text so that the paper is effectively organized.
- In drafting, the students write a rough copy of their text with citations included.
- Once the draft is complete, the work is revised to clarify ideas and organize paragraphs.
- The revised work is then edited for grammatical, mechanical, and spelling errors.
- Finally, the published copy is created.

ALERT

Middle school research should involve the use of books, websites, databases, and periodicals. All sources should be reliable and must be properly and accurately cited in the paper. Work that is not sourced is plagiarism, and plagiarized work is a form of cheating.

Gathering, Using, and Presenting Sources

The Common Core State Standards say that your child should be able to "gather relevant information from multiple print and digital sources, using search terms effectively; assess the credibility and accuracy of each source;

and quote or paraphrase the data and conclusions of others while avoiding plagiarism and following a standard format for citation."

Sources used in writing science papers must be credible and accurate. In order to determine their validity and accuracy, students must use their critical thinking skills to evaluate the sources. This involves assessing the credibility, accuracy, reliability, relevance, date, and source as well as the scope and purpose of the sources.

- In evaluating the **credibility**, students judge the quality of the author by researching his credentials, education, experience, and connections.
- The **accuracy** of the source refers to the facts, statistics, and data that are presented.
- Students evaluate **reliability** by checking for any bias or particular perspective in the information provided.
- The **relevance** of the source is verified in looking for connections between the topic and the thesis statement of the paper being written.
- Outdated sources have reduced validity, so verifying the **date** of publication is essential.
- The **source** itself must be determined to be either a primary or secondary source. As a secondary source, the reliability of the primary information must be checked.
- Finally, the ability to clearly understand the source and its possible range of data must be considered.

Once the sources have been determined to be acceptable, the information must be summarized. Students use the source information through quotations, paraphrasing, and summarizing. Quotations are the direct use of someone else's work word for word. These must be cited. Paraphrasing involves putting someone else's ideas into your own words. It is a form of rewriting text. These must also be cited. Summarizing involves creating a short version of original source that includes just the main points. These too must be cited.

Using Evidence from Texts

According to the Common Core State Standards, students must "draw evidence from informational texts to support analysis, reflection, and research."

Students refer to the evidence presented in informational texts as evidence for their analyses and research. In order to effectively use the information for support, students must know how to effectively find the ideas and data they need, and then provide it effectively as evidence. In some cases the information is directly within the text, but in other texts the students must make inferences to make determinations.

Range of Writing

The standard presented under the range of writing section explains the range of writing your child will develop over the course of his middle school classes. According to the standards, your child should be able to "write routinely over extended time frames (time for reflection and revision) and shorter time frames (a single sitting or a day or two) for a range of discipline-specific tasks, purposes, and audiences."

The narrative abilities of students develop through middle school. Students will be asked to incorporate aspects of narrative writing into their argument, explanatory, and informative texts. Students must show that they are able to precisely describe the procedures they follow in their scientific investigations and design work so that others can reach similar results by following the instructions provided.

CHAPTER 5

Reading in Science

The Common Core standards for literacy in science and the technical subjects are grouped under the ELA (English language arts) standards. The standards define college- and career-readiness expectations so your child will be prepared for the rigors of higher education and requirements in the workforce. There are three central components of the English language arts standards: reading, writing, and listening and speaking. The reading standards include literary and informational texts. The writing standards include argument, explanatory, informative, narrative, and opinion texts. As your child progresses from one grade to the next, her performance expectations and reading requirements in the sciences will increase.

Develop a Love of Reading

The Common Core standards require your child to read books and passages of increasing complexity in all subjects as she progresses through grade levels. You can help your child with her ability to read more complex texts in the science fields by developing her love of reading. Be sure she has access to all sorts of reading materials. They can be books, magazines, Internet content, or newspapers—anything that interests her and that she can read will help. Take a trip to your local library and have her choose books and magazines to borrow. The English language arts standards put an emphasis on reading informational text throughout a range of topics, including science, so choose reading material that is both fictional and informational. As your child reads more complex texts, her vocabulary will improve, and ultimately she'll become a better learner.

Read aloud with her. Listen to her and have her listen to you. Shared reading experiences will help you see where she is excelling and where she might need help. Your reading model will help her understand the importance of voice and fluency.

ESSENTIAL

Pictures communicate strong messages, and this is particularly important when explaining abstract topics in the sciences. Take time to look at all of the images you come across. Illustrations, charts, and diagrams provide a lot of information, so be sure to take the time to talk about them too.

When you have finished a read-aloud session, ask each other questions—not just about what you've read, but about *why* things in the text occurred, and what will happen next. This skill will be particularly important when she is required to formulate and test hypotheses in her science classes. Ask your child to find evidence in the text to support the answers she gives to your questions.

Tips for Reading Through Science Textbooks

Your child will be required to read through his science textbooks and fully comprehend the information presented. Science texts can be a bit complicated compared to narrative literature, and they grow in complexity as your child progresses through the grade levels. Share these instructions with your child to help prepare him for homework and reading assignments.

When reading through science texts, it's a good idea for your child to read through the passages several times in order to make sure he understands all of the information that is being provided. The first time he goes through the text, he should read to get an idea of the main points and to determine if there is anything he doesn't understand. Science texts provide a great deal of new concepts that can be complicated at times. Typically, the text is set out to provide more and more complex ideas the further he reads through a section.

Have your child read through each paragraph slowly, staying focused on the ideas being presented. He shouldn't try to read straight through a paragraph. Make sure he pauses at the end of each sentence to make sure he understands what he just read. If possible, he should read the text aloud to himself. If his teacher has provided a copy of the text that he can keep, have him take out a highlighter and use it to indicate the main points within the text. If he is reading from a school textbook, then he should write down the key points from the passage.

ALERT

Have your child look to the graphics on the page as he finishes a paragraph. The graphics are included to provide more information. He should carefully look at the images and read any captions that are provided. The graphics on the page may include illustrations, graphs, charts, and maps.

If your child seems distracted from the text on the page, have him stop reading. Try and determine why he's lost focus. If the words on the page are too difficult, have him make a list of the words that are giving him trouble in his interactive science notebook. Then he can use the textbook glossary to determine the definitions of the words or add illustrations and synonyms to help him better understand and remember the words. Once he is sure of their meaning, he can go back and continue reading.

If your child seems to be growing tired of reading, have him stop and take a break. Have your child get up and move around or get a snack. Let him do something different for about five minutes and then go back to the text. By getting up and moving around, he'll give his brain a bit of a break. This break will make it easier to get back to reading, and to better understanding the passages in the text.

Once he has read through the entire section of required text and understands the concepts being presented, he should go back and read it again. The second time through, he should have a lot more confidence as he reads. At this point, he should understand the concepts and be reading for review.

Key Ideas and Details

The Common Core science standards covered under Key Ideas and Details determine how your child will cite evidence taken from scientific texts, draw conclusions and make summaries of those texts, and follow precise steps and procedures when performing experiments and recording results. These basic concepts form the foundation upon which your child will build his understanding of scientific texts, learn the importance of citing evidence, and maintain precision when performing and recording experiments.

Citing Textual Evidence

The Common Core State Standards state that your child should "cite specific textual evidence to support analysis of science and technical texts." Students will read and investigate text structures and use text features to better understand the concepts. They will also cite evidence as they read through passages.

To accomplish this, your child will:

- Read text passages and cite evidence from that text to support the findings of the author.
- Find evidence within the article to answer questions being posed.
- Determine the main idea of the text by providing examples that give support. He will also cite the page numbers of the text from which he found the evidence.
- Determine a claim by giving examples that support the argument.

- Make conclusions about a text by providing the words and details that give evidence for the analysis.
- Make inferences about a text by telling what was expressed in the text, the details that back up the communication, how the text relates to the known, and what questions still need to be answered.

Drawing Conclusions from Text

Your child will need to draw conclusions from the scientific text she has read. To do this, she will first need to discover the main points in the text. She can identify the major points in a text by reading through passages and finding the central concepts. She may then choose several main ideas she learned from the passage and write them down in her notebook. She may write three or four examples that support each of the main ideas she listed. Once she has the central ideas and supporting details outlined, she can re-write her findings in a paragraph format.

FACT

The concept of drawing conclusions is stated by the Common Core State Standards as the ability to "determine the central ideas or conclusions of a text; provide an accurate summary of the text distinct from prior knowledge or opinions."

In summarizing the main ideas, she should write down the central concept in her own words, citing the page numbers from the text. Then, once the summary is complete, she can determine the conclusion that is made from the text, using a direct quotation that serves as evidence. She can then make connections from the text to other concepts she has already learned.

Standards for Experiments, Measurements, and Technical Tasks

According to the Common Core State Standards, students should be able to "follow precisely a multistep procedure when carrying out experiments, taking measurements, or performing technical tasks."

Your child will read through procedures and be able to accurately follow each step in order to complete an experiment or class activity. These activities will include science lab instructions that need to followed in the specific order in which they are given. For instance, the beginning steps in a science lab include making a hypothesis about what results might occur. If this step is not completed prior to the experiment, the hypothesis will become invalid. As a course of study, science is a precise subject that requires students to follow directions properly.

Craft and Structure

The Common Core science standards covered under Craft and Structure explain how students will decipher key terms and determine their contextual relevance. They also show how the particular structure and organization of a text contribute to the understanding of the text as a whole. Finally, the standards explain how text is organized and how to determine the author's purpose of the piece (explain, describe, or discuss).

Determining Relevant Terms

In order to fully understand the scientific text, your child must be able to decipher all the relevant scientific terms within it. The Common Core State Standards say that your child should be able to "determine the meaning of symbols, key terms, and other domain-specific words and phrases as they are used in a specific scientific or technical context relevant to grades 6–8 texts and topics."

In determining the meaning of science terms, your child will practice several vocabulary-building strategies. He will create charts that include a science term, his thoughts on the meaning of the term based on its context, and the actual definition of the word.

Text Structure and Organization

Authors use a variety of structures in organizing texts. Your child will determine the type of structure that is being used based on specific features of text. Here are some of the most common text structures and how your child should approach each of them:

- **Chronological text** organizes a series of events in their order of occurrence. Your child will analyze the structure, listing each of the main points as they appear in the text.
- **Compare and contrast text** explains the similarities and differences between two concepts. Your child will interpret the structure, writing the topics that are being compared and contrasted, and listing the similarities and differences between each of them.
- **Order of importance text** is written with the most important concepts coming first and the least important ideas coming last. Your child will investigate the structure, listing the main points in their order of importance.
- **Sequence text** provides the directions of a process in the order in which they occur. Your child will analyze the text, listing the main concepts in their proper sequence.
- **Spatial text** is written in such a way as to give a description that enables the reader to picture the concept being discussed. Your child will create an illustration of the idea described in the text that includes a title and labels of all of the important components.
- **Cause and effect text** explains the reason for an occurrence. The words "because" and "as a result" provide clues to this text format. Your child will investigate the structure, listing the causes and effects that are included in the text.
- **Problem and solution text** explains a problem and offers several possible solutions. Your child will analyze the text, writing the problem in the center of a page and adding the solutions around it.

Determining the Author's Purpose

The author's purpose tells the reader why the text was written. An author writes to entertain, to explain, to inform, and to persuade. The focus of a scientific text may be to provide an explanation, to discuss an experiment, or to describe a procedure.

FACT

The Common Core State Standards for author's purpose state that your child should be able to "analyze the author's purpose in providing an explanation, describing a procedure, or discussing an experiment in a text."

Your child will be asked to determine the author's purpose in writing the text she has read. She may read two passages and develop a fact and opinion chart to identify the purpose of the author in describing theories within the text. Your child will then explain how the author's purpose helped her to learn something new or to understand something better.

Integration of Knowledge and Ideas

The Common Core science standards covered under Integration of Knowledge and Ideas explain how students will explain texts visually, distinguish facts in the texts they read, and compare and contrast their findings from experiments with those that they have read about in their texts. They also state that students should be able to use a variety of multimedia options to demonstrate what they are learning from their texts.

Explaining Text Visually

The Common Core State Standards state that your child should be able to "integrate quantitative or technical information expressed in words in a text with a version of that information expressed visually (e.g., in a flowchart, diagram, model, graph, or table)."

Your child may follow a procedure or use a technology device, collect information, and then represent the findings using graphs, charts, and illustrations. He may then compare the data that he collected to the data from the device of another student in order to find out how valid the results are. He will then use all of the valid results that have been found to create a design solution for the problem.

Distinguishing Facts

The Common Core standards say that students should "distinguish among facts, reasoned judgment based on research findings, and speculation in a text."

Your child will need to identify whether the text she is reading is giving her facts, judgments, or speculations. As she reads through a particular passage, she could create and fill out a chart with the headings "Fact," "Judgment," and "Speculation." She can then write an example of each and a short explanation of why she believes certain statements fall under each category determination.

Comparing and Contrasting Information

Common Core State Standard ELA-LITERACY.RST.6-8.9 reads, "compare and contrast the information gained from experiments, simulations, video, or multimedia sources with that gained from reading a text on the same topic."

Your child will use hands-on activities and multimedia programs to support the concepts he is learning through the passages in his textbook. Reading about a concept informs your child about a scientific concept but applying the concepts through experiments helps your child better develop a deeper understanding of the scientific principles he is studying.

CHAPTER 6

The Three Dimensions of Science

The framework of the Next Generation Science Standards is built around three important dimensions: scientific and engineering practices, crosscutting concepts, and core ideas. These dimensions provide a broad outline of the scientific applications and concepts that students will understand and use effectively by the end of high school.

What Are the Scientific and Engineering Practices?

The first dimension, science and engineering practices, describes the practices that scientists and engineers use to investigate phenomena, design systems, solve problems, and develop theories about the world around us. Students become engaged in investigation and demonstrate their knowledge and skills connected with each specific practice. They're required to demonstrate their scientific understanding through real-world applications.

FACT

The Three Dimensions of the Next Generation Science Standards can be read in detail at *www.nextgenscience.org/three-dimensions.*

Asking Questions and Defining Problems

In science, your child will learn to ask questions that can be tested and that generate explanations and descriptions of the workings of the natural and man-made worlds. While researching and reporting findings, students are required to be specific in describing the relationships among variables and analyzing models and arguments. The learning process continues after experiments are concluded: students will formulate questions that come out of a conscientious observation of results, models, and phenomena so that they can define and research more data.

As your child works to define appropriate questions and problems, he will also:

- Make a claim about a particular scientific phenomenon and find evidence to support his claim.
- Establish relationships among dependent and independent variables and models. The independent variable is the one factor being changed by the person doing the experiment. The dependent variable is the factor being measured when the change is made.

- Analyze an explanation he has found for a particular scientific phenomenon and modify the explanation to meet the specific experiment or design he is investigating.
- Understand that when he is answering a scientific question he needs to give proof that is valid and that includes observations and facts.
- Understand that he can explore science problems in the classroom and in other non-classroom places in order to perform the best investigation possible.
- Ask questions that challenge the foundation of an argument or the analysis of set information.
- Describe a design problem that can be solved with a tool, a process, or a system that involves several criteria and limitations, and includes the incorporation of scientific knowledge that could restrict the solution possibilities.

Developing and Using Models

Developing and utilizing models is applicable in both the scientific and engineering process. This practice enables your child to build models that will help him to represent his explanations and ideas. These models might include illustrations, diagrams, computer simulations, mathematical representations, and replicas.

ESSENTIAL

The term "practices" is used in the NGSS in place of the term "skills" that was used in previous state standards in order to emphasize the understanding that successful scientific inquiry uses knowledge and skill at the same time.

Your child will develop, utilize, and revise models so that he can define and evaluate his research. In addition, he will:

- Assess the limitations of his models as a tool
- Develop and refine his model, based on the proof obtained, to correspond with the results of a change in a system

- Develop and utilize a model of a basic system with unpredictable and unclear factors
- Develop and modify a model to demonstrate the relationship between variables, both observable and predictable
- Develop and utilize a model that will help him predict and define phenomena
- Develop a model to explain mechanisms that cannot be observed
- Develop and utilize a model to formulate data to evaluate ideas regarding phenomena in designed and natural systems

Planning and Carrying Out Investigations

Scientists and engineers develop and implement investigations that are systematic. These investigations require clarification of what information is valuable and determine limitations and variables. Your child will investigate using several variables and provide proof to support his solutions and explanation, and will:

- Develop an investigation on his own and with others
- Determine dependent and independent variables, the tools he needs to collect information, how he will record his results, and how much information he will need to support his hypothesis
- Implement his investigation, and assess and revise the design of his experiment so that he can produce information as evidence for his investigation
- Gather information to use as evidence to solve scientific questions or evaluate solutions to designs under several conditions
- Gather information about the effectiveness of an object, process, system, or tool

Analyzing and Interpreting Data

Investigations in science generate information that your child must analyze so that he can acquire meaning from the exploration. Since information trends are sometimes difficult to see, your child may use visualization, graphic interpretation, and analysis of statistics so that he can determine the important factors and patterns in the information. He will determine any origins of errors in the investigation and determine the validity of the results. Your child will:

- Extend quantitative analysis to investigations, differentiating between causes and correlations, and basic information analysis
- Create, analyze, and interpret graphical exhibits of information to determine nonlinear and linear connections
- Use charts, graphs, maps, and tables to determine spatial and temporal connections
- Differentiate between correlation and causal connections of information
- Analyze and interpret information to provide proof for a particular phenomenon
- Use digital tools to apply statistical concepts and probability to evaluate information
- Consider the constraints of information analysis and explore ways to produce more precise and accurate data using more advanced methods and tools
- Analyze and interpret information to establish differences and similarities in results
- Analyze information to determine the best practical use of an object, process, tool, or system

Using Mathematics and Computational Thinking

Mathematics and computation are important tools that are used to represent variables and relationships. They are used to analyze information, construct simulations, and explore quantitative relationships. Your child will identify patterns in large sets of information and use mathematical theories to support his arguments and explanations, and will:

- Utilize digital tools to analyze the information, looking for trends and patterns
- Utilize mathematical representations to explain and support scientific conclusions and design solutions
- Construct algorithms to solve problems
- Apply mathematical theories and processes to scientific and engineering problems and questions
- Utilize digital tools and mathematical theories to assess and compare proposed solutions to design problems

Constructing Explanations and Designing Solutions

In science, the products that are developed are referred to as explanations. In engineering, the products are called solutions. Your child will build explanations and design solutions that are supported by several sources of proof that is developed through scientific theories, ideas, and principles. In addition, he will:

- Construct explanations involving quantitative and qualitative connections between variables that predict and explain phenomena
- Use representations and models to build his explanations
- Build scientific explanations on the basis of valid proof that is acquired from sources
- Conduct investigations under the assumption that scientific laws and theories are valid throughout history
- Apply scientific principles, proof, and ideas to build, revise, and utilize explanations for phenomena that exist in the real world
- Apply scientific reasoning to demonstrate how his evidence is sufficient for his conclusion or explanation
- Apply scientific principles and ideas in order to develop, build, and evaluate his design of an object, process, system, or tool
- Complete a design project using the design cycle to build and exercise a solution that matches particular limitations and criteria
- Improve his design performance through criteria prioritizing, assessing, revising, and reassessing

Engaging in Argument from Evidence

Solutions and explanations are reached through argumentation. Your child will build a credible argument refuting or supporting assertions for solutions and explanations in the real world. As such, he will:

- Make a comparison and examination of two arguments of the same subject and explore the similarities or differences in evidence and fact interpretation
- Courteously receive and provide critiques about his explanations, models, processes, and questions by citing pertinent proof, and asking and answering questions that evoke relevant discussion and explanation

- Build, utilize, and present a written and oral argument that is supported by scientific reasoning and empirical evidence that will be used to refute or support his model or explanation of a problem, phenomenon, or solution
- Create a written or oral argument that refutes or supports the publicized performance of a particular device, system, or process on the basis of empirical evidence regarding the capacity of the technology to meet pertinent limitations or criteria
- Assess competing design solutions on the basis of collaboratively developed design criteria

Obtaining, Evaluating, and Communicating Information

Engineers and scientists have to clearly and effectively communicate their ideas and methods. They also communicate and analyze their ideas in groups or individually. In order to master these skills, your child will:

- Evaluate the value and merit of methods and ideas
- Critically read scientific texts, identify the main ideas, and acquire scientific understanding
- Incorporate quantitative and qualitative scientific and technical information in media text and graphic displays to define results and claims
- Collect, read, and analyze information from several sources and evaluate the reliability, accuracy, potential bias, and methods utilized so that he can explain the support provided by the evidence
- Assess information, hypotheses, and conclusions in technical and scientific texts for competing data
- Communicate technical and scientific information in written assignments and oral presentations

FACT

Paul Anderson at Bozemanscience provides a clear outline of the Three Dimensions that form the Next Generation Science Standards. Visit the site at: *www.bozemanscience.com/next-generation-science-standards*.

What Are Crosscutting Concepts?

The second dimension, crosscutting concepts, describes the connections of scientific practice through all science domains and across other subject areas. These concepts provide an organized system for relating understanding of various science domains with real world applications and knowledge.

Patterns

Patterns of events and forms that we can observe help to guide our classification and organization. They trigger questioning about connections and relationships and the components that impact them. For example, your child will begin to see the patterns between microscopic and atomic structures.

By the end of middle school, she will be able to:

- Recognize that macroscopic patterns are related to the nature of microscopic and atomic-level structure
- Identify patterns in rates of change and other numerical relationships that provide information about natural and human-designed systems
- Use patterns to identify cause-and-effect relationships, and use graphs and charts to identify patterns in data

Cause and Effect: Mechanism and Explanation

Events that take place have causes, and these causes can be simple or complex. A principal activity in science is the investigation and explanation of the relationship between the cause and its effect: essentially, between factors and specific phenomenon. Scientists also investigate and explain the mechanisms that mediate the relationships between cause and effect.

Scientists test these mechanisms over particular contexts and use them in predictions and explanations of particular events in new contexts. In school, your child will argue her own cause-and-effect explanations. She will also compare the various scientific theories that explain causal mechanisms.

By the end of 8th grade, she will be able to:

- Classify relationships as causal or co-relational, and recognize that correlation does not necessarily imply causation. (Causation refers to the relationship between cause and effect; an action causes something else to occur.)

- Use cause-and-effect relationships to predict phenomena in natural or designed systems
- Understand that phenomena may have more than one cause, and that some cause-and-effect relationships in systems can only be described using probability

ESSENTIAL

Crosscutting concepts give students the tools they need to relate the content they learn in science across other subject areas and to connect the ideas they learn in other subjects to their science studies.

Scale, Proportion, and Quantity

When you consider phenomena, it is crucial to recognize the relevance of various measures of energy, size, and time. It is also important to recognize the effects of changes in quantity, proportion, and scale on the structure and performance of a system.

Your child will begin to understand the process of estimation across contexts and scales, and will use estimation in her analysis of information. The process of estimation also includes:

- Questioning whether her numerical results make sense
- Developing a grasp of the power-of-10 scales and using them in analyzing phenomena
- Applying algebraic reasoning while investigating scientific information, and predicting the impact that changes to one variable will have on another variable

By the end of middle school, she will be able to:

- Observe time, space, and energy phenomena at various scales using models to study systems that are too large or too small
- Understand that phenomena observed at one scale may not be observable at another scale, and that the function of natural and designed systems may change with scale

- Use proportional relationships to gather information about the magnitude of properties and processes
- Represent scientific relationships through the use of algebraic expressions and equations

Systems and System Models

By defining a particular system, specifying its limits, and creating explicit models of the system, scientists produce tools that help us understand and test ideas that can be applied across science and engineering. Graphs, ratios, and other mathematical ideas are tools that are used for creating models. Your child will use her mathematical abilities to explore relationships and analyze patterns between variables, and will use models to reveal problems and progress in her understanding of systems.

By the end of middle school, she will be able to:

- Understand that systems may interact with other systems; they may have sub-systems and be a part of larger complex systems
- Use models to represent systems and their interactions—such as inputs, processes, and outputs—and energy, matter, and information flows within systems
- Understand that models are limited in that they only represent certain aspects of the system under study

Energy and Matter: Flows, Cycles, and Conservation

Following fluctuations of matter and energy as they move within, into, and out of systems makes it possible for scientists to understand the possibilities and limitations of a particular system. Your child will be introduced to the role that energy transfers play in the flow of matter. She will differentiate between weight and mass, gain an understanding of atoms and their property of conservation, and investigate the core ideas of energy and matter of the systems in the life and earth and space sciences.

By the end of 8th grade, she will be able to:

- Understand that matter is conserved because atoms are conserved in physical and chemical processes

- Understand that within a natural or designed system, the transfer of energy drives motion and matter cycling
- Understand that energy may take different forms such as thermal energy, fields of energy, and energy of motion
- Understand that the transfer of energy can be tracked as energy flows through a designed or natural system

Structure and Function

Many of the functions and properties of living and nonliving things are determined by their substructure and their shape. Your child will be able to model, visualize, and apply her understanding of function and structure to more complicated systems and processes.

By the time she finishes 8th grade, she will be able to:

- Model complex and microscopic structures and systems and visualize how their function depends on the shapes, composition, and relationships among its parts
- Analyze many complex natural and designed structures and systems to determine how they function
- Design structures to serve particular functions by taking into account properties of different materials, and how materials can be shaped and used

Stability and Change

Determinants of rates of change or evolution and conditions of stability are crucial elements to the study of both natural and constructed systems. Your child will develop her understanding of matter, the atomic scale, and the importance of using models to explain stability and change.

By the end of middle school, your child will be able to:

- Explain stability and change in natural or designed systems by examining changes over time, and considering forces at different scales, including the atomic scale
- Understand that changes in one part of a system might cause large changes in another part, systems in dynamic equilibrium are stable due

to a balance of feedback mechanisms, and stability might be disturbed by either sudden events or gradual changes that accumulate over time

- Understand that uses of technologies and any limitations on their use are driven by individual or societal needs, desires, and values; by the findings of scientific research; and by differences in such factors as climate, natural resources, and economic conditions
- Understand that technology use varies over time and from region to region

What Are the Disciplinary Core Ideas?

The third dimension, disciplinary core ideas, describes the key ideas that students need at specific grade levels. These core ideas are key principles across several science disciplines that offer vital tools for solving problems and analyzing complicated concepts, are relevant to the lives of students, and can be studied and applied at increasing levels of complexity over several years of learning. These ideas are divided into the four domains of science: the life sciences; the physical sciences; the earth and space sciences; and engineering, technology, and applications of science.

CHAPTER 7

Matter and Its Interactions

Matter is the material that makes up everything in our universe. From the tiniest seed in the soil to the highest peak in the mountains, from the magma within the earth's core to the galaxies above, all things are made of matter. This chapter will give you a better understanding of the way that matter is organized. You'll learn more about why the organization of matter affects the interactions of substances and how you can make predictions based on that understanding. The concepts considered are based on the Next Generation Science Standards.

What Should My Child Already Understand?

By the time your child finishes 5th grade, she understands that matter is made up of very small particles that are too difficult to see with the human eye. While you can't see these particles, they do exist, and you can use ways other than your sense of sight to detect them. You can weigh the particles or observe how they affect other things. For example, you can't see the particles in air, but you can see how a balloon changes when it is filled and how it changes again when the air is removed. Your child understands that it doesn't matter what changes take place, the weight of matter stays the same. This fact is referred to as the conservation of mass. Her past experiences in science included measuring the properties of matter in order to determine how an object can be identified. Your child knows that mixing two substances together creates a new substance with different properties and that temperature plays a large role in the mixing process. Again, she also understands that even through these processes, the weight of the matter does not change.

FACT

Two volatile elements come together to produce something we eat every day. How is that possible? Well, sodium is a metal that can produce an explosive reaction, and chlorine is a hazardous substance that can be quite deadly. However, when these two elements are combined into a compound, they lose their dangerous properties and become something quite common, table salt.

Disciplinary Core Ideas

The following concepts have been established by the Next Generation Science Standards as some of the important points of understanding in studying matter and its interactions. Following are some of the topics your child will learn about and discuss in school.

Structure and Properties of Matter

All substances are made up of different atoms that are combined in a variety of ways. Together these atoms form molecules. These molecules can range from two atoms to thousands in size. Every pure substance has specific chemical and physical properties.

These properties can help to identify the substance. All liquids and gases are made from inert atoms or molecules that move. The molecules in liquids are always in contact with other molecules. The molecules in gases are spaced apart except when they collide with one another. The molecules in solids are spaced closely and do not change their relative locations. Solids can be made from molecules or they can be extended structures with subunits that repeat. The changes of states of matter caused by temperature and pressure variations can be described; through the use of models of matter, they can also be predicted.

Chemical Reactions

All substances have characteristic chemical reactions. During a chemical process, the atoms within the substance become regrouped into different molecules. These newly formed substances generate new and different properties from the ones of the reactants.

ALERT

Chemical reactions are interactions. They happen when at least two molecules interact with each other. This interaction causes the molecules to change. The bonds between the atoms within the molecules become broken. The atoms then create new bonds and create new molecules.

In the process, the total number of each of the types of atoms remains the same and there is no change in mass. Some chemical reactions store energy and some chemical reactions release energy.

Key Matter Terms

These terms are important for your child to learn; they'll help her gain a good understanding of matter:

- Change of State—A physical change of a substance from one state to another. The changes of state include boiling, condensation, evaporation, freezing, melting, sublimation, and vaporization.
- Chemical Change—Chemical change happens when substances become completely new substances that have different properties. Chemical changes are usually irreversible.
- Chemical Property—A property of matter that identifies a particular substance based on how it changes into a new substance with different properties.
- Density—The amount of matter in a unit volume. It is an intensive property of matter that can be calculated by dividing mass by volume.
- Gravity—The force of attraction between objects. The strength of gravity is based on the distance between the objects and their masses.
- Intensive or Characteristic Property—A characteristic of matter that does not change regardless of the size of the sample of matter. It is used to identify the types of matter.

ESSENTIAL

Everything that has weight and takes up space is made up of matter. Matter is made up of atoms that are about a hundred times smaller than the distance across a human hair. Atoms in their purest forms are called elements, and these elements are determined by their physical states.

- Mass—The amount of matter within an object.
- Matter—Anything with a volume and mass that can be measured.
- Physical Change—Change that affects physical properties and can usually be reversed.
- Physical Property—A property of matter that is observed or measured and that does not involve a change in the substance.

- States of Matter—The physical forms that substances are in. These states include gas, solid, and liquid. The state of matter does not chemically change the substance.
- Volume—The amount of three-dimensional space that an object occupies.
- Weight—The measure of the force of gravity on objects.

Key Matter Concepts

Everything around you is made of matter. This section will explore what matter is and its different properties and states.

What Is Matter?

Matter is *everywhere*. Matter is made up of atoms, which contain particles. The particles within these atoms are constantly moving. Everything that has mass and volume is matter. Matter is organized by the types of atoms inside an object and the way the atoms interact with one another. Matter can be characterized for its states, properties, and reactions. These states, properties, and reactions can be explained and predicted based on the atoms within the matter and the way they interact. Energy, space, antimatter, and forces are not forms of matter because they do not have a mass or volume that can be measured.

How Is Matter Measured?

Matter must have volume and mass. An object must be measured for its volume and mass to determine if it is matter. *Volume* is the amount of three-dimensional space that is taken up by an object. *Mass* is the amount of matter that an object has. Measurement tests can be used to determine whether an object has matter. Volume is measured using a graduated cylinder, calculations, or water displacement. A graduated cylinder is used to measure the volume of liquids. Calculations are used to measure the volume of rectangular prisms. Water displacement is used to measure the volume of objects that have an irregular shape. Mass is measured using a triple beam balance.

Mass and weight are different. *Mass* is the amount of space an object occupies, and *weight* is the amount of gravitational pull applied to that object. The mass of an object is always the same because the number of particles that are inside it do not change, even when the object changes its location. The amount of gravity that is applied (the weight) depends on the mass of two objects and the distance between them.

Mass is measured on a balance using grams. Weight is measured with a spring scale using Newtons. Weight is calculated by multiplying the mass of an object by the gravitational pull.

$$Mass \times gravity = weight$$

The States of Matter Q&A

The states of matter are the physical forms that matter exists in. While matter has four states, only the three main states will be investigated in middle school. These states include: solid, liquid, and gas. Matter can change from one state to another. When matter changes from one state to another, it does not chemically change.

A solid has a specific volume and shape. Its particles have low energy and they vibrate locked in place. A liquid has no specific volume or shape. Its particles move around each other and are more widely spaced than those in a solid. Particles have less energy than a gas and more than a solid. A gas has no defined shape or volume. Its particles move about freely at a very quick pace.

Q: What are changes of state in physical science?
A: Changes of state are changes in matter from one physical state to another. Changes in state include: boiling, condensation, evaporation, freezing, melting, sublimation, and vaporization.

Q: What is density?
A: Density measures how much matter occupies a specific space. Density is calculated by dividing mass by volume. Mass/volume = density. Its measurement units are g/cm^3 or g/mL.

Q: Why is density important to science?
A: Density is important to understanding matter because it helps in identifying specific types of matter. Density identifies whether some-

thing will float or sink, which has an impact on many physical processes, including ocean currents and weather. Objects float or sink because of their density. Objects that are denser than the liquid they are in will sink. Objects that are less dense than the liquid they are in will float.

Q: What are the properties of matter?
A: The properties of matter are ways to describe matter. There are chemical and physical properties.

Q: What are chemical properties?
A: Chemical properties can only be observed when matter is reacting with other matter and forming into a new type of matter. Chemical properties describe how the forms of matter react. Chemical properties include explosivity, flammability, radioactivity, reactivity with acid, reactivity with oxygen, and reactivity with water.

Q: What are the physical properties of matter?
A: Physical properties can be observed without the matter forming into a new type of matter. *Intensive properties* of matter are properties that are constant regardless of the amount of matter available. They are used to determine different types of matter when some of the other properties are unknown. *Physical properties* include color, density, ductility, electrical conductivity, flexibility, hardness, malleability, mass, odor, shape, solubility, weight, and volume.

Q: What are physical processes?
A: The melting point is when enough pressure or heat is added to change matter from a solid state to a liquid state. The melting process is when matter changes from a solid state to a liquid state. The freezing point is when enough heat is removed to change matter from a liquid to a solid. The freezing process is when matter changes from a liquid state to a solid state. The boiling point is when enough pressure or heat is added to change matter from a liquid state to a gas state. The boiling/evaporation process is when matter changes from a liquid state to a gas state. The condensation point is when enough energy is

removed to change matter from a gas state to a liquid state. The sublimation state is when matter changes from a solid state to a gas state.

Q: How does thermal energy affect matter?
A: When energy is added to a solid, the particles inside it begin to get farther apart and move faster. When energy is taken from a gas, the particles inside it begin to get closer together and move more slowly.

FACT

Matter can be broken into two different groups: living matter and nonliving matter. Living matter grows and reproduces and includes things like plants, animals, and microorganisms. Nonliving matter does not grow or reproduce and includes things like rocks and minerals.

Key Atomic Terms

These terms are important to a strong understanding of atoms:

- Atom—The smallest unit of matter.
- Atomic Mass Unit—The metric unit that is used to express the mass of particles within an atom. A proton and neutron each have a mass of 1 amu.
- Atomic Number—The number of protons within the nucleus of an atom. Atomic numbers are used in the periodic table to arrange the elements.
- Electron—A negatively charged particle that orbits the nucleus in the electron cloud of the atom.
- Element—A pure substance that cannot be separated into simpler substances by a physical or chemical change.
- Group—On the periodic table, "group" refers to the vertical columns of elements. Similar chemical and physical properties are found in the elements of the same group.
- Mass Number—The total sum of the protons and neutrons within an atom.

- Neutron—A particle that has no charge and is also found in the nucleus of an atom.
- Nucleus—The tiny center inside an atom. It has a positive charge and contains most of the mass of the atom.
- Period—On the periodic table, "period" refers to the horizontal rows of elements. The properties in each row follow repeating patterns across the period.
- Periodic Table—A chart that organizes the elements by regular and repeating patterns. Arranged by increased atomic masses, it is possible to see similar chemical and physical properties every eight elements.
- Proton—A positively charged particle that is located in the nucleus of an atom.
- Pure Substance—A substance that is made up of one type of particle.

FACT

You wouldn't be able to see an atom under a typical microscope because they are far too small. Instead, you could use an STM or AFM device. An STM, or scanning tunneling microscope, and an AFM, or atomic force microscope, bounce light off of atom particles and change the beams of light into an image of the atoms.

Key Atomic Concepts

Atoms are the smallest forms of matter. Liquids, solids, and gases are made up of atoms. This section will explore what atoms are and their interactions within matter.

Atoms Q&A

Q: What is an atom?
A: Atoms are the basic units that make up matter. They can come together to create molecules that make up the objects around you. Every atom has three types of particles: protons, neutrons, and electrons. Every atom has a nucleus. The nucleus is the smallest part of

the atom but it contains most of the mass of the atom because it contains the protons and neutrons. Most of the space surrounding the nucleus is empty. The number of protons in the nucleus of an atom determines the type of atom that it is.

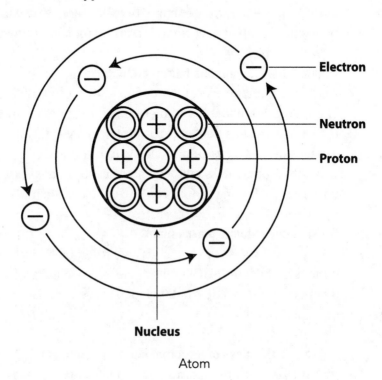

Atom

Q: What are protons?

A: Protons are particles that have a positive charge. They are found inside the nucleus of an atom. Each specific element has the same number of protons in each of its atoms. The number of protons in an atom is referred to as its atomic number.

Q: What are neutrons?

A: Neutrons are also located in the nucleus of an atom. Neutrons have no electrical charges and are neutral. There is not always the same number of neutrons in the atoms of each specific element. When the atoms of an element have a different number of neutrons, they are referred to as isotopes.

Q: What are electrons?

A: Electrons orbit around the nucleus. Electrons are particles that have a negative charge. Electrons are much smaller than protons and neutrons. Their mass is about $\frac{1}{2000}$ of the mass of protons and neutrons. When electrons are shared between atoms, they form chemical bonds that result in new compounds and molecules being formed.

Q: What does atomic number mean?

A: Atomic number refers to the number of protons inside the nucleus of an atom. Atoms are extremely small, making it impossible to use milligrams to measure them. The atomic mass unit, amu, was created to measure the mass of particles within an atom. The proton has a mass of 1 atomic mass unit. The neutron has a mass of 1 atomic mass unit. The electron has a mass of $\frac{1}{2000}$ of an atomic mass unit.

Q: What does atomic mass mean?

A: The atomic mass of an atom is calculated by adding the number of protons and neutrons within its nucleus. Since electrons are so small, their atomic mass unit is not included in the calculation of the atomic mass of an atom.

Q: What is the mass of a proton, neutron, and electron?

A: A proton has a mass of 1 amu. A neutron has a mass of 1 amu. An electron has a mass of $\frac{1}{2000}$ of an amu.

Q: Where is most of the mass of an atom located?

A: Most of the mass of an atom is located in the nucleus, where the protons and neutrons are found.

Q: What are the charges on a proton, neutron, and electron?

A: Protons have a charge of +1. Neutrons have no charge. Electrons have a charge of -1.

Q: What is the overall charge of an atom?

A: Typical atoms are neutral because the opposing protons and electrons balance each other and the neutrons have no charge at all.

Q: What is a molecule?

A: A molecule is a group of two or more atoms that are chemically bonded.

Q: What is an element?

A: An element is a pure substance that cannot be separated into simpler substances through any physical or chemical changes.

Q: What is the periodic table?

A: The periodic table is a chart that organizes all of the elements. Every element is positioned in a particular place on the chart based on its atomic structure. It has rows that read from left to right and columns that go up and down. Elements with similar properties share the same row or column. Each row is called a period and has specific characteristics. Each column is called a group and has specific characteristics as well.

Q: What are some of the patterns on the periodic table?

A: Moving downward through a group of elements, the atomic radius increases, the number of energy levels increases, and the reactivity remains the same, as does the number of valence electrons. Moving across through a period on the table, the number of valence electrons increases, and the number of energy levels remains the same.

Q: How are the different types of elements determined?

A: The atomic number of a substance determines the number of protons. The number of protons in an atom determines the type of element the substance is. Every element has a different number of protons.

ALERT

Energy and matter are not the same. Matter takes up volume and space. Energy does not. Matter makes up the things in the universe. Energy is something that these things in the universe have. Energy is a property of a specific type of matter and characterizes how these types of matter function and interact.

Key Chemical Reaction Terms

These terms are important to developing a good understanding of chemical reactions:

- Chemical—Everything that is made up of matter is a chemical.
- Chemical Bonding—The force of attraction that pulls two or more atoms together to form a new substance.
- Chemical Equation—A brief description of a chemical reaction that includes symbols and formulas.
- Chemical Formula—A symbolic expression of chemical bonding between atoms.
- Chemical Reaction—A process through which one or more substances become changed and create one or more new substances.
- Compound—A pure substance that is made of two or more elements that have been chemically bonded.
- Ion—A charged particle that is created during a chemical change when one or more valence electrons transfer to another atom. Ions of opposite charges are attracted to each other to form ionic bonds.
- Law of Conservation of Mass—The mass of matter cannot be created or destroyed through a typical chemical or physical change.
- Mixture—A combination of two or more substances that have not been chemically bonded.
- Molecule—A neutral group of atoms that is kept together through a covalent bond.
- Product—The new substance that is created by a chemical reaction.
- Reactant—An original substance before it is changed by a chemical reaction.
- Solubility—The ability of a substance to dissolve in another substance.
- Solution—A mixture of two or more evenly distributed substances that appears to be one single substance.

Key Chemical Reaction Concepts

Chemical reactions take place all around you. Let's find out how these reactions occur and what happens when the process is complete.

Chemical Reaction Q&A

Q: What is a chemical?
A: Anything in the universe that is made up of matter is a chemical.

Q: What is a chemical formula?
A: A chemical formula is a symbolic expression of a bond between atoms.

Q: How are chemical symbols and numbers used?
A: The symbols and numbers can be used to determine the number of atoms of different elements that are bonded through a chemical process.

Q: What are the results of a chemical mixture?
A: There are three results of a chemical mixture: mixing, non-mixing, or a chemical reaction.

Q: What are mixtures?
A: There are three types of mixtures: solutions, colloids, and suspensions. A *solution* contains very small particles that are homogeneous in nature. There is no light scattering or particle settling in a solution. A *colloid* contains small particles that are homogeneous in nature. There is light scattering but no particle settling in a colloid. A *suspension* contains larger particles that are heterogeneous in nature. There is light scattering and particle settling in a suspension.

Q: What do heterogeneous and homogeneous mean?
A: It is possible to observe the different parts of a mixture when a mixture is heterogeneous. An example of a heterogeneous mixture is vegetable soup. You can see every vegetable and distinguish them from the broth. A homogeneous mixture appears as one single substance.

An example of a homogeneous mixture is something around you all of the time, air! It's clear, never changes color, and contains oxygen, nitrogen, and carbon.

Q: How can mixtures be separated?
A: Colloids and solutions can be separated through evaporation because their particles are not chemically combined. By evaporating a colloid or solution, one of the parts will be left behind. Filters, magnets, and screens can be used to separate suspensions because their particles are larger.

Q: What are solutes and solvents?
A: A *solute* is a substance that is dissolved into a solvent and forms a solution. It typically has a smaller amount than the solvent. A *solvent* is the substance in which a solute is dissolved and forms a solution; it typically has a greater amount than the solute. If you were to mix salt with water, the salt would be the solute and the water would be the solvent.

Q: What does soluble mean?
A: When a chemical is able to dissolve in another substance, it is soluble. The ability to be dissolved is referred to as solubility. Solubility is a physical property of matter. Dissolving a chemical into another substance does not create a new substance. There is no chemical bonding involved because the particles are dispersed without bonding.

Q: What happens when a solute dissolves into a solvent?
A: When a solute dissolves into a solvent, the particles of each substance combine equally. It is a physical change because there is not chemical bonding involved.

Q: What is the law of conservation of mass?
A: Matter cannot be created or destroyed through chemical and physical changes. The atoms may move or become recombined to create a new substance, or they can change form, but the total of the atoms remains the same.

Q: What are chemical reactions?

A: There are many substances that react chemically when they combine with other substances. This chemical reaction causes them to form new substances that have different properties. The change to the properties of a substance takes place because of the ways that the atoms from the initial substance are rearranged and combined through the chemical reaction process. There are some reactions that require energy and some that release energy. The outcomes of reactions can be described and predicted using the property of conservation and the knowledge of the chemical properties of specific elements.

Q: How do chemical reactions affect the structure of an atom?

A: The change created by the chemical reaction does not affect the total number of each type of atom in the substance. The total number of atoms is conserved in a chemical reaction. Since the number of atoms stays the same, the mass stays the same as well.

Q: What are the outcomes of a chemical reaction?

A: The outcomes of reactions can be described and predicted using the property of conservation and the knowledge of the chemical properties of specific elements. It is easier to reverse these changes than ones that occur through chemical reactions. Changes in matter can take place where the molecules remain the same but their motion and positions change, such as making a solution.

Q: Which clues indicate that a chemical reaction has taken place?

A: When a chemical reaction has occurred, there are several results that may take place, including bubbling, color changes that are unexpected, energy changes, foaming, formation of new gas, and odor changes that are unexpected.

Q: How can a chemical reaction be sped up or slowed down?

A: By adding energy, increasing the surface area, or adding a catalyst, a chemical reaction can be sped up. Energy can be added through heat, the surface area can be increased through crushing and stirring, and the catalyst might be a chemical that makes the reaction faster.

By removing energy or decreasing the surface area, a chemical reaction can be slowed down.

Q: What role does energy play in chemical reactions?

A: All chemical reactions require energy to take place. An exothermic reaction releases energy. An endothermic reaction continues absorbing energy.

Q: Why is it important to understand chemical reactions?

A: A strong understanding of the properties of elements and of chemical reactions is crucial to developing a good foundation in the physical, life, and earth and space sciences. Matter cycling and energy transfers within systems are based on physical and chemical processes.

Q: How are new substances formed?

A: When two substances react with each other, the bonds between the atoms of the substances may be broken. The two substances that react are called reactants. The new substance that is formed is called the product. The breaking of the bonds takes energy. The initial atoms may move or recombine with other atoms. New bonds are then formed, and this also takes energy. The new product is different from the reactants. Due to the conservation of mass, no atoms are destroyed in the reaction. A chemical reaction can be expressed by a chemical formula.

Q: How do atoms, elements, compounds, molecules, and mixtures compare?

A: An atom is a basic unit of matter. An element has a specific type of atom that contains different numbers of electrons, neutrons, and protons. An element has unique physical and chemical properties. A compound is a combination of two or more different elements that have been chemically bonded to form a new substance. A molecule is a combination of elements that have been chemically bonded to either form the same substance or a new substance. A mixture is a combination of two or more substances without any chemical bonding.

ESSENTIAL

The electron cloud model describes where the electrons go when they move around the nucleus of an atom. This model explains that there is no set place where an electron is in a particular moment but that there is a probable area where it will be.

Science and Engineering Practices

In learning about matter and its interactions, your child will use science and engineering practices to better understand the ideas that relate to matter and its interactions. These practices might include:

- Asking and solving questions about the properties of matter, substances, atoms, chemical reactions, elements, and compounds.
- Analyzing and interpreting data in order to design a solution that helps him identify the substances contained within an unknown mixture.
- Analyzing and interpreting data to identify the properties of particular materials in order to determine the best way the material can be used.
- Using mathematics to calculate the mass, volume, and density of a variety of objects.
- Using mathematics to compare the mass of various reactants and products that support the law of conservation of matter.
- Constructing an explanation that defines how a substance's characteristic properties remain constant regardless of the sample amount.
- Engaging in an argument that uses evidence to debate the best means of disposing of hazardous materials.
- Obtaining, evaluating, and communicating information about the properties of various substances and using that information to group the properties.
- Defining problems that come up when the properties of a material limit a product design solution.
- Developing and using models that represent atoms, molecules, elements, and compounds and their relative systems.
- Planning and carrying out investigations that demonstrate the law of conservation of matter or the law of conservation of mass.

Next Generation Science Standards Performance Expectations

These performance expectations describe what your child should be able to demonstrate and understand about the specific science unit he is studying in middle school. From these expectations your child's teachers will determine how successfully he understands and can apply the concepts that have been covered.

Developing Models to Describe Atoms

Performance expectation MS.PS1.1 states that students should be able to "develop models to describe the atomic composition of simple molecules and extended structures." As previously discussed, basic atomic composition comprises three subatomic particles: the proton, neutron, and electron. These particles are arranged much like our solar system, with the protons and neutrons arranged at the center providing the main characteristics of the atom, much like our sun in the solar system, with outer electrons orbiting like planets, but also emanating like waves.

Molecules, however, are clusters of atoms brought together by things called bonds. *Bonds* are electron interactions between two atoms, which can involve the giving, taking, or sharing of electrons between two atoms. Molecules are formed in many different shapes and sizes, but are all chains of different atoms.

The characteristics of different elements (different atoms) determine the characteristics of the molecules that they make up. For instance, a molecule composed of elements that are gaseous at room temperature is likely to be gaseous at room temperature. In the same way, molecules composed of solid elements like metals are likely to be solid at room temperature. All molecules depend on the characteristics of the elements that they are composed of.

Your child will develop models that will be used to describe how simple molecules and extended structures are composed. The types of models will differ in how complex they are. Simple molecules might include water and sodium chloride. Extended structures might include ethanol or ammonia. The model assignments might be drawings or computer-generated representations that show a variety of molecules with different atom types.

Determine Chemical Reactions

According to performance expectation MS.PS1.2, students should be able to "analyze and interpret data on the properties of substances before and after the substances interact to determine if a chemical reaction has occurred."

Molecules are created by reactions. These reactions involve all atoms included in the molecules or atoms involved. To deduce that there has been a reaction by the contact of two types of molecules, you must refer back to the bonds that hold these molecules together.

To create a bond between two elements, energy must be taken in by the molecule. This process is called endothermy. To break a bond, energy will be released. Therefore, one of the ways you can deduce that a chemical reaction has occurred is to observe temperature. If there is a temperature increase as a function of adding two molecule substances together, then there is an obvious chemical reaction.

However, not all reactions have temperature changes that are immediately obvious. Other indicators of chemical reactions are things called precipitates. *Precipitates* are a function of two molecules coming together to form two new elements, each with different physical states (solid, liquid, and gas). These two states show an obvious chemical reaction occurrence, as a solid will begin to fall from within the liquid.

FACT

Similar to precipitates is the formation of lattices within liquids, as well as gases released into the air from within the reacting liquid, which may be visible in bubbles.

Your child will analyze and interpret information on the properties of specific substances both before they have interacted, and after an interaction has occurred, to discover whether a chemical reaction has taken place. Reactions that are studied might include heating sugar, mixing hydrogen chloride with zinc, and sodium hydroxide reacting with fat. Your child will analyze properties for density, boiling points, solubility, melting points, odor, and flammability.

Predict Changes in Particles

Performance expectation MS.PS1.4 states that your child should "develop a model that predicts and describes changes in particle motion, temperature, and state of a pure substance when thermal energy is added or removed."

The characteristics of atoms are determined by the subatomic particles that were previously mentioned. These characteristics include things like freezing point, boiling point, and other ways that the element has a change of phase (solid, liquid, gas). Each one of these characteristics is unique to each element, and no two elements are the same (although they can be extremely similar).

In terms of phase change, an element in a pure state (a mass containing only the same atoms or molecules), depending on its characteristics and limits, will be in one of the three states (phases) of matter: solid, liquid, or gas, depending on how much energy has been applied to this mass. This energy is usually thermal, or what we know as heat.

As heat is applied or removed from a substance, the atoms in the substance will either become more excited or more dormant. The less energy these atoms have, the less they will move. As atoms slow down, they begin to take up less space, and will tend to stick together. This is how a substance goes from an excited gaseous state, with dispersed molecules, to a more calm state with condensed molecules in a liquid, to a dormant state with extremely little movement, as the molecules form a solid. Inversely, the heating and energizing of these molecules will cause them to begin to move, and break the mold of a solid, becoming a liquid. As they continue to heat up and gain energy, they break the forces, keeping the liquid molecules together and dispersing into a gas.

To visualize this, you can observe water in our own environment. During the cold seasons, water is cooled below its freezing point, becoming ice. As the season warms the environment, temperatures increase above this point, causing the ice to melt. The heat energy from the environment causes the ice to become liquid water. As you progress toward summer, you see the liquid water evaporate into the air as it becomes a gas (although it has not actually reached its boiling point yet, there are other factors that induce evaporation).

Middle school students will create a model that they will use to predict and describe changes in the motion and temperature of particles. It will also be used to demonstrate the effects that the addition or removal of thermal energy has on a pure substance. The types of models developed might include drawings and diagrams. The particles might include inert atoms and molecules. The pure substances could include helium, water, and carbon dioxide.

Portray Conservation of Mass

According to performance expectation MS.PS1.5, students should be able to "develop and use a model to describe how the total number of atoms does not change in a chemical reaction and thus mass is conserved."

As previously discussed, to indicate that a chemical reaction has occurred, you can observe precipitates as new elements have been formed. However, if you are to weigh the total mass of the products in the reactions, as well as the reactants, you will find that the totals of each are the same. This is thanks to the law of conservation of mass.

Your child might create and use a model to describe how the number of atoms in matter does not change during a chemical reaction and the conservation of mass. The models might include drawings and digital forms.

Test Thermal Energy

Performance expectation MS.PS1.6 states that your child should be able to "undertake a design project to construct, test, and modify a device that either releases or absorbs thermal energy by chemical processes."

In order to understand the process of heat and energy transfer in our universe, we should take a look at real-world examples by creating an experiment. You can do this very simply, by creating a device that uses chemical energy derived from a reaction in order to melt ice. To do this, you must use a small amount of combustible fuel, such as kerosene, and a source of heat, which is best found in fire, usually from a match. You must have an object to contain the heat energy, so you will use a can with the top removed. You then place the ice around the can. As you place the kerosene in the can and light it, you can immediately feel the heat emanating from the flame. Be careful, as this can burn you very easily. As the kerosene undergoes a combustion reaction, it creates heat. The heat then transfers to the walls of the can. As the ice begins to melt, and the kerosene burns to completion, the walls of the can will begin to become cold, as the can begins to absorb the heat energy released from the ice as it melts. Both processes, both chemical and physical (combustion and melting), cause the can to absorb energy that is the result in a change of molecular shape and composition.

Matter Experiment

For this experiment, a question has been provided for you. Work with your child to come up with a hypothesis and then perform the experiment together.

Question

What will happen to the states of matter when sugar, corn syrup, water, and baking soda are placed over a heat source?

Materials

- Baking sheet
- Butter
- Aluminum foil
- 125 mL corn syrup
- 500 mL white sugar
- 60 mL water
- Whisk
- 1 (3-liter) saucepan
- Cooking thermometer
- 10 mL baking soda

Method

1. Grease the baking sheet with butter.
2. Lay aluminum foil over the bottom of the greased baking sheet.
3. Place the corn syrup, sugar, and water into the saucepan. Use the whisk to combine.

4. Place the saucepan onto a burner on the stove, and heat the mixture over medium heat. Place the cooking thermometer into the saucepan so you can easily read the liquid's temperature.
5. Let the mixture heat until all of the sugar has dissolved.
6. Let the mixture come to a boil, but do not stir.
7. When the mixture reaches 150°C, remove the saucepan from the burner.
8. Add the baking soda to the mixture. Whisk it in. Observe the results.
9. Pour the mixture onto the baking sheet, and allow the mixture to cool for 2 hours.
10. Observe and record the results.
11. Divide the mixture into edible pieces. (This is a recipe for sponge toffee. It can be eaten if desired.)

Consider Testing . . .

- What happens if you change the amount of baking soda?
- What happens if you change the amount of sugar?
- What happens if you change the amount of corn syrup?
- What happens if you change the amount of water?
- What happens if you change the heat level?

Let's Review—Checklist

Now that you've covered the important aspects of matter and its interactions, here are some important points to remember as you help your child:

- Moving particles make up matter.
- Matter is anything that has a measurable volume and mass.
- The properties of matter are mass, volume, weight, and density. These properties make it possible to identify and classify matter.
- Density is an intensive property of matter and is the ratio between mass and volume.
- Mass, weight, volume, and density are different and can be measured.
- The physical state of matter is determined by the speed of the particles moving within the substance.

- Physical changes to matter do not create new substances and include boiling, condensation, evaporation, freezing, melting, sublimation, and vaporization. Physical changes can usually be reversed.
- Changes of energy affect the changes of state in matter.
- Chemical changes to matter create new substances that have new properties. Chemical changes are usually irreversible.
- The size of a sample does not affect the properties of a substance; these properties are always constant.
- Mixtures can be separated into their initial substances.
- Matter has specific physical and chemical properties.
- Matter can change chemically and physically.
- Matter is not lost through a chemical reaction but rather changes its form.
- The mass, weight, volume, and density of matter can be measured.
- The Periodic Table of Elements organizes matter by its characteristics and atomic mass.
- The properties of a particular material can create limitations in the product design process.
- Elements are substances that have only one type of atom.
- Elements have specific chemical and physical properties.
- The elements are classified into families on the basis of their properties.
- Elements have characteristic physical and chemical properties.
- Typical reactions will not break down elements.
- When elements are combined, they create new compounds that have characteristic properties.
- Atoms that are kept together through a chemical bond create molecules.
- Compounds are created when substances that have atoms with two or more elements are bonded together to make molecules.
- The physical properties of a substance affect its chemical structure.
- The total weight of a substance does not change even if it has been broken apart or combined with another substance.
- The conservation of matter states that if the total number of atoms remains the same regardless of their arrangement, then the total mass also remains the same.

CHAPTER 8

Motion and Stability—Forces and Interactions

When two different objects are interacting with one another, changes can take place. Your child will need to understand why these changes take place. She will need to understand what creates the changes so that she can describe what is happening and so that she can predict whether the objects are stable or unstable. Forces between objects create change. These forces begin with the interactions that take place because of gravity and electromagnetism. This chapter will describe the concepts of force and what your child will be learning about it.

What Should My Child Already Understand?

By the time your child begins 6th grade, he understands that a force can be a pull or a push. He knows that objects can move in a variety of ways, including backward, forward, slow, and fast. He recognizes that specific forces exerted on an object can change its motion, including its direction and speed. He has learned that the greater the force that is exerted on an object, the greater the change in its motion. He grasps that every force has direction and strength and acts on a specific object.

An object that is at rest usually has several forces acting on it but those forces have a net force of zero. Forces that do not total to zero can result in changes to the speed or direction of motion of a particular object. It is possible to observe and measure the patterns of the motion of an object in different conditions. When an object's past motion has displayed a regular pattern, the future motion of the object can be predicted using the pattern. Objects that are contacting each other are also exerting forces on each other. These forces include elastic pushes and pulls as well as friction.

Objects do not have to be in contact for electric, gravitational, and magnetic forces to function. Magnets can pull an item from a distance. The force size in each situation is based on the properties of the objects and the distance between them. Magnetic force size is also based on the orientation of each object relative to the other. The earth's gravitational force acts on objects near its surface and pulls the object toward the center of the planet.

FACT

Gravity is the force that makes all of the planets in the solar system orbit the sun. It also keeps the moon rotating around the earth. The force of gravity on the earth is six times greater than gravity on the moon. If a person weighed 66 kilograms on the earth, he would weigh only 11 kilograms on the moon. The gravity on the earth is greater because the earth is a hundred times larger in mass than the moon.

Disciplinary Core Ideas

The following components have been established by the Next Generation Science Standards as some of the important points of understanding in studying force and motion. Following are some of the topics your child will learn about and discuss in school.

Force and Motion

How can you predict how stable an object is? How can you determine whether its movement will continue or change? In any changes of motion, the mass of the object must be qualitatively clarified due to the force's application. When pairs of objects interact, the force that is exerted by one object on the other is equal to the force that is exerted by the other object, in the opposite direction. This is referred to as Newton's third law. You can determine the motion of a particular object by calculating the sum of the forces that are acting on it. If the total force on a particular object is not zero, then there will be a change in its motion. The greater the mass of a particular object, the greater the force necessary to make the same changes in motion. Regardless of the particular object, a greater force results in a greater change in its motion. It is necessary to describe every position of an object along with the directions of motions and forces in a randomly chosen frame of reference and size units. When sharing the data, the choices must be shared as well.

Types of Interactions

Which forces explain the activities that take place between particular objects? All of the forces between objects begin with electromagnetism, gravity, or nuclear interactions. When objects collide, the forces acting between them can create changes in the movements of these objects. When objects are in contact, they exert their forces on one another. Forces that function at a distance use fields that you can map by the relative effects and strength of them on a particular object. Electric and magnetic forces are referred to as being electromagnetic.

ALERT

The mass of an object is not the same as the weight of an object. The mass of a particular object remains constant wherever it may be in the universe because the amount of mass within an object never changes. Weight is the force of gravity pulling on an object. So weight changes depending on where in the universe an object might be and the pull of gravity that is acting on it.

Electromagnetic forces can attract or repel. The size of electromagnetic forces is based on the magnitude of the currents, charges, or magnetic powers that are involved, as well as the distances that exist between the objects that are interacting. All gravitational forces are attractive. A gravitational force exists between any two masses. This force is quite small except when the mass of at least one of the objects is quite large, as is the case with the sun and the earth.

Key Force and Motion Terms

These terms are important to a solid understanding of force and motion:

- Acceleration—The amount an object increases or decreases its speed, or changes direction. It measures the rate of change of velocity or speed as it relates to time.
- Centripetal Force—The force that is exerted on an object that is moving in a curvilinear motion and is being directed to the center of curvature. This force makes an object move in a circular motion.
- Force—A pull or a push that is exerted on an object (force has direction and size).
- Friction—The opposite force that is exerted by one surface on another when two surfaces are rubbing together.
- Gravity—The force that attracts two objects together. Its strength is based on the mass of the objects and the distance between them.
- Inertia—An object's resistance to a change in motion. A body at rest stays at rest; a body in motion stays in motion unless a force acts on it and changes its motion.
- Mass—The amount of matter within an object.
- Motion—A change in the position or place of an object.
- Newton's Laws—The three laws discovered by Sir Isaac Newton that define and describe force and motion. These three laws are the foundation of mechanics.
- Speed—The distance an object moves from a point of reference over a specific unit of time.
- Vector—A quantity that measures both magnitude and direction. It is represented with an arrow symbol.

- Velocity—The speed of a particular object in a specific direction.
- Weight—The measure of the gravitational force on a particular object.

ESSENTIAL

Normal force is a support force that is applied when one object comes into contact with something else that is stable. For example, a plate sitting on a table is supported by the normal force of the table. The table is exerting an upward normal force on the plate.

Key Force and Motion Concepts

Force and motion are important to science and everyday life. Motion is what happens when you move from one place to another, and force is what causes the movement to occur.

Force and Motion Q&A

Q: How can we describe the motion of an object?
A: Motion is described as a change in distance between one object and another object. Example: A horse running across a field.

Q: What is speed and velocity?
A: Speed refers to the distance an object moves over a specific period of time. Velocity refers to the speed that an object travels in a specific direction. Example: The speed at which a horse is running across a field.

Q: What is distance and displacement?
A: Distance refers to the amount of space an object travels or how far it goes. Displacement refers to the direction and change in position of an object. Example: The length from one town to another town.

Q: How do we calculate speed and velocity?
A: We calculate speed by dividing the distance an object traveled by the time it took to get there (distance/time = speed). We calculate the

velocity of an object by dividing the change in position of an object by the time it took to get there (displacement/time = velocity). Example: Traveling 5 miles in 5 hours would mean your speed was 1 mile per hour (mph). Traveling 5 miles in 5 hours north would mean your northbound velocity was 1 mph.

Q: How are speed and velocity different?
A: Speed is a measurement that describes only how fast an object is moving. Velocity is a measurement that describes both the speed of an object and its direction.

Q: What is acceleration?
A: Acceleration measures the amount an object is speeding up, slowing down, or changing its direction. It refers to the rate of change of the speed or the velocity of a particular object. Example: How fast it takes a car to go from not moving, to moving as fast as it can.

Q: Are there different types of acceleration?
A: There are four different types of acceleration: constant, nonconstant, positive, and negative. Constant acceleration happens when the velocity of an object is changing over equal increases in time. Non-constant acceleration is when the velocity of an object is changing over unequal increases in time. Positive acceleration occurs when an object speeds up. Negative acceleration happens when an object slows down.

Examples: Constant acceleration would come from a car with the pedal firmly pressed to the floor. Non-constant would come from a car with the pedal gradually pressed over time. Positive acceleration would come from a car accelerating from a still position. Negative acceleration would come from a car braking to a stop.

Q: How do we calculate acceleration?
A: We calculate acceleration by dividing the change in velocity by time (change in velocity/time = acceleration). Example: The change in speed of a sprinter from his starting position to 10 meters into his run.

Q: What is a force?

A: A force is a push or pull that acts on a particular object or a group of objects. A force can be measured for both its direction and magnitude. Example: How hard you swing a baseball bat.

Q: How do we calculate force?

A: We calculate force by multiplying mass by acceleration (mass × acceleration = force). Example: A runner's force is equal to his mass times how fast he is accelerating.

Q: What does mass have to do with an object?

A: The mass of an object is the amount of matter that is contained within it. Example: How much gas is contained inside of our sun.

Q: Which force is opposite to motion?

A: Friction is a force that is opposite to motion. It happens when two objects are rubbing against one another. Each object exerts a force over the other, causing a change in the movement of the objects. Example: The skid marks on the street are caused by friction between the road and car tires.

Q: What is gravity?

A: Gravity is a force that attracts and pulls two objects together. The strength of this force is based on the mass of the objects and the distance between them. Here on earth, the force of gravity pulls objects down toward the center of the planet. Example: Gravity is the force that makes apples fall from trees.

Q: What does weight have to do with an object?

A: Weight is the measurement of the force of gravity that is being exerted on the mass of an object. You measure weight by multiplying the mass of an object by its acceleration. Example: Your weight is equal to your mass multiplied by the force of gravity.

Q: What is a scalar quantity?

A: A scalar quantity refers to the amount of measurement only. Length, mass, speed, and temperature are scalar quantities because they refer to the amount of measurement only. Example: The height of a tree.

Q: What is a vector quantity?

A: A vector quantity refers to both the amount of measurement and direction. Acceleration, force, and velocity are vector quantities because they refer to both the amount of measurement and direction. Example: The rate of speed at which a plane is traveling west.

Q: Who was Sir Isaac Newton?

A: Sir Isaac Newton was an influential physicist and mathematician whose discoveries became the principles of modern physics.

Q: What are Newton's Laws of Motion?

A: Newton's first law of motion states that an object that is at rest will stay at rest, and an object that is moving at a velocity that is constant will keep moving at that velocity, unless an unbalanced force acts on it. This is referred to as the law of inertia. Newton's second law of motion states that the acceleration of an object is based on its mass and the net force acting on it. Newton's third law states that if two objects are exerting forces on each other, the strength of the force of the second object is equal and opposite to the strength of the force of the first object.

Q: What is net force?

A: The total net force is the sum of all of the forces that are acting on an object. If there is a net force that is greater than zero Newtons, then the object will move. If there is a net force of zero, the object will not move. Example: Particles stand still in space because the net forces acting on them are zero.

Q: When forces are balanced, what happens to an object?

A: When forces are balanced, the movement of an object will remain the same. If it is resting, it will stay resting. If it is moving, it will continue moving at a velocity that is constant. Example: A wall does not topple over because the forces acting on it are balanced.

Q: When forces are unbalanced, what happens to an object?
A: When forces are unbalanced, the movement of an object will change. The object will change either its direction or its speed. Example: When the friction force of a car's tires are greater than that of its forward motion, the friction force will cause opposite directional force until the car is stopped.

Q: Which tools do we use to measure force and motion?
A: In order to measure force and motion, you need to use specific tools and units of measure. You determine distance and length with a metric ruler or a meter stick that measures in millimeters, centimeters, meters, or kilometers. You determine mass with a triple beam balance that measures in milligrams, grams, and kilograms. You determine force using a spring scale that measures in Newtons.

FACT

Magnets create a force called a magnetic field that attracts specific types of metal. Cobalt, iron, and nickel are all types of metal that are attracted to magnets. Aluminum, copper, gold, silver, and platinum are not attracted to magnets but can become somewhat magnetized if they are within a magnetic field.

Science and Engineering Practices

In learning about motion and stability, your child will use science and engineering practices to better understand the ideas that relate to forces and interactions. These practices might include:

- Asking questions before planning and carrying out investigations that determine how force, mass, and speed relate.
- Using force diagram models to describe whether an object is moving or not.

- Analyzing and interpreting data about distance and time through the calculation of the speed of an object.
- Designing solutions that make an object increase the speed and reduce the friction of its movement.
- Engaging in arguments using support from graphs that explain Newton's second law that force equals mass times acceleration.
- Obtaining, evaluating, and communicating a strong understanding of the connection between motion and force.

Next Generation Science Standards Performance Expectations

These performance expectations describe what your child should be able to demonstrate and understand about the specific science unit he is studying in middle school. From these expectations your child's teachers will determine how successfully he understands and can apply the concepts that have been covered.

The Problem of Colliding Objects

According to performance expectation MS.PS2.1, your child should be able to "apply Newton's third law to design a solution to a problem involving the motion of two colliding objects."

Newton's third law states that every action has an equal and opposite reaction. For every force exerted in the universe, there is a counterforce pushing back against it. Therefore, this property allows you to break down the concepts of forces that you observe in your life. For example, you notice basic forces exerted between two humans. If two similar (same mass, height, strength) persons stand next to each other, and one pushes the other with a considerable amount of force, then the person pushed will be knocked back by the force of the pusher, and the pusher will feel the recoil of his strike.

However, due to the fact that mechanical (human) force is proportional to mass, you find that when a larger object or being exerts force on that of a smaller one, recoiling forces are negligible. This is thanks to the equation of forces (force = mass × acceleration). A more massive object or person will absorb greater amounts of force than that of a smaller one. This is why people view trains and transport trucks to be more dangerous than regular cars and trucks, even if they are traveling at an equal, or potentially slower, rate. These large vehicles pose a hazard to others due to their massive size and weight, being able to negate impact forces in accidents and barrel on through collisions.

ESSENTIAL

Applied force is a type of force that is exerted on an object. This force can be a push or a pull and can be applied by a person or another object. A person that is pulling a wagon is exerting an applied force on the wagon.

We can investigate this information by testing it. Students will place textbooks of equal weight one by one on two separate carts. They will then collide these carts from a distance of one meter, and record the results based upon the cart distance after the collision and the number of textbooks on each cart at the point of impact. Students will find in their results that carts containing more textbooks (mass) will absorb more force and travel farther, pushing through opposing forces, than those of smaller mass.

Middle school students will apply Newton's third law to solve a problem that involves the motion of two colliding objects. The problem might include the impact of two colliding cars, between one car and an object that is not moving, and between a space vehicle and a meteor moving through space.

Prove Force Affects Motion

Performance expectation MS.PS2.2 states that students should "plan an investigation to provide evidence that the change in an object's motion depends on the sum of the forces on the object and the mass of the object."

Further expanding on the topic and lessons learned about forces in the last segment, students will now turn their focus to direction and motion pertaining to forces. Everything on our planet is affected by forces, whether they be mechanical, electromagnetic, magnetic, gravitational, and so on. Forces are a part of our everyday lives, and not just the force of gravity, which keeps our feet firmly planted on the ground. This is especially true in terms of motion. Without the amount of force required to break counterforces as seen in the previous section, there would be no motion in the universe.

ALERT

Inertia is a property of matter, not a force. This property will resist any change in movement whenever a force is applied to it. Any object that has mass will slow down from its weight. The more mass an object has, the more inertia it has, and the more force is required to get it to move.

For humans, we must use the force of friction on the ground we walk on to gain enough traction to move forward against the force of gravity, wind, etc. Without the combined force of friction and the force exerted by our bodies, we would not be able to move. The sum of these forces gives us motion. If we have one without the other, we wouldn't be going anywhere anytime soon. Without our bodies to move us, we would stand still and stiff. Without friction, we would do nothing but slip and slide all over the material we were standing on, but in no particular direction.

This applies to static (non-moving) objects as well. For example, for a wall to stand straight up and down, it must have forces acting upon it at all times to keep it balanced. Mostly this is downward force due to mass.

To test this, students will experiment with the sum of forces on an object. A Styrofoam block will be placed in between four students, who will all equally push on this block centrally. The demonstrator will then have students carefully be removed from applying forces to show that the block will fall over due to forces not being in summated equilibrium.

Your child will plan an investigation to provide proof that the sum of the forces on a particular object along with its mass will directly impact the motion of that object. Students will work with balanced and unbalanced forces as well as qualitative comparisons of mass, forces, and changes in motion.

Determine Electric and Magnetic Forces

According to performance expectation MS.PS2.3, students should be able to "ask questions about data to determine the factors that affect the strength of electric and magnetic forces."

With regards to electricity, you should refer back to the concepts of atoms and their structure. The term electricity is derived from the word electron. This is due to properties of electricity stemming from the behavior of electrons. Electric current comes from the flow of electrons through a substance. Electricity has the potential to flow through all elements and materials. However, certain elements are more conductive than others. This depends on many factors, such as molecular and atomic structure. Certain types of molecules can increase the conductivity of other molecules.

For instance, we think of water as a dangerous substance to introduce electricity to; for example, bathtub electrocution could occur. However, this is due to molecules called electrolytes, not water. Pure water molecules have very little conductivity. A container of nothing but pure H_2O water molecules would not conduct electricity at all. However, when humans, as well as soaps, are introduced, acids, salts, and bases from the body and chemicals allow electrolytes to increase the conductivity of the water, making it dangerous.

Magnetic forces, however, have two vastly different characteristics to take into account. Magnetism is the attractive force emanated by a particular object composed of specific substances. The earth itself has a magnetic field, and certain elements have stronger magnetic forces than others. Neodymium, for instance, is a rare earth metal used to make permanent magnets.

Every magnet has a north pole and south pole. If you put two magnets together so that the north poles were close together, the magnets would repel and push away from each other. If you put two magnets together so that the north pole and the south pole were close together, the magnets would attract and pull together.

But what is a permanent magnet? A permanent magnet is a magnet that has a constant magnetic field. This is in comparison to an electromagnet. Electromagnetism is the process of creating a magnetic field around a metal by passing electrons through it.

For example, by wrapping copper wire (which has a high conductivity) around a metallic core that has a low amount of carbon, and by flowing a great deal of electric current through the wire, you can create a magnetic field around the core, with strength depending on the amount of electric current flowing through the wire.

Students will pose questions about information to determine the factors that influence the strength of magnetic and electric forces. The devices they might use include electric motors, electromagnets, and generators. The data collected could include the impact that the number of wire turns has on an electromagnet, or the impact that the strength and number of magnets might have on an electric motor's speed.

Prove That Gravity Depends on Mass

According to performance expectation MS.PS2.4, students should "construct and present arguments using evidence to support the claim that gravitational interactions are attractive and depend on the masses of interacting objects."

Gravity is one of the many laws of our universe that depend on certain characteristics of objects. Much like magnetism, gravity causes other objects to be drawn toward the central object that has a gravitational pull. But what causes objects to have gravity?

The answer to this is mass. The more mass an object has, the greater gravitational pull it will have. By nature, all objects, including humans, have a magnetic pull. However, being as small as we are compared to other things in our universe, our pull is negligible. To have a pull that is noticeable in the universe, an object must have great mass.

Our moon, for instance, has its own gravitational pull, though not as strong as the earth's due to its mass not being as great (thankfully, because if these two masses were equal, they would collide catastrophically); however, our moon still has enough gravitational force to influence the tides on earth, which change with the rise and fall of earth's only natural satellite.

To prove that mass is the culprit for gravitational force, we can turn to our own solar system and galaxy for evidence. As planets orbit our sun, they have their own gravitational pull, which allows for them to have moons held in orbit due to gravity. In this same way, the planets in the system orbit the sun, which is considerably more massive than all of the planets in the system. This shows that gravity is dependent on mass.

However, further proof is shown by our galaxy, which features a super-massive black hole in the center, causing all systems in the galaxy to orbit it as the gravitational pull of the hole inches each system closer to destruction. Unlike other massive centers of orbit, the black hole is so great that nothing in our galaxy can escape its pull.

If we would like to visualize such a concept, the best way to do this would be to use a trampoline. If we imagine that the trampoline is the fabric of our universe, and that people on the trampoline are massive objects within it, we can see the effects of gravity. As more and more mass (people) are placed in a concentrated area of the trampoline, the material begins to sag and deepen. As a deeper rift occurs, other masses on the trampoline will begin to shift toward this increasing depth. If too much mass is concentrated, the fabric of the trampoline would rip, and much like a black hole, all matter would be sucked into and through the hole.

Your child will build and present arguments using proof as support of a claim that gravitational interactions are both attractive and depend on the individual masses of the interacting objects. The evidence used might include charts displaying the strength of the interactions, and data generated from digital simulations.

Prove Objects Exert Force Without Touching

Performance expectation MS.PS2.5 states that your child should "conduct an investigation and evaluate the experimental design to provide evidence that fields exist between objects exerting forces on each other even though the objects are not in contact."

To test on a smaller scale the existence of fields between non-contacting objects, you can perform a minor electromagnetic experiment. Using an AA battery, a nail, some metal filings, and copper wire, you can illustrate how the electromagnet process works. You must first wind the copper wire from the base of the nail to the top, making sure that your windings (coils) are tight. By removing slack, you allow more electrons to circulate around the nail due to the conductivity of the wire. The more electrons there are, the greater the magnetic field. As you attach the battery to the system, you induce a field. Therefore, by placing the now magnetized nail next to the filings, the filings will become attracted, and stick to the nail. When you remove the source of the electrons, the current will be removed, and the magnetic force will stop, causing the filings to fall off.

Furthermore, if you are to take the ends of the battery and flip them, you will change the behavior of the magnetic field. By reversing the polarity of the magnet, you will still induce a field. However, this time, instead of attracting forces, the field generated will have a repulsion force. Now when the magnetized nail is placed near the filings, the filings will seem to shy away from the nail, getting out of the way whenever the nail is near. This is due to the repulsion force pushing the filings.

Middle school students will conduct an investigation and analyze the experimental design to provide proof that fields do exist between objects that are exerting forces on each other even if there is no contact between them. These investigations might include simulations and involve the interactions of electrically charged objects and magnets.

Forces and Motion Experiment

For this experiment, a question has been provided for you. Work with your child to come up with a hypothesis and then perform the experiment together.

Question

How does the ramp affect the movement of the car?

Materials

- Cardboard box
- Scissors
- Toy car
- 5 books
- Scotch tape
- Timer
- Measuring tape

Method

1. Use the cardboard box to create a ramp for your car: Using the scissors, cut the box into a long strip of cardboard that is wide enough for the car.
2. Stack your books into a pile on the floor, preferably on a floor without carpeting.
3. Attach one end of your cardboard ramp to the top of the book pile with tape so that the other end is able to reach the floor.
4. Place your car at the top of the ramp.
5. Set your timer.
6. Start the timer as you let go of the car.
7. Measure the time it takes until the car stops moving after going down the ramp and onto the floor. When the car stops, stop the timer.
8. Use measuring tape to measure how far the car travels when it comes off the ramp.
9. Record the results.

Consider Testing . . .

- What happens when you add more books to the pile, and the angle of the ramp incline is changed?
- What happens when you add fabric to the surface of the ramp? (Try gluing strips of fabric to the cardboard ramp.)
- What happens when you use a larger toy car?

Let's Review—Checklist

To help your child in her studies, there are several key points you'll need to remember on the concepts of forces and interactions:

- You can describe an object's motion in a variety of ways, including acceleration, deceleration, direction, position, and speed.
- You relate the motion of a particular object to a frame of reference.
- You can graphically analyze motion using speed in reference to time and distance relating to time graphs.
- You can assume that when an object's mass remains constant, the greater the force that is applied to it, the greater its motion will change.

- More massive objects require larger forces to change their motion.
- When you want to change the motion of an object, you have to apply a force to it. This is called Newton's first law. It is also called the law of inertia.
- A force that acts on a particular object can change the orientation and shape of that object.
- You can calculate the magnitude of an object's motion change with this equation: Force equals mass times acceleration, or $F = ma$. This is referred to as Newton's second law.
- You measure force in Newtons, mass in grams, and acceleration in m/s^2.
- When two objects are interacting and object one exerts force on object two, object two exerts an equal and opposite force on object one. This is referred to as Newton's third law.
- You have to take into account properties of materials, construction techniques, engineering principles, and scientific laws when you design solutions to problems.
- Friction is an opposite force that results in speed changes of a particular object.
- Forces that are acting in the same direction reinforce each other, and forces that are acting in opposing directions cancel each other out.
- Forces that are unbalanced have a net force of zero.
- Unbalanced forces cause objects to change their motion, including direction and speed.
- You can determine the motion of a particular object by the sum of all of the forces that are acting on it.
- You can use force diagrams to represent the motion and forces on an object.
- An object will change its motion if the total force that is acting on it is not equal to zero.
- There are various types of forces, including electric, electromagnetic, gravitational, magnetic, and nuclear.
- Gravity is a force that always attracts.
- The strength of gravity is based on the mass of the interacting objects.
- Objects with a greater mass have a strong gravitational force.
- Some forces can act from a distance.
- Forces can lead to stability and instability in particular physical systems.

CHAPTER 9

Energy

You can better understand the interactions of particular objects by taking a look at the energy that is transferred from one object to another. Energy can only be transferred; it cannot be destroyed. The energy of an object changes only when it transfers into or out of that particular object.

What Should My Child Already Understand?

By the time your child reaches middle school, he should have a basic understanding of energy and its properties. Some things he will already know include:

- Magnets attract and repel each other and certain kinds of other materials.
- A magnet can exert a force on another magnet or magnetized material resulting in a transfer of energy between the objects even though they are not in contact with each other.
- A warmer object can warm a cooler object by direct contact or at a distance. When two objects of different temperatures are near each other, the cooler one becomes warmer and the warmer one becomes cooler until they are the same temperature.
- Heat is transferred from a warmer object to a cooler one.
- Heating and cooling change the properties of materials.
- The faster a particular object moves, the more energy it has.
- Energy can be moved from one place to another through the movement of objects, or through electric currents, light, or sound. Wherever there are objects in motion, heat, light, or sound, energy is also there.
- When objects collide, energy can transfer from one object to the other, which in turn can change the movement of both objects. In these collisions, some of the energy also transfers to the air around the objects, which causes the air to heat and sound to be produced. Light can also transfer from one place to another.

FACT

The amount of kinetic energy in an object stays the same unless it slows down or speeds up. Kinetic energy occurs in any direction that an object is moving. So long as you know the mass of a particular object and its speed, you can calculate its kinetic energy. Students are learning more about the relationship between kinetic energy and the mass of an object. They learn that as the mass doubles, so does the kinetic energy, and that as the mass halves, so does the kinetic energy. The equation for kinetic energy is $KE = \frac{1}{2} mv^2$.

Energy from the sun is transferred as light to the earth. This light is then absorbed and warms the air, land, and water, enabling plants to grow. Energy can transfer from one place to another through electric currents.

This energy can be used to create heat, light, and sound. The transformation of motion energy from electrical energy can generate electric currents.

Disciplinary Core Ideas

The following concepts have been established by the Next Generation Science Standards as some of the important points of understanding in studying energy. Following are some of the topics your child will learn about and discuss in school.

Definitions of Energy

Just what is energy anyway? While energy is the ability to do work, it is difficult to give it one simple definition because it has many different forms. Each type of energy is either kinetic or potential. You can track changes in energy from and to each type through chemical and physical interactions. The relationship between the total energy and the temperature of a specific system is based on the amounts, states, and types of matter. Motion energy is referred to as *kinetic energy*. Kinetic energy corresponds to the mass of an object in motion and grows with its rate of speed squared.

A system of objects can have stored energy based on their relative positions. This stored energy is also referred to as *potential energy*. Temperature measures the mean kinetic energy of matter particles. The word heat that we use in our daily language refers to radiation and thermal motion (or the motion of molecules or atoms inside a substance). The term heat that is used in science refers to the energy that is transferred when two systems or two objects are at differing temperature levels.

Conservation of Energy and Energy Transfer

What does conservation of energy mean and how does energy become transferred? Energy transfers occur in all forms; from the physical, to the observable (light), and those that occur from temperature. Other changes in energy occur in an object when its motion energy changes. An energy transfer must occur to change the temperature of matter by a specific amount. The amount of energy transfer that is needed is based on the nature, size, and environment of the matter. Energy automatically transfers into colder objects or regions from hotter ones.

Relationship Between Energy and Forces

How do energy and forces relate to each other? When there is an interaction between two objects, each of the objects exerts force on the other one. The forces between two interacting objects are able to transfer energy between the objects.

ALERT

Heat is a form of energy, not a substance. Temperature is not a property of an object or a material. An object within specific temperature conditions will gain the same temperature level. Cold is not the opposite of heat; cold is the absence of heat.

Key Energy Terms

These terms are important to a strong understanding of energy:

- Acceleration—The speed an object moves in a specific direction.
- Conservation of Energy—The law of conservation of energy states that energy can be transferred and transformed but never destroyed.
- Energy—The ability to do work.
- Energy Transfer—The process of moving energy from one object to another.
- Energy Transformation—The change of energy from one form to another.
- Force—The size and direction of a push or pull.
- Forms of Energy—There are several forms of energy, including chemical, electrical, light, sound, and thermal.

  1. Chemical: The energy of a compound that changes as its atoms are rearranged to make a new compound; a form of potential energy.
  2. Electrical: The energy of electrical charges.
  3. Light: The energy produced by the vibrations of electrically charged particles.
  4. Sound: The energy caused by an object's vibrations.

- Kinetic Energy—Energy of motion; based on the speed and mass of an object.

- Mechanical Energy—An object's total energy. It is the energy of motion plus the energy of position of a particular object. The formula for calculating mechanical energy is kinetic energy plus potential energy equals mechanical energy.
- Potential Energy—Energy of position.
- Speed/Velocity—Measurements of the rate of movement of an object. Speed is based on the distance traveled, and velocity is based on the speed and direction of movement.
- Wave—The vibration transfer of energy from one location to another.
- Work—Action that takes place when a force makes an object move in a particular direction.

ESSENTIAL

Energy can be separated into two groups: kinetic and potential. Kinetic energy is of movement. Any object that is moving has kinetic energy. Kinetic energy is based on an object's mass and velocity. Potential energy is energy that is stored in an object based on its specific position.

Key Energy Concepts

Energy is everywhere. Everything that has been produced needed energy to make it happen. It is an essential part of life.

Energy Q&A

Q: What is energy?
A: Energy is used by every living organism every day to be able to do anything. Energy is the power that creates change. It is defined as the ability to do work.

Q: How is energy categorized?
A: There are several forms of energy that are divided into two categories: working and stored. Working energy is referred to as kinetic energy, and stored energy is referred to as potential. Kinetic energy relates to the speed of a particular object. Potential energy relates to an object's height above a point of reference.

Q: What forms of kinetic energy are there?

A: Kinetic energy involves atoms, electrons, molecules, objects, substances, and waves. Kinetic energy includes electrical, motion, radiant, sound, and thermal. Electrical energy is created through charged electrons that move through wires. Motion energy involves the energy stored in moving objects. When objects move faster, there is more energy stored within them. Wind is a form of motion energy. Radiant energy involves electromagnetic energy that moves through transverse waves and includes light, sunshine, radio, and x-rays. Sound involves energy moving through waves. This energy is generated when a force makes an object vibrate. Thermal energy involves heat. This energy is generated through vibrating and moving atoms and molecules contained in substances. When heat is applied to an object, the atoms and molecules within it begin to move faster and collide. Geothermal energy is generated from the center of the earth.

Q: What forms of potential energy are there?

A: Potential energy involves energy related to position and stored energy. Potential energy includes chemical, gravitational, mechanical, and nuclear. Chemical energy involves energy that is stored within the bonds of molecules and atoms. Natural gas, batteries, and biomass are forms of chemical energy. Gravitational energy involves energy that is stored in the height of an object. The higher the position of an object, the more energy is stored within it. A waterfall is a form of gravitational energy. Mechanical energy involves energy that is stored in an object through tension. Stretched elastics are a form of mechanical energy. Nuclear energy involves the energy stored in an atom's nucleus that holds it together.

Q: What is the law of conservation of energy?

A: The law of conservation of energy states that energy cannot be created or destroyed; it can only be transformed.

Q: What is energy transformation?

A: Energy transformation refers to the change of energy from one type to another. For instance, when people eat food, they take in chemical energy. They then use the energy in daily activities through motion energy. Plants take in the sun through radiant energy, then process and use it through chemical energy. Car drivers buy gasoline to put in their cars to be used as chemical energy. This energy is changed to motion energy as the car moves. Electrical energy is used to make an oven work. The oven then transforms the energy to thermal energy to cook food.

Q: What are natural resources?
A: Natural resources are materials that occur naturally and that are used by people. Examples of natural resources include the sun, air, water, wood, wind, waves, and minerals.

Q: What are renewable resources?
A: Energy sources are either renewable or nonrenewable. Renewable energy can be easily replaced. These sources include biomass, geothermal, hydropower, solar, and wind energy. Biomass energy comes from plants. Geothermal energy comes from the heat within the earth. Hydropower is generated from hydroelectricity.

Q: What are nonrenewable resources?
A: Nonrenewable energy cannot be replaced. These sources include fossil fuels and uranium. Fossil fuels are generated from the forces of heat and pressure on the remains of living organisms over millions of years.

Q: What is photosynthesis?
A: Plants are living organisms and need energy to move, transform glucose into energy, react to their environment, produce offspring, excrete waste, and make food. Plants use sunlight to make food. Solar energy is trapped in the leaves of the plant and is transformed through the process of photosynthesis. The energy from the plants is transferred to animals that eat the plants. Photosynthesis starts with carbon dioxide and water that plants take in through their leaves. The plants use energy they get from the sun to turn the carbon dioxide and water into glucose. As the glucose is made, oxygen is also generated. Some of the oxygen is released into the air that living organisms

breathe in. Photosynthesis occurs in the green leaves of plants. The leaves contain chlorophyll, which absorbs the light from the sun.

Q: What is cellular respiration?

A: Through photosynthesis, plants produce glucose. This glucose is turned into energy through the process of respiration. Cellular respiration refers to the process where cells release energy from food molecules and then use that energy for the functions of life. Every living organism experiences cellular respiration, which can be either aerobic or anaerobic. Aerobic cellular respiration utilizes oxygen and thus creates a greater amount of energy. There is no oxygen involved in anaerobic cellular respiration but energy is still produced.

FACT

An object gains kinetic energy when it begins to move faster or it gains mass. Speed and mass have different effects on the increase in kinetic energy. An object that doubles in mass will double its kinetic energy. An object that doubles its speed will quadruple its kinetic energy.

Science and Engineering Practices

In learning about energy, your child will use science and engineering practices to better understand the ideas that relate to energy transfer and energy conservation. These practices might include:

- Asking and answering questions to understand how energy moves.
- Developing and using models to show that the movement of heat is predictable.
- Planning and carrying out investigations to discover how heat moves in a particular system.
- Analyzing and interpreting data to find out the causes and results of heat movement.
- Using mathematics to create graphs, histograms, and tables, and to calculate energy transfer.

- Designing solutions to increase the efficiency of a heating system in a home or school.
- Engaging in an argument using evidence collected through an investigation on which design solution was best and why.
- Obtaining, evaluating, and communicating information that explains the law of conservation of energy.

Next Generation Science Standards Performance Expectations

These performance expectations describe what your child should be able to demonstrate and understand about the specific science unit he is studying in middle school. From these expectations your child's teachers will determine how successfully he understands and can apply the concepts that have been covered.

Show the Relation of Kinetic Energy to Mass and Speed

According to Performance expectation MS.PS3.1, your child should be able to "construct and interpret graphical displays of data to describe the relationships of kinetic energy to the mass of an object and to the speed of an object."

Kinetic energy is a function directly related to the forces discussed earlier. Kinetic energy is the measurement of energy that an object has in motion. It is given by the equation: Kinetic Energy (KE) = one half times the product of mass times velocity squared. Obviously, then, we see that mass is the most major component of this equation. Objects with the most mass will have the most energy, given that both objects are moving at a constant speed. For example, if two vehicles were traveling down a road at the same speed, the larger one will have more kinetic energy than the other. A transport truck will have more energy than a compact car, and in this way, you can see the danger of the accidents between such differences in mass. A collision between these two vehicles will not end in a standstill, as the more massive and higher-energy truck will barrel through the accident without stopping, as opposed to the smaller vehicle, which will be stopped instantaneously.

Students will build and interpret graphical displays of information to describe the relationships between kinetic energy and object mass or object speed. Focus is on separately describing relationships between kinetic energy and speed, and kinetic energy and mass. Examples might include rolling balls of varying sizes downhill, and riding a bike at varying speeds.

Research Potential Energy

Performance expectation MS.PS3.2 states that students should "develop a model to describe that when the arrangement of objects interacting at a distance changes, different amounts of potential energy are stored in the system."

ESSENTIAL

Gravitational energy is a type of potential energy. An object's mass and height off of the ground affect the amount of gravitational potential energy it has. As its mass and its height off the ground increase, so does its gravitational potential energy.

Directly related to kinetic energy is potential energy. Potential energy is the energy that an object has when at rest. When objects are not in motion, the main component of their energy is still their mass, but this is multiplied by how high they are from the ground, as well as the acceleration of gravity. Due to gravity with relation to height not being constant throughout the universe, we focus more attention on the mass of an object in relation to its potential energy. The function of potential energy is the attractive force of gravity. Therefore, you find varying potential energies throughout the globe, as different areas of our planet have different heights, also known as altitudes. These two variables, mass and height, give different potential energies to different natural occurrences throughout the world. This is true for events like avalanches, volcanoes, and even rain. These different natural precipitates and projectiles have great potential energies due to their heights and masses, even in rain, which has great energy relative to its size.

Your child will develop a model to describe how the change in object arrangement interactions at a distance causes them to store varying amounts of potential energy in the system. She will develop a model to describe that when the arrangement of objects interacting at a distance changes, different amounts of potential energy are stored in the system. Examples might include a roller-coaster car at different positions on a track or books at varying heights on a shelf. Models might include diagrams, written descriptions, and pictures.

Experiment with Thermal Energy Transfer

According to Performance expectation MS.PS3.3, your child will "apply scientific principles to design, construct, and test a device that either minimizes or maximizes thermal energy transfer."

Some of the factors that influence motion in our universe tie back into what you learned about atomic character. Specifically, temperature—a function of energy and proponent that correlates with a substance's characteristics such as boiling and freezing point—influences all aspects of our everyday environment.

What you must focus on, then, is how temperature influences substances in an environment, and how that environment applies heat energy to the substance. For example, a humid day feels hotter due to a greater concentration of water vapor in the air, which applies more heat to the body, even though the air temperature stays the same. Due to the water vapor, different levels of heat energy are transferred in the air. The water vapor acts as an insulator. This is the same concept that we see in coffee mugs and cups, as the material around the liquid slows the rate of heat dissipation, keeping the liquid at the temperature it currently is, either hot or cold, for longer.

To demonstrate, you can create a device that will minimize the loss of heat. The simplest way to do this is to use a refractor with an insulator. By placing tinfoil within Styrofoam, you can keep a hot object hot for longer periods of time than just simple insulation foam. You can use this device, in comparison with regular Styrofoam, to see how adding or subtracting different elements to and from insulators can alter the amount of insulation a device has.

Your child will apply some of the principles of science to design, build, and evaluate a device that maximizes or minimizes the transfer of thermal energy. Some of the devices might include a solar cooker or an insulated container.

Investigate Energy Transfer

Performance expectation MS.PS3.4 states that your child will "plan an investigation to determine the relationships among the energy transferred, the type of matter, the mass, and the change in the average kinetic energy of the particles as measured by the temperature of the sample."

To tie in all of the information your child will learn about temperature and potential and kinetic energies, it is good to look at a system that incorporates all of these aspects. The best way to do this is to turn to nature. If you look at the water cycle in your environment, you can see how energies and temperature affect the precipitates you see in nature.

FACT

The term potential energy refers to the potential of the stored energy being used at some point. The potential energy of a moving object increases when it begins to slow down. When the object begins to speed up, its potential energy is reduced.

The potential energy of the water you see in rain begins very low, as precipitates in the sky begin their life as frozen water lattices in the clouds. Due to the small mass of the crystals, the potential energy is not great within the precipitate. However, as the water falls from the sky and transfers into kinetic energy, the speed of the slow-falling snow keeps energy low, and thanks to the heat energy of the system, the frozen water will turn to liquid, which has a higher concentration than the crystal. Although the mass does not change, as the snow becomes a water droplet, there is less air resistance on the object, allowing it to fall faster than snow, giving it more potential energy. In this way, you see how natural systems are an all-encapsulating combination of aspects that change temperature and energy outcomes based upon the very variables that act upon them.

In school, your child will plan an investigation so that she can determine the relationships among the matter type, the transferred energy, the mass, and the change in the average particle kinetic energy measured by the sample's temperature. Experiments might include comparing the impact on water temperatures of varying masses of ice melted.

Investigate Changes in Kinetic Energy

Performance expectation MS.PS3.5 reads: "construct, use, and present arguments to support the claim that when the kinetic energy of an object changes, energy is transferred to or from the object."

By Newton's first law, an object in motion will stay in motion, and an object at rest must stay at rest. By the function of this statement, as well as the equation for kinetic energy and the law of conservation of energy, you see that for an object to begin, increase, or change direction of motion speed, energy must be applied or removed from an object. As an object in motion is slowed, its velocity decreases. Due to a decrease in velocity, there is a decrease in the kinetic energy of the object. Since energy cannot be created or destroyed, this means that the energy of the object must be transferred to the system in which it is moving. For example, as a car brakes along a road, energy is removed from the system of the car and transferred to its environment in several ways. The most noticeable of these transfers is the audible screech of the tires, and the skid marks left upon the ground due to the heating of the tires enough for molten rubber to be scraped along the road. For a car to increase its speed, it must burn gasoline, drawing in energy from the combustion of fuel within the engine. This is one of the many ways you can observe energy transfer in our universe.

ALERT

An object that is at rest and not moving still has energy. The molecules within the object are moving and have kinetic energy. The object itself has the potential to move and therefore has potential energy.

Your child will build, use, and present arguments in support of the claim that a change in kinetic energy of an object results in the energy being transferred to or from another object.

Energy Experiment

For this experiment, a question has been provided for you. Work with your child to come up with a hypothesis and then perform the experiment together.

Question:

What will happen to the rope of beads when pulled out of a glass cylinder vase?

Materials

- Rope of beads 5 meters long
- Glass cylinder vase

Method

1. Place the rope of beads in a circular pattern into the cylinder vase.
2. Hold the vase up high with one hand.
3. Pull the end of the rope of beads out of the vase with a quick motion using the other hand.
4. Observe and record the results.

Consider Testing . . .

- What happens when you use a longer rope of beads?
- What happens when you use a shorter rope of beads?
- What happens when you use a plastic vase?
- What happens when you use a rope with larger beads?

Let's Review—Checklist

When exploring the world of energy with your child, you'll need to remember some key facts:

- When objects interact, one object can exert force on another and transfer energy.
- Energy exists in several forms that include chemical, electrical, nuclear, and thermal.
- Energy can be changed from one form to another within a particular system. For instance, it can transform from potential to kinetic energy.
- Energy can be transferred, but it cannot be destroyed. This is the law of conservation of energy.

- Energy transfers through conduction, convection, and radiation from an area with more heat to an area with less heat.
- A significant number of the changes to the surface of the earth are a result of the energy from the sun.
- Objects can have stored energy based on their relative positions.
- The stored energy of an object is referred to as potential energy.
- The movement of an object is referred to as kinetic energy.
- Kinetic energy involves the speed of a particular object.
- The temperature of an object is referred to as thermal energy.
- The term heat is used in everyday language to talk about energy transfer and thermal energy, but in science the term heat refers only to heat transfer.
- Heat transfer involves a difference in temperature between two objects.
- Temperature measures the average kinetic energy of particles within matter.
- Temperature and total energy are related based on the amount, state, and type of the matter samples.
- Gravitational energy is connected to potential energy.
- Elastic energy refers to how an elastic object is able to compress and stretch.
- Chemical energy refers to a substance's composition.
- Electrical energy involves the electric current within a circuit.
- Light energy involves the frequency of electromagnetic waves.
- The movement of heat is predictable.
- Energy is transferred into and out of systems through most reactions.
- The law of conservation of energy states that the total energy of the universe is constant.
- Light interacts with matter by absorption, reflection, scattering, and transmission.
- When an object's motion energy changes, other changes occur as well.
- When friction is applied to a moving object, the object's speed decreases and its thermal energy increases.

CHAPTER 10

Waves and Their Applications

How do waves transfer information and energy? Waves are a form of disturbance that creates a repeating motion pattern. This motion carries energy from one place to another without moving any matter. Light is a phenomenon that has wavelike properties. Understanding the properties of waves and the activity of electromagnetic radiation makes it possible for systems to be designed that carry information over great distances, store data, and investigate nature.

What Should My Child Already Understand?

At the beginning of middle school, your child should already understand that waves have different amplitudes and wavelengths. He should know that waves can be added on or canceled out based on the position of the parts of a wave and their relation to other waves.

Other wave-related facts your child will already know include:

- Light waves move throughout space and can travel great distances.
- People are able to see objects because of the reflection of light off of surfaces.
- Lenses are able to bend the beams of light and make it possible to see small things through magnifying glasses. Lenses are also found in microscopes, telescopes, and eyeglasses.
- Technology uses digitized data to receive, decode, and store information, and this digitized information can be carried over great distances in waves. Receptors pick up on different waveforms and translate the data into what we can physically recognize.

ESSENTIAL

Waves are vibrations that travel through space and time. Light and sound are different types of waves. Light is caused by the vibration of energy, and sound is caused by the vibration of matter. Light moves faster than sound and does not need a medium to travel. Light is made of transverse waves and sound is made of longitudinal waves.

Disciplinary Core Ideas

The following concepts have been established by the Next Generation Science Standards as some of the important points of understanding in studying waves. Following are some of the topics your child will learn about and discuss in school.

Wave Properties

Simple wave models have repeating patterns with particular amplitudes, frequencies, and wavelengths and are used to explain phenomena including light and sound. While mechanical waves can only be transmitted through a medium, sound waves need mediums in order to be transmitted. Energy can be transmitted through waves.

ALERT

Sound waves travel faster through liquids than through air. They travel even faster through solids. The molecules within solids are more compact than those in liquids. The molecules in liquids are more compact than those in gases. Sound waves move faster when molecules are closer together.

Electromagnetic Spectrum

The design of a wave can model the interaction between light and objects. When light shines on objects, it becomes absorbed, reflected, or transmitted through the objects. The absorption, reflection, or transmission is based on the light's frequency and the object's material. Light travels in a straight line except when it meets surfaces between differing transparent materials. When light bends, it passes between differing transparent materials. A model of light waves can be used to explain color, brightness, and bending of light. Light waves travel through space unlike sound waves, which do not.

FACT

Light travels incredibly fast. Its speed in an area without any matter is about three hundred thousand kilometers per second. The speed of light is not constant, however, and changes depending on where it is traveling. It slows down as it moves through a transparent medium like water.

Information Technologies and Instrumentation

Digitized signals are transmitted as wave pulses. Digitized signals are reliable for encoding and transmitting data. You can use waves to transmit digital data. Digitized data is made up of a pattern of 0s and 1s.

Key Wave Terms

These terms are important to a good understanding of waves:

- Amplitude—The distance that medium particles move from their resting points when waves pass through them.
- Compression—A force exerted that shortens length.
- Concave Lens—A type of lens with an inwardly curved center through which objects appear to be smaller.
- Convex Lens—A type of lens with an outwardly curved center through which objects appear to be larger.
- Crest—The highest point of a wave.
- Electromagnetic Spectrum—The range of long-to-short wavelengths or frequencies.
- Energy—Ability to do work that can lead to changes in matter.
- Frequency—The number of crest-to-crest cycles of a wave that take place in one second.
- Light—Electromagnetic radiation that can be observed through sight.
- Longitudinal Wave—A wave with medium particles that vibrate parallel to the direction of the wave.
- Medium—A gas, liquid, or solid through which a wave and energy is transmitted.
- Opaque—A material through which light does not travel.
- Rarefaction—A reduction in a medium's density and pressure.
- Reflection—The bouncing of light off of a surface.
- Refraction—The bending of a wave as it passes through mediums in which its speed of travel differs.
- Sound—The transfer of a vibrating object's energy in the form of waves traveling through matter.
- Translucent—A material through which light passes and is scattered.
- Transparent—A material through which light passes.
- Transverse—Waves with medium particles that vibrate perpendicular to the direction of the wave.
- Trough—The lowest point of a wave.
- Vibration—Oscillation that results in a disturbance of equilibrium.
- Wave—A vibration or disturbance.
- Wavelength—The distance between the same two points of adjacent waves.

Key Wave Concepts

Understanding waves and how they move is important to studying physical sciences and engineering.

Wave Q&A

Q: What is a wave?

A: Waves have repeated patterns and specific amplitudes, frequencies, and wavelengths. They are vibrations or disturbances that transmit energy through space or matter. Waves travel through material referred to as the medium. The medium through which the wave travels can be a gas, liquid, or solid. The medium through which the wave travels does not move with the energy that is transmitted. Mechanical waves need a medium to travel. Electromagnetic waves do not need a medium to travel. These waves travel the fastest when moving through an empty space.

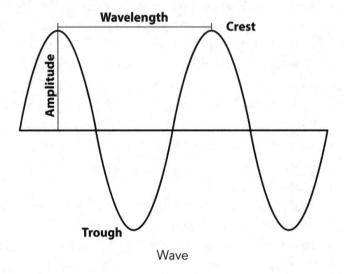

Wave

Q: What are the types of waves?

A: Waves are categorized by the direction in which the medium particles vibrate. Transverse waves have medium particles that vibrate perpendicular to the direction of the wave. Electromagnetic waves are transverse waves. The highest point in a wave is called the crest. The lowest point in a wave is called the *trough*. Longitudinal waves have medium particles that vibrate parallel to the direction of the wave. Sound waves are longitudinal waves. Surface waves are a combination of transverse and longitudinal waves. Seismic waves are surface waves.

Q: What are the properties of waves?

A: The properties of a wave are based on the type of energy that produces it. The amplitude of waves is the greatest distance they vibrate from their resting positions. The greater the amplitude, the greater the energy carried by the wave. The *wavelength* of waves is the distance between two crests that are adjacent to one another. The *frequency* of waves is the number of waves that are generated in a specific time period. It can be determined by counting the crests or troughs as they pass a particular point over a specific period of time. It is measured in Hertz. The greater the frequency, the greater the energy. Wave speed is how fast the wave travels. The speed is based on the medium through which the wave travels. Sound waves travel at the greatest speed through solids and at the next greatest speed through liquids. Sound waves travel at the lowest speed through gases. The speed of a wave is determined by multiplying the wavelength by the wave frequency.

Q: How do waves interact?

A: Waves can interact with other waves or objects. Reflection takes place when waves bounce back from hitting a barrier. Echoes are examples of reflected sound. Mirror images are examples of reflected light. Refraction occurs when waves bend as they go through one medium to another medium at an angle. Diffraction takes place when waves bend through an opening. Interference happens when at least two waves overlap. Waves do not share space, meet, or pass through one another. Constructive interference increases amplitude. When two crests come together, one overlaps the other and causes additional waves that increase amplitude. Destructive interference reduces amplitude. When crests and troughs overlap, waves with smaller amplitudes are produced. Interference refers to standing waves in which a stationary pattern is created. Resonance happens when objects vibrate at a frequency near the frequency of another object, causing the other object to vibrate as well. A compression is a section of a longitudinal wave where the particles are crowded together. A rarefaction is a section of the wave where particles are less crowded than normal.

Q: How do waves change direction?
A: Reflection takes places when a wave bounces off of a surface. The angle that the wave hits and leaves a flat surface is the same. This is referred to as the law of reflection. Refraction refers to the bending of waves and occurs when the speed of a wave changes as it enters a particular medium. The medium being entered affects the amount of bending that takes place. Diffraction refers to waves bending around objects. The size of the obstacle and the waves affect the amount of bending that occurs. A wave with a small wavelength bending around a large object creates low diffraction. A wave with a large wavelength bending around a small object creates a large diffraction.

Q: What are the properties of light?
A: Light is a form of energy that you are able to see. Light travels in straight lines. It reflects off of flat, shiny, or smooth surfaces in a pattern of regular reflection. It reflects off of rough, shiny, or uneven surfaces in a pattern of diffused reflection. When light cannot be reflected, it is absorbed. As light passes through water, it bends.

Q: What are the properties of sound?
A: Sound is a wave that can be heard. It is caused by vibrations and transmits through gases, liquids, and solids. Sound travels and can be absorbed, modified, or reflected. Reflected sound bounces off of an object; absorbed sound does not. The pitch and loudness of a sound can be modified.

Q: What are seismic waves?
A: Seismic waves are vibrations with low frequencies that transmit throughout the earth. They are usually caused by explosions, earthquakes, and volcanoes. When these events take place, energy is

released through radiating waves. The waves are categorized as P-waves and S-waves. P-waves refer to primary waves. They move the fastest, traveling through liquids and solids. They compress and expand material that is found in the same direction they are traveling. S-waves refer to secondary waves. They move more slowly than P-waves, traveling only through solids. They vibrate the ground that is perpendicular to the direction they are traveling.

Q: What are digitized signals?

A: Electric devices transform electricity to other energy forms. An oven changes electrical energy to thermal energy. Some devices use electrical energy to encode information. The voltage of an electric current is repeatedly changed to encode the data. Encoded information is referred to as an electronic signal. There are two types of electronic signals: analog and digital. Analog signals use continuous voltage changes to encode information. This type of signal can experience distortions and outside noises, making it less efficient for transmitting information. Digital signals use quick voltage pulses to encode data. This type of signal is easier and more efficient for transmitting information.

FACT

Sir Isaac Newton noticed that a single ray of sunlight traveling at an angle through a glass prism created a band of colors. These colors included red, orange, yellow, green, blue, indigo, and violet. Different colors move through glass at different speeds, making them separate.

Science and Engineering Practices

In learning about waves, your child will use science and engineering practices to better understand the ideas that relate to sound, light, and energy. These practices might include:

- Explaining why colors can be seen in space but sounds cannot be heard
- Creating and presenting ray diagrams to demonstrate and explain how light is refracted and reflected

- Explaining how the properties of light make it possible for distant objects to appear closer and small objects appear larger
- Constructing a model to explain the function of wave pulses and their use in receiving, storing, and transmitting information
- Describing and predicting how waves will interact with matter based on their characteristic behaviors and properties
- Asking and answering questions in writing to identify and clarify evidence about waves
- Developing and presenting a labeled model to predict and describe wave patterns
- Analyzing and interpreting data to determine and provide a model that details, describes, and supports the principles of the interactions of waves
- Using mathematical representations to support scientific conclusions and explanations about waves
- Providing a written description for the properties and behaviors of specific types of waves
- Constructing a model that communicates information about waves and identifies patterns of waves

Next Generation Science Standards Performance Expectations

These performance expectations describe what your child should be able to demonstrate and understand about the specific science unit he is studying in middle school. From these expectations your child's teachers will determine how successfully he understands and can apply the concepts that have been covered.

Explain Wave Amplitude in Relation to Energy

Performance expectation MS.PS4.1 states that your child should be able to "use mathematical representations to describe a simple model for waves that includes how the amplitude of a wave is related to the energy in a wave."

The energy of a wave is dependent on its length (wavelength) and its height (amplitude). Waves occur in several ways in nature, most notably the visual wave you can see in water. The equation given for the energy of these waves is: Energy equals the density of water, multiplied by gravity, as well as amplitude squared. This is all divided by two. In this way, you can see that the energy of a wave is most dependent on its amplitude, as density and gravity are both constant numbers.

Another way to visualize the energy of waves being dependent on amplitude is to refer back to the equation of potential energy. If you recall that potential energy is dependent on the height of an object, you can see that the height of a wave, being momentarily still, and therefore having potential energy, will have a great effect on the overall energy of the wave. Additionally, as potential energy becomes kinetic with the fall of the wave, the decrease of height adds to velocity, giving energy to the wave.

ALERT

Waves do not transport matter from one place to another. Waves are patterns of crest and trough movements. These movement patterns cause energy to move, but particles of matter do not move; they vibrate in place.

Your child will use mathematical representations to describe a basic model for waves. This model will include the relationship between the wave's amplitude and its energy.

Explore How Waves Are Transmitted

According to Performance expectation MS.PS4.2, students should "develop and use a model to describe that waves are reflected, absorbed, or transmitted through various materials."

To demonstrate the plethora of waves that occur in nature, you can look to your senses to observe different waves around you. Both light and sound are waves. Light comes from several sources, but the best way to observe light as a wave is through an old light bulb. By applying power to a light bulb that is on the verge of going out, you can observe waves in the oscillation of the filament. A flickering light bulb is proof of the wave nature of light, as the small vibrations coming from the source destroy the central filament. The properties of light are what (usually) cause light bulbs to go out.

Another way to observe waves is to look at how sound works. Sound waves are compressed air traveling through the medium to your eardrums, which take the vibrations and translate the waves to the sound you hear in your head. These waves can be observed in a variety of ways. For example, if you turn on the radio in your vehicle, and place yourself near the sub-woofer coupled with the speakers (if you have one), you can feel the vibrations of the low tones created.

ESSENTIAL

Electromagnetic waves can transmit energy without a medium through empty spaces. Mechanical waves need a medium to transmit energy and cannot move through an empty space. Light waves are electromagnetic, and sound waves are mechanical.

Additionally, there are ways to convert sound through materials other than air. The soup-can telephone functions in this way. By connecting two empty soup cans with a string in the center of the bases, one can speak to another person by talking into the can while the recipient puts the other can up to his or her ear. This is due to sound traveling through the string as a wave. It isn't visible, but it is audible.

Your child will develop and utilize a model to describe the reflection, absorption, and transmission of waves through a variety of materials. Focus is on both mechanical and light waves. Models might include simulations, text descriptions, and illustrations.

Delve Into Digitized Signals

Performance expectation MS.PS4.3 states that your child should "integrate qualitative scientific and technical information to support the claim that digitized signals are a more reliable way to encode and transmit information than analog signals."

Due to the constants regarding waves and their energy, you can create reliable and constant means of transferring information. For example, as opposed to sending a letter by mail, modern technology has allowed you to send information wirelessly. Not simply this, but also we have the evolution of modern technologies like the telephone.

The telephone, when used in a landline configuration, as it was originally invented, required the sending of audible data along cords to other phones. In the modern age, you rarely see the use of cords due to the fact that we can transfer waves through the medium of air. Cell phones, thanks to these waves, are the most common means of communication. Even home phones, which use a landline, are usually cordless.

FACT

Seismic waves are produced by earthquakes. They are caused by the energy that is released from the interior of the earth through the surface. There are two types of seismic waves: body and surface. Body waves travel through the interior of the planet. Surface waves move along its surface.

Additionally, data can be sent digitally, and thanks to the use of light waves in lasers to collect mass amounts of data, we can send and receive more data than humans previously could with say, libraries and archives. A simple disc can hold countless amounts of information and be placed within a computer, and thanks to light waves, be read and transferred into physical information that the computer will display. In turn, different waves can transfer this information over networks to other computers.

In this way, the most efficient way to transfer information is with the use of waves. Additionally, due to the scientific and mathematical nature of these waves, it is also the most reliable. So long as the mathematics regarding the waves that carry information is correct, the data transfer will be reliable.

Your child will incorporate technical data and qualitative information to support the assertion that digitized signals are more effective and reliable means of encoding and transmitting information than analog ones. Focus is on basic comprehension that waves can be utilized to communicate. Wave examples include the use of fiber optic cables in the transmission of radio waves and light pulses in Wi-Fi components.

Waves Experiment

For this experiment, a question has been provided for you. Work with your child to come up with a hypothesis and then perform the experiment together.

Question

Does the presence of water in a glass affect the sound of rubbing the rim?

Materials

- 2 drinking glasses with thin rims
- Water
- Paper towels

Method

1. Pour water into one of the glasses until it is half full.
2. Place your index finger into the water.
3. Rub your finger along the rim of the glass without stopping. Observe and record results.
4. Wipe your finger dry with a paper towel. Place the empty glass in front of you.
5. Dip your finger into the water again, and rub your finger along the rim of the second (empty) glass without stopping. Observe and record results.

Consider Testing . . .

- What happens when you change the amount of water in the glass?
- What happens when you change the thickness of the glass?
- What happens when you change the temperature level of the water?

Let's Review—Checklist

As your child is learning about waves in school, here are some points you should know to assist her in her knowledge:

- Waves have repeating patterns with specific amplitudes, wavelengths, and frequencies.
- Sound waves need a medium to transmit.
- Seismic waves are used by geologists to study the structures within the earth.
- Light waves can be absorbed or reflected when they strike a surface.
- Light waves can be transmitted through objects based on the light frequency and the material of the object.
- Light waves travel in a straight line except between surfaces of transparent materials including air and water. Light bends when it passes between air and water.
- The bending of light can be observed with lenses and prisms.
- Models of light waves can help to demonstrate and explain the bending of light.
- Some technologies can detect and analyze digitized signals that cannot be experienced through typical senses.
- Digitized signals are used in communication devices to reliably transmit and encode information.

CHAPTER 11

From Molecules to Organisms—Structures and Processes

Every living organism is made from cells that are organized by their structure and function. The more complex an organism is, the more complex its cell system. Cells work together within the living organisms of algae, animals, plants, and microorganisms and respond to the environment in which they live. Cells grow and reproduce, creating offspring with their genetic information. In order to survive, cells need energy and matter from their environment. This chapter will discuss what your child will be learning about cells and the organisms they create.

What Should My Child Already Understand?

At the beginning of middle school, your child should understand that there are some living organisms that are made of one cell. These single-cell organisms also need air, food, water, a way to get rid of their waste, and an environment in which they can live. It is possible to see that living organisms contain many cells through the use of a microscope. Some living things have cells that cooperate. The cells of some living things appear different and perform different jobs inside the organism. All parts of the body send signals to the brain about what is happening. The brain sends signals to influence the body parts. These sensory receptors in the human body play an important role in telling body parts how to develop, function, and heal.

FACT

Carbohydrates, lipids, nucleic acids, and proteins are organic molecules that are important for life. Carbohydrates are used to make energy. Lipids store energy and produce hormones. Nucleic acids transmit information, and proteins build and repair tissues.

Disciplinary Core Ideas

The following concepts have been established by the Next Generation Science Standards as some of the important points of understanding in studying molecules and organisms. Following are some of the topics your child will learn about and discuss in school.

Structure and Functions

How are life's functions made possible through an organism's structure? Every living thing is composed of cells. The cell is the smallest living organism. Cells work together in organisms to build organs and tissues for specific bodily functions. Some organisms contain only one cell and are called *unicellular*. Some organisms contain different types and numbers of cells and are called *multicellular*. All organisms are able to reproduce asexually or sexually, and they transfer their genetic data to their offspring.

Inside cells there are structures that perform specific functions. The cell membrane surrounds the cell as a boundary and controls everything that enters and exits the cell. The body of a multicellular organism contains a system of several subsystems that interact with each other. The subsystems are sets of cells that work together to build organs and tissues that perform specific bodily functions.

Growth and Development of Organisms

How are organisms able to grow and develop? Living organisms reproduce through a sexual or an asexual process. Through reproduction the parents are able to transfer their genetic information to their offspring. All animals participate in activities that increase the probability of reproducing. The growth of organisms is influenced by environmental and genetic factors.

Organization for Matter and Energy Flow in Organisms

How do organisms get the energy and matter that they need to grow and survive? Plants use energy that they get from light to make sugar. This process is called photosynthesis. Many microorganisms, including algae and plants, use the energy they get from light to make sugar. They use the sugar as food either immediately or at a later time. Through the process of photosynthesis, they use carbon dioxide that they get from the atmosphere and combine it with water. Photosynthesis releases oxygen into the atmosphere.

ALERT

Whether they are part of a plant or an animal, all cells perform the basic functions of life. These functions include taking in fuel, converting it to energy, eliminating waste, and reproducing.

Individual organisms break down food through a process of chemical reactions that reorganize molecules, enabling energy to be released. The chemical reactions break down the food and rearrange it to create new molecules, support development, or release energy.

Key Molecule Terms

These terms are important to a good understanding of molecules:

- Active Transport—The process where cells use energy to transport chemical substances from a low concentration to a high concentration
- Adapt—Making an adjustment to be more suitable for a particular situation
- Amoeba—A unicellular organism with a jelly-like body that has no fixed form
- Asexual—A process where reproduction takes place without the joining of female and male gametes
- Carrier Proteins—Membrane proteins with a high affinity for certain solutes that help the solutes pass through membrane barriers
- Cell—The smallest unit of structure within an organism that can function independently and that has at least one nucleus, a cytoplasm, and several organelles enclosed by a semipermeable membrane
- Cell Membrane—A semipermeable membrane that surrounds the cytoplasm in a cell
- Cell Theory—A principle describing the cell as the basic unit of living things and stating that the properties of an organism are built on the properties of the cells within it
- Cell Wall—A rigid layer of cellulose that protects cells found in plants
- Centrioles—Cylindrical-shaped cell structures that form asters during the process of mitosis
- Chlorophyll—A group of green pigments that is located in the chloroplasts of plant life
- Chloroplasts—Located in green and algal plant cells; a plastid that contains chlorophyll
- Chromatin—A complex of proteins and nucleic acids found in the nucleus of the cell
- Chromosomes—A linear strand of DNA that is found in the nucleus of a eukaryotic cell; it transmits the functions and genes of heredity information
- Cytoplasm—The protoplasm that is found outside of the nucleus of cells

- Deoxyribonucleic Acid (DNA)—A nucleic acid that transmits the genetic information of the cell
- Endocytosis—Cellular ingestion where the plasma membrane bends inward to move substances into cells
- Endoplasmic Reticulum—A network of membranes inside the cytoplasm of a cell that is related to modification, synthesis, and the transport of cell materials
- Energy—The ability of one system to work on another
- Enzymes—A variety of proteins that function as biochemical catalysts and are the product of living organisms
- Eukaryotic Cells—Single or multicellular organisms with cells that have a nucleus surrounded by a membrane
- Exocytosis—Cellular excretion or secretion where substances in vesicles are discharged through the fusion of the outer membrane with the vesicular membrane
- Facilitated Transport—The transport of specific materials down a concentration gradient across the membrane of a cell with help from certain proteins contained in the membrane and without the explicit use of energy
- Fertilization—The creation of a zygote through the joining of female and male gametes
- Fission—A process of asexual reproduction where a single-celled organism divides into a minimum of two independently developing cells
- Genetic Code—The sequence of nucleotides found in RNA or DNA, determining the particular sequence of amino acids in protein synthesis; it is universal in almost all organisms and is the biochemical foundation of heredity
- Golgi Complex—A complex of flattened and parallel saccules, vacuoles, and vesicles that are found next to a cell's nucleus and are involved in secretion formation inside the cell
- Homeostasis—The ability of a cell or living organism to keep its internal equilibrium through an adjustment of its physiological processes
- Hypertonic—A fluid with a higher osmotic pressure than another fluid
- Hypotonic—A fluid with a lower osmotic pressure than another fluid
- Isotonic—Solutions with the same osmotic pressures
- Lysosomes—A single membrane-bound sac containing digestive enzymes

- Metamorphosis—A change to the form and habits of animals as they develop from the embryonic stage
- Mitochondria—A sphere-shaped organelle that is found in the cytoplasm of almost all eukaryotic cells and contains the enzymes and genetic information necessary for the metabolism of cells
- Multicellular—Having many cells
- Mutation—The process of being changed
- Nucleolus—A small, round body made of RNA and protein in the cell's nucleus
- Nucleus—A large, membrane-bound structure inside a living cell that contains hereditary material and controls growth, metabolism, and reproduction
- Nutrients—Nourishing ingredients
- Organ—A specific part of an organism that has a particular function
- Organ System—A group of organs within the body that work with each other to perform necessary functions of the body
- Organelles—Structures inside a cell, including chloroplast, mitochondrion, or vacuole, that have a specific function
- Organism—An individual living form
- Osmosis—The movement of fluid through a membrane that is semipermeable from a low solute to a higher solute solution, until the liquid on both sides has an equal level of concentration
- Passive Transport—The movement of chemical substances across the membrane of a cell without the use of energy
- Photosynthesis—A process that takes place in green plant life that involves the synthesis of carbohydrates from water and carbon dioxide using light as its source of energy; this process releases oxygen
- Plasma Membrane—The semipermeable membrane that surrounds a cell's cytoplasm
- Prokaryotic Cell—A cell without organelles and a distinct membrane-bound nucleus
- Protein—A group of complex macromolecules that have carbon, hydrogen, nitrogen, oxygen, and sulfur and are made of at least one chain of amino acids
- Ribosome—Large numbers of small particles contained in living cells that convert genetic information into protein molecules

- Sexual—A process where reproduction takes place through the joining of female and male gametes
- Solute—A substance that is dissolved into another substance
- Solvent—Able to dissolve another substance
- Stimulus—Something that causes a response
- Tissue—Morphologically similar cells and intercellular cells that work together to carry out specific bodily functions
- Unicellular—Having one cell
- Vacuole—The membrane-bound organelle located in particular protists that move fluid from the inside to the outside of a cell
- Waste—Body excretion
- Zygote—A cell that is created through the joining of two gametes, in particular a fertilized ovum prior to cleavage

ESSENTIAL

An organism is not determined to be alive by its physical features. A living organism is anything that is able to eat, grow, perform respiration, and reproduce. Most of them are able to move, but not all. There are more than ten million types of organisms on the planet ranging in size from the microscopic to gigantic.

Key Molecule Concepts

Understanding molecules is fundamental to the study of organisms and life sciences.

Molecule Q&A

Q: What makes up all living things?
A: All living things are made of cells. This includes the human body. Cells can differ in their size, shape, and function. A cell is the smallest functional and structural unit of a living thing. Some living things actu-

ally have only one cell. Larger living things have millions and millions of cells. While these organisms are very different in size and shape, the structure of their cells can be similar.

Q: How are the structures of living organisms organized?
A: Specialized cells come together to form groups that perform specific functions. These groups are organized into different types of tissue that make up the organs of an organism. These organs work together to create a system within an organism. For instance, specialized nerve cells join together to form nerves that work together within the nervous system. Living things have many levels of organization.

Q: What are the levels of organization in living things?
A: Beginning with the smallest unit: the atom, the molecule, the organelle, the cell, the tissue, the organ, the organ system, and the organism. The cell is the basic unit of structure and function in all living organisms. Cells working together to perform specific functions form tissue. Tissues working together to perform particular jobs form organs. Organs working together to perform specialized tasks form organ systems. Organ systems working together form organisms.

Q: What is cell theory?
A: Cell theory is a principle that states that every organism is made up of cells, cells are the basic organizational units of all organisms, and all cells are made from other cells.

Q: What are cells?
A: Most cells contain a nucleus that contains DNA. The nucleus is found in the cytoplasm and is enclosed by a membrane. There are two types of cells: prokaryotic cells and eukaryotic cells. Prokaryotic cells have no nucleus. Their DNA is found in the cytoplasm and not in the membrane of the nucleus. These cells are found in unicellular organisms. Organisms that have prokaryotic cells are referred to as prokaryotes. Bacteria contain prokaryotic cells.

Eukaryotic cells have a nucleus. These cells are generally bigger than prokaryotic cells. Eukaryotic cells are found in multicellular organisms. Organisms with these cells are referred to as eukaryotes. Eukaryotes also have organelles. Organelles are structures inside the cytoplasm that carry out specific functions. These parts of the cell make it possible for eukaryotes to perform more jobs than prokaryotes.

Q: What are the parts of a cell?

A: While there is diversity among cells, all of them have common parts. These parts include cytoplasm, DNA, ribosomes, and plasma membrane. The plasma membrane is also referred to as the cell membrane. The cell membrane encloses the cell with a thin layer of lipids. It forms a barrier between the cell and the environment around it. Cytoplasm is the cell material that is found inside the cell membrane. It contains ribosomes and other cell structures. Proteins are formed in the ribosomes of the cell. DNA holds the genetic information that cells require to produce proteins. All cells contain these parts. This fact is evidence that all living organisms on planet Earth evolved from common connections.

Q: What are organelles?

A: Eukaryotic cells also contain organelles that include the nucleus, mitochondria, vesicles, vacuoles, lysosomes, ribosomes, endoplasmic reticulum, and Golgi apparatus. The nucleus holds the genetic information needed to produce proteins. The mitochondria provide the necessary energy for chemical reactions. Vesicles transport materials throughout the cell and to the membrane of the cell. Vacuoles store nutrients and water. Lysosomes use enzymes to break up and recycle molecules. Ribosomes produce proteins, which is the main job of the cell. Some ribosomes are located in endoplasmic reticulum and some move about the cytoplasm. Golgi apparatus accept the proteins and send them to the proper place within or outside the cell.

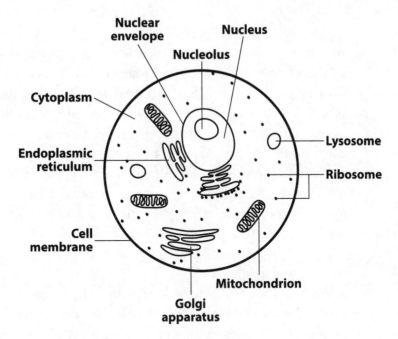

Animal cell

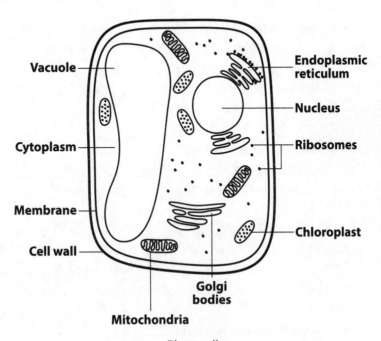

Plant cell

Q: What is the plasma membrane?

A: Your cells have to be protected from unwanted materials getting into them and from becoming destroyed by their environment. All cells have a protective barrier called the plasma membrane. The plasma membrane, also called the cell membrane, is made from a layer of phospholipids. Phospholipids are a type of molecule that creates a barrier, keeping water from the cell environment out of the cell itself. The job of the plasma membrane is to regulate what enters and exits the cell. There are some molecules that are able to pass through the membrane and others that are not, making the membrane semipermeable.

Q: What is cytosol?

A: All cells have a jelly type of substance that is called cytosol. It is made of water and molecules. All of the contents of the cell are held in the cytosol. The cytosol and the organelles together make up the cytoplasm of the cell.

Q: What is the nucleus?

A: Only eukaryotic cells have a nucleus. The nucleus holds the genetic information that instructs the cell on forming the molecules they need to function. The nucleus is found inside a membrane that regulates what enters and exits.

Q: What are chromosomes?

A: Chromosomes are located inside the nucleus and contain genetic material. They are lengths of DNA that encase proteins.

Q: What is the nucleolus?

A: Many cells have a nucleus that contains a nucleolus. The nucleolus forms ribosomes that move out of the pores of the nucleus and into the cytoplasm. Inside the cytoplasm, the ribosomes produce proteins.

Q: What is the cell membrane?

A: Cells are located in many different environments and require a means of being protected. The job of the protector goes to the cell membrane. The semipermeable cell membrane allows some molecules to go through but not others in order to keep a stable environment within the cell. This stable state is referred to as homeostasis. Cells need to maintain homeostasis in order to survive.

Q: How does the cell membrane protect the cell?

A: The cell membrane is able to protect the cell by allowing necessary molecules to pass into it but not dangerous ones. The membrane is able to do this because of its composition. The cell membrane is made up of two layers of phospholipids that act as a protective barrier. Phospholipids have two parts: a hydrophilic head and a hydrophobic tail. The head loves water and the tail fears it. Since there is water inside the cell and in the environment around it, the heads of the phospholipids are directed toward the water and the tails are directed toward each other in the area inside the cell without water. This enables the cell to survive. Some molecules like carbon dioxide and oxygen are able to move through the membrane but others need proteins to get through the barrier.

Q: What does active transport mean?

A: Active transport refers to the movement of molecules from a region of low concentration to high concentration. Energy is necessary to move molecules using this form of transport. In order to move against concentration gradients, molecules use a special protein that provides the energy needed to move across the membrane.

Q: What does passive transport mean?

A: While some molecules need protein to give them the energy to move across the cell membrane, others do not. Passive transport refers to movement across the membrane without the need for energy. Diffusion is a type of passive transport. Through the process of diffusion, molecules are able to go from a region of high concentration to one of low concentration, moving down the concentration gradient. No protein-produced energy is needed for this process.

Q: Why do cells divide?

A: Some organisms contain only one cell but others are made up of trillions of cells. In order for an organism to develop into so many cells, the first cell has to divide into two cells. After that the cells continue dividing through the process of cell division. Cell division is one component of the cell cycle of eukaryotic cells. The process of mitosis ensures that each newly created cell contains cells that are genetically identical to the ones from which they developed. Cell division allows for the growth and development of parts of living organisms. It also helps in repairing damage to injured parts. Without cell division there would be no growth, development, or healing, and cells would not survive.

Q: What is the cell cycle?

A: The cell cycle refers to a cell's life cycle. As with any cycle, there are different phases of the cell cycle. The two main phases are the interphase and the mitotic phase. The interphase stage occurs when a cell is performing its typical jobs and consists of the first growth, synthesis, and the second growth phases. During first growth, the cell doubles its organelles and size. In the synthesis phase, it replicates its DNA. The second growth phase is when it synthesizes proteins and becomes ready for mitosis. The nucleus divides in mitosis, creating two identical nuclei. Cytokinesis takes place after mitosis, and this is when the cell itself divides into two cells and the cycle is complete.

Science and Engineering Practices

In learning about molecules and organisms, your child will use science and engineering practices to better understand the ideas that relate to structures and processes. These practices might include:

- Asking and answering questions about the causes of disease in humans and how they can be prevented.
- Developing and using models to show the structure, size, and functions of specific cells, and to distinguish between plant and animal cells.

- Planning and carrying out investigations using a microscope to observe, identify, and classify the structures of microbes.
- Analyzing and interpreting data to discover patterns in the different structures and functions of various cells.
- Using mathematics to calculate the magnification of a lens of a microscope.
- Constructing explanations that compare and contrast organisms with single and multiple cells.
- Engaging in arguments using evidence to demonstrate that every living thing is made of cells.
- Obtaining, evaluating, and communicating information to show that humans are made of thousands of individual cells.
- Creating a model of a cell to show the function and structure of organelles.
- Drawing and labeling organisms with single cells.
- Researching diseases that are caused by microbes.

Next Generation Science Standards Performance Expectations

These performance expectations describe what your child should be able to demonstrate and understand about the specific science unit he is studying in middle school. From these expectations your child's teachers will determine how successfully he understands and can apply the concepts that have been covered.

Investigate Proof of Cells

According to performance expectation MS.LS1.1, students will be able to "conduct an investigation to provide evidence that living things are made of cells; either one cell or many different numbers and types of cells."

Expanding on the concept of atomic and molecular structure, we have the assertion that all living things are composed of cells. Cells are the intermediary step between molecules and tissues. The order goes as follows: subatom, atom, molecule, cell, tissue, organ, system. In this way, cells are the things that differentiate all living things from nonliving things. Things that are alive are composed of cells, and cells are composed of molecules and therefore atoms. Nonliving things are composed of molecules and atoms and are as such, nonliving.

ESSENTIAL

In living organisms that are multicellular, their structures are all made of cells. It does not matter if it is a plant or animal; all of their structures contain cells. The stems, leaves, and flowers in a plant are made of cells. The skin, muscles, heart, and brain of animals are all made of cells.

Cells are a collection of living molecule systems working together in tandem to accomplish a task. Cells require a source of energy to complete said task, and in this way they must absorb nutrients from the elements around the cell. This is the reason that cells become tissues, as cells benefit from the presence of other cells that contribute to longevity, specifically similar cells.

However, some organisms are unicellular. This means that the whole "animal" is just one large cell. On such a large scale, cells like this can thrive in their environment as their size allows for them to contact copious amounts of nutrients.

Your child will carry out an investigation to provide proof that living things are composed of cells. Using a microscope, students will be able to observe the cells within onion plants and small aquatic animals.

Explore How Cells Function

Performance expectation MS.LS1.2 states that students will "develop and use a model to describe the function of a cell as a whole and ways parts of cells contribute to the function."

The function of a cell is to carry out a task. Each cell has a purpose. The first and foremost purpose of a cell is to reproduce. If cells are not reproducing, then they cannot continue to fulfill their function. Cells, especially those within a multicellular organism, do not have very long lifespans. In fact, every time you rub your arm, approximately one million dead skin cells are removed from your body. And yet, you are not missing any large portion of your skin. This is due to the fact that cells are constantly reproducing and dying within your body. Multicellular organisms tend to do this because if cells lived forever, they could potentially continue to form incorrectly or be a sap of nutrients. This is the exact reason that cancer cells are so dangerous. They continue to live and form improperly, stealing healthy components from the rest of the body.

ALERT

Proteins are a type of molecule that cells need to grow and repair. These proteins are not made from special cells but are created by each individual cell. Each cell makes its own protein molecules and uses them to function and live.

Just like cells have different types and designations to function and run tissues and organisms inside of a living thing, cells also have different parts inside of them to actuate their potential functions. For example, the DNA inside of a cell allows for different signals to be sent around the cell to activate different functions, such as synthesizing proteins, which is carried out by the mitochondria. There is a plethora of different cell parts and systems that make up the cells that make up organisms.

Students will develop and utilize a model to express the functions of cell parts and whole cells. Focus is on the function of cells within a system and the main role of cell parts, including the cell wall, cell membrane, chloroplasts, mitochondria, and nucleus.

Show the Body Is Composed of Cells

According to performance expectation MS.LS1.3, students should "use argument supported by evidence for how the body is a system of interacting subsystems composed of groups of cells."

As previously discussed, cell systems make up different tissues in the body. These tissues in turn make up different organs, and finally, these organs make up entire bodily systems. These different levels all work together to keep the body running, and alive.

For example, cells make up the muscular system in the body. The body's muscles require nutrients to survive, but in order for the body to get these nutrients, it must use muscles to take them in from the environment. In this way, all of the body systems must work together for the body to live. The body requires muscles to pump the heart (which is a muscle), to open and compress the lung cavities, and to actively search for and digest food. In turn, the body processes the raw material into energy to power the muscles so that the body can repeat the process.

The nervous system also works in tandem with these in order to maintain balance and control of the processes. The nervous system allows for the body to safely and accurately continue functioning in a dangerous environment. Much like a security system, the nervous system records input from the environment, such as touches, tastes, and smells, and by relaying reflexes to the muscles, can either continue or cancel functions. For example, if you are feeling pain, your body is taking in the input of a situation dangerous to your well-being, which causes you to recoil and discontinue your detrimental actions.

FACT

Organisms are grouped into two major groups: eukaryotes and prokaryotes. Eukaryotes are made of cells that contain a nucleus and other cell parts called organelles. Animals and plants are in this category of organisms. Prokaryotes contain a cell or cells with no nucleus or major organelles. Bacteria are considered prokaryotes.

Your child will argue how the groups of cells within the body interact in subsystems. Focus is on the concept that the organs within the body are formed from tissues, which are formed from cells. Examples include circulatory, digestive, excretory, muscular, nervous, and respiratory systems.

How Behaviors Affect Reproduction

Performance expectation MS.LS1.4 states that your child should be able to "use argument based on empirical evidence and scientific reasoning to support an explanation for how characteristic animal behaviors and specialized plant structures affect the probability of successful reproduction of animals and plants respectively."

Your child will use sound arguments supported by scientific reasoning and empirical evidence to explain how specific structures of plants and behaviors of animals influence the probability of reproduction. Examples include nest building, animal herding, plumage coloring, pollen transfer, seed germination, flower odors, and hard shell coverings.

Show How Genetics Influences Growth

According to performance expectation MS.LS1.5, students should "construct a scientific explanation based on evidence for how environmental and genetic factors influence the growth of organisms."

Furthering the discussion on the survival of the fittest, evolution shows how the adaptation of animals to an environment will weed out inconsistencies. For example, if the climate changes around an organism, natural genetic mutation will occur due to reproduction between two different gene sets. If the mutation is not well suited for the environment, then the organism will die, and vice versa. This is the current concern surrounding the use of pesticides. As bugs are placed in an adverse situation, the fear is that they will adapt to survive through common pesticides and become an unstoppable (or at least hard to stop within a given time frame) force.

Middle school students will develop a scientific explanation using proof to detail how genetic and environmental factors impact how organisms grow. Examples of environmental factors include the availability of water, food, space, and light. Examples of genetic factors include large-breed farming animals and grain growth. Examples of evidence include the effects of drought and fertilizer on plant growth, and rates of seed growth in various conditions.

Investigate Photosynthesis

Performance expectation MS.LS1.6 states that your child should be able to "construct a scientific explanation based on evidence for the role of photosynthesis in the cycling of matter and flow of energy into and out of organisms."

Cells take in nutrients in order to live. For an organism to live, its cells must live. In this way, cells must live in order for the organism to live. In some organisms like plants, cells do not simply take in the nutrients required for function, like in organisms that do eat. In order for plants to live, organisms like plants must take in minerals and other things that they use to synthesize into nutrients that they use to live. This is why plants thrive upon water and sunlight, as opposed to organisms that thrive on other organisms.

FACT

Living organisms are divided into five kingdoms based on their characteristics, including the monera, the protist, the fungi, the plant, and the animal kingdom. Organisms in the monera kingdom are prokaryotic. The fungi kingdom includes plant-like organisms that do not make their own food. The plant kingdom has organisms that make their own food but cannot move. Organisms in the animal kingdom cannot make their own food but are able to move.

Plants use things called chloroplasts in their leaves to collect sunlight, which they use to synthesize the sugars that they use to survive. These chloroplasts are what give the plant the green color that it has in its leaves. As the chloroplasts die due to lack of nutrients and sun absorption, the leaves change color and begin to die, falling off as the plant goes into hibernation for the seasons that do not provide ample resources for it to live.

In addition to these systems, you can see how plants play a larger role in the ecosystem. As plants perform photosynthesis, they take in carbon dioxide and release oxygen gas, whereas aspirating (breathing) animals take in oxygen and expel carbon dioxide. Therefore, you can see the relation between animals and plants, and how they work in tandem in the ecosystem.

Students will develop a scientific explanation using proof to detail how photosynthesis affects energy flow and matter cycling, both out of and into organisms.

Show How Food Converts to Energy

Performance expectation MS.LS1.7 states that your child should be able to "develop a model to describe how food is rearranged through chemical reactions forming new molecules that support growth and/or release energy as this matter moves through an organism."

Plant cells take in carbon dioxide, light energy, and water to create the products oxygen and nutrient-rich sugars, which the plant needs to live. It is within the plant's cells that these reactions occur, specifically in the roots and leaves. The nutrients are then fed up and down the stem to facilitate the health of the plant.

Just like humans eat food to be broken down in the stomach and then dispersed around the body, cells undergo similar processes to stay alive. Cells take in nutrients to be converted into adenosine triphosphate, also known as ATP. ATP is sent throughout the cell as a means of energy for the cell to function. ATP is much like the sugars that plants create from the resources around them to stay alive.

Middle school students will create a model to describe the rearrangement of food through chemical reactions. The model will also be used to describe how the chemical reactions lead to the formation of new molecules that generate energy release and growth. Focus is on detailing how molecules release energy as they break apart and go back together.

Prove That the Brain Reacts to Stimuli to Form Memories

According to performance expectation MS.LS1.8, students should "gather and synthesize information that sensory receptors respond to stimuli by sending messages to the brain for immediate behavior or storage as memories."

How does the mind gather and store data about experiences? Human beings have this brain function primarily for survival. Human beings can remember what hurts them, and what makes them feel good. In this way, a human will recognize that fire will harm and burn him, so by being burned one time, a human will remember not to get near fire, for fear of being burned. This is not true for all organisms, as fish tend to bite multiple times on baited hooks, not remembering that the trap can kill them.

Additionally, humans do the opposite about things that make them feel good. Human beings have different taste buds on their tongues to evaluate the foods that they consume. Sweet and hearty foods taste good to you, because the body dictates this as a flavor you like. The body does this because it knows that sugars, fats, and proteins are good for the body, and therefore humans grow to like the foods that are associated with nutrients that they need. In the same way, foods that are acidic or basic do not generally taste good to humans in their most basic form, as they are sour (acidic) and bitter (basic), and can throw off the natural pH levels of the body.

Expanding further is the joy that most humans feel from company. This happy feeling is associated with safety, as humans are safer in groups than they are on their own. Therefore, the body will remember good memories of the happy feelings brought on by good company with people that they like. This is yet another aspect of the evolutionary aspect of humans known as the senses and feelings, which aid us as organisms in our environment so that we can survive and live optimally.

Students will collect and synthesize information that describes how sensory receptors react to stimuli through the transmission of messages to the brain. The information will also detail how the messages lead to immediate behaviors or memory stores.

Organism Experiment

For this experiment, a question has been provided for you. Work with your child to come up with a hypothesis and then perform the experiment together.

Question

Is the yeast alive?

Materials

- Funnel
- Measuring cup
- Warm water
- Clear plastic bottle
- Yeast
- Sugar
- Balloon

Method

1. Using the funnel, pour 20 mL of warm water into the plastic bottle.
2. Pour the yeast into the warm water.
3. Move the bottle in circular motions to combine the water and yeast.
4. Add the sugar to the yeast and water mixture.
5. Move the bottle in circular motions to combine the sugar with the yeast and water mixture.

6. Stretch the opening of the balloon and place it over the top of the bottle.
7. Observe the mixture and the balloon.
8. Let the bottle sit in a warm location for 20 minutes.
9. Observe what happens over time.

Consider Testing . . .

- What happens when you change the amount of yeast?
- What happens when you change the amount of water?
- What happens when you change the temperature of the water?
- What happens when you change the size of the balloon?

Let's Review—Checklist

As you are helping your child with the world of organisms, here are some key points to keep in mind:

- Every living organism is made up of cells that can only be seen through a microscope.
- Cells are living and can perform similar functions.
- Cells have similar structures that include a cytoplasm, membrane, nucleus, and nuclear membrane.
- Size, shape, and structure are used to identify single-cell organisms.
- Living organisms can be simple or complex; with a single cell or millions of cells.
- Organisms are able to detect and use information they get from their environments.
- Disease occurs when the structure and function of an organism breaks down.
- Lifestyle, viruses, genes, and the environment can cause disease.
- Microbes are the cause of most of the infectious diseases.
- The human body can defend itself from infectious diseases.
- The body is able to build an immunity to bacterial and viral disease through vaccines.
- Bacterial infections can be effectively fought with antibiotics but not viral infections.

CHAPTER 12

Ecosystems—Interactions, Energy, and Dynamics

How do organisms interact with and affect the environment around them? An ecosystem is an interactive network that involves biotic and abiotic components. There is a hierarchy to the structure of an ecosystem that enables it to survive and develop. Organisms form species, species form populations, populations form communities, communities form ecosystems, and these ecosystems come together to make our biosphere. Organisms within the ecosystem get the materials and energy they need to develop and reproduce. As the interactions develop, the characteristics of an ecosystem change. Over a period of time, these changes can influence whether an ecosystem remains viable or not.

What Should My Child Already Understand?

By the time your child reaches middle school, he should have a good understanding of ecosystems. He should know that:

- Most of the food that animals eat initially came from a plant source.
- Organisms will only survive within their ecosystem if it meets all of their needs.
- Living things can be divided into many groups based on a variety of characteristics.
- Matter that exists within an ecosystem cycles from the air through the soil and among all of the organisms as they live and die. These organisms get the materials they need to survive and excrete their waste into their environment.
- Changes to the physical characteristics of an environment will influence the organisms living there.

FACT

When talking about ecosystems, the term *competition* does not necessarily mean physical fighting between plants and animals. It refers to an organism's efforts to get a resource that is limited. It can sometimes mean being able to find and use a resource before another plant or animal can get to it.

Disciplinary Core Ideas

The following concepts have been established by the Next Generation Science Standards as some of the important points of understanding in studying ecosystems. Following are some of the topics your child will learn about and discuss in school.

Interdependent Relationships in Ecosystems

Populations and organisms depend on interactions with living and nonliving factors within their environments. These interactions can limit the growth of these organisms and populations. There are different types of interactions; they include: competitive, mutually beneficial, and predatory. These interactions may vary through ecosystems, but they share patterns.

Organisms and populations within an ecosystem that share similar needs for food, oxygen, and water can compete for limited resources. Access to limited resources can limit the growth and reproduction of an organism or population. Predatory interactions can decrease or eliminate the number of organisms in a population. Interactions that are mutually beneficial can lead to each organism needing the others in order to survive. The organisms involved in different interactions may vary, but their patterns of interacting with the environment are shared.

Cycles of Matter and Energy Transfer in Ecosystems

Organisms contain atoms. These atoms are continually cycled among living and nonliving components of an ecosystem. Food webs illustrate the transfer of matter and energy among consumers, decomposers, and producers as these groups interact with each other and the environment in an ecosystem. Matter transfers in and out of physical environments at every level. Nutrients from dead animal and plant life are recycled by decomposers back into terrestrial environments in the soil and aquatic environments in the water.

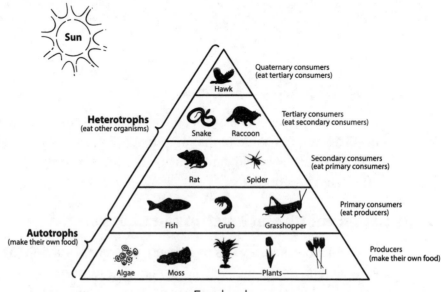

Food web

Food webs include producers, consumers, and decomposers. Producers are all forms of plants that make their own food. Consumers do not make their own food. They get their food from plants and animals. Consumers include herbivores, carnivores, and omnivores. Herbivores eat only plants. Carnivores eat only other animals. Omnivores eat both plants and animals.

Ecosystem Dynamics, Functioning, and Resilience

Over periods of time, the characteristics of an ecosystem will vary. Shifts in populations can occur if disruptions within any part of an ecosystem take place. The level of health of the biodiversity within an ecosystem is often measured by its integrity or completeness. Ecosystems are by nature dynamic, and their attributes vary over periods of time. Shifts in an ecosystem's population will occur with disruptions to its biological and physical characteristics. Biodiversity refers to the range of species found in the oceanic and terrestrial ecosystems of the earth.

Social Interactions and Group Behavior

Alterations in biodiversity may impact the resources needed by humans, including energy, food, and medical materials. These changes can also affect the ecosystem services that humans need, including recycling and the purification of water.

ALERT

The flow of energy within an ecosystem is best demonstrated through a food web, not a food chain. Food webs show the complex nature of the relationships that exist in an ecosystem. They demonstrate how plants and animals within an ecosystem are connected and rely on each other to survive.

Key Ecosystem Terms

These terms are important to a good understanding of ecosystems:

- Abiotic—Nonliving factors within an ecosystem that include air, sunlight, and weather
- Adaptations—Attributes that enable organisms to survive in a specific ecosystem
- Bacteria—A decomposer that is the simplest group of the five kingdoms of life and that has one cell and no membrane-bound nucleus
- Biotic—Living factors within an ecosystem that include decomposers, consumers, and producers
- Carbon Dioxide—A nutrient that plants need for photosynthesis
- Carnivores—Animals that do eat other animals and do not eat plants
- Consumers—Animals that need to eat other organisms to live
- Decomposers—Organisms that do not eat but rather break down dead material by secreting enzymes on them and then absorb nutrients from the material
- Earthworm—An organism that is an omnivore and a scavenger animal
- Ecosystem—All living and nonliving things in a specific region
- Enzyme—A biological substance that increases the speed of chemical reactions and that decomposers use to get nutrients from dead materials
- Food Chain—A linear connection showing the transfer of energy and nutrients through an ecosystem
- Food Web—A complex network containing many food chains that shows the transfer of energy and nutrients through the interactions within an ecosystem
- Herbivores—Animals that eat plants but not animals
- Kingdom—One of five broad groups of organisms including animals, bacteria, fungi, plants, and protists
- Litter—Dead material that is decomposing
- Omnivores—Animals that eat plants and other animals
- Photosynthesis—The process that takes place in chloroplasts and is used by plants to produce their own energy
- Predator—An animal that hunts and kills other animals for food
- Prey—Animals that are hunted and killed by predators for food
- Producers—Organisms that use photosynthesis to make their own food

- Protists—A group within the five kingdoms of life that lives in aquatic habitats and has one cell with a membrane-bound nucleus
- Scavengers—Animals that eat organisms that are dead for food
- Species—A category of organism with specific characteristics; two organisms within the same species must be able to reproduce fertile offspring

Key Ecosystem Concepts

Ecosystems help you learn more about organisms and their relationships within their environments.

Ecosystem Q&A

Q: What do living organisms need to survive?
A: All living organisms need nonliving things to survive in their environments, including air, sunlight, and water. Without these nonliving things, living organisms would not be able to grow, develop, and reproduce, and they would eventually die.

Q: What is an ecosystem?
A: Every living organism grows and reproduces. In order to do this, they interact with the environment to get the energy and materials they need. Ecosystems are made up of all of the biotic and abiotic factors that exist within a particular habitat. Living factors are referred to as biotic and include animals, plants, and microorganisms. Nonliving factors are called abiotic and include the air, atmosphere, climate, earth, soil, sun, temperature, and water. Each organism has its own niche in an ecosystem. A niche is a particular role to play. As biotic and abiotic factors interact within an ecosystem, carbon and nitrogen are recycled, and energy flows. Ecosystems range from small fish bowls to large lakes, from the space under a rock to an open field in the country. Every ecosystem needs energy to survive. Many of them get it from the sun through the process of photosynthesis. The energy from photosynthesis flows from the producers to the consumers, from plants to the animals that eat the plants, within the ecosystem. Within ecosystems, the

recycling of matter also takes place. Nutrients such as carbon, nitrogen, and water are all constantly recycled. The recycling of nutrients and the flow of energy are evidence of the interactions between biotic and abiotic factors and between organisms and their environments.

Q: How is an ecosystem organized?

A: Ecosystems are divided into several levels of organization. A group of individuals that are connected by genetics and that produce offspring are members of a species. A group of organisms that are part of the same species and are living and interacting in the same region are referred to as a population. All of the populations of various species living and interacting in the same region are called a community. All of the populations and all of the nonliving factors of a particular region are called an ecosystem.

Q: What is a niche?

A: Every organism within a particular ecosystem has a role to play. *Niche* refers to the particular role that an organism plays. These roles include the flow of energy within the ecosystem. The flow of energy involves the food eaten by an organism and the passage of this energy as the organism is eaten by something else. A niche also involves the interactions between organisms in recycling nutrients within the ecosystem.

Q: What is a habitat?

A: Habitat refers to the physical place in which a species lives. There are many factors that characterize a habitat, including rainfall, sunlight, and air temperatures. These factors affect the traits that are needed for plants and animals to be able to survive in that area.

Q: What is a biome?

A: A biome is a large community of similar organism populations that live in the same area. A forest, desert, tundra, and ocean are all examples of biomes. Biomes differ by their abiotic factors, in particular their climate. These differences influence the plants and animals that live within them.

Q: What is an energy pyramid?

A: Plants produce their own energy by converting sunlight into glucose through the process of photosynthesis. Herbivores eat the plants and the energy contained in them. Any leftover energy that the plant did not use in its development is then available for the herbivore to use as it forms tissue and lives. As the herbivore uses the energy, it is released as heat. Other organisms eat the herbivores and the energy contained in them. Any leftover energy that the herbivore did not use in its development is then available for the organism to use as it forms tissue and lives. At each stage of energy transfer from one organism to another, there is some energy loss. The energy pyramid is made up of steps referred to as trophic levels. Organisms that produce energy through photosynthesis are called *autotrophs* and are found on the first trophic level. Organisms that eat producers are called *primary consumers* and are found on the second trophic level. Organisms that eat primary consumers are called *secondary consumers* and are found on the third trophic level. Organisms that eat secondary consumers are called *tertiary consumers* and are found on the fourth trophic level. As an example, grass is eaten by a mouse, which is eaten by a snake, which is then eaten by a hawk.

Q: How does matter move through an ecosystem?

A: Living organisms need energy and nonliving matter to survive. The matter is used to grow, reproduce, and perform the functions of life and is referred to as nutrients. As the nutrients are received and used, they become recycled in the ecosystem. Decomposers release nutrients into the soil. The nutrients are then taken through roots into plants. When the plants are eaten, the nutrients are passed to primary consumers. As consumers higher on the energy pyramid eat the primary consumers, the energy is passed on. When a living organism dies, its body is broken down by decomposers and the cycle continues.

Q: How does energy flow through an ecosystem?

A: Every living organism needs energy to survive. They use energy to grow, reproduce, and perform the functions of life. Energy cannot be created or destroyed; it can only change its form. As energy flows through an ecosystem, its form changes. The sun provides energy to most ecosystems. Producers use the sunlight to make energy. The sunlight is converted into glucose and is used by producers to grow, reproduce, and live. When consumers eat producers, they get some of that energy. Consumers that are eaten by other consumers pass the remaining energy on.

Q: What is a food chain?
A: A food chain is a diagram model that demonstrates how energy flows from one organism to another within an ecosystem. At each step of the chain, there is a loss of energy. About ten percent of the initial energy flows to the next level.

Q: What is a food web?
A: A food chain is a basic link within a food web. A food web demonstrates the complexity of the interactions among decomposers, producers, and consumers within an ecosystem.

Q: What is the nitrogen cycle?
A: Every living organism needs nitrogen to survive. Nitrogen is a nutrient that is a vital component of protein. The nitrogen cycle includes air, living organisms, and soil. About 78 percent of air is nitrogen. It is released into the air through the waste of dead organisms. Many producers cannot use this form of nitrogen. They need the nitrogen to be mixed with other elements before it can be used. The first step in the nitrogen cycle is fixation. During this step, bacteria change the nitrogen into ammonium. The second step is nitrification. During this step, the ammonium is changed into nitrates that plants can absorb and use. The third step involves assimilation, where plants absorb the nitrates into their roots to be used in their development. The fourth step involves the decaying process of ammonification, which takes place when a plant or animal dies. Decomposers change the nitrogen into ammonium and then it returns to the nitrogen cycle. Finally denitrification takes place, where extra nitrogen from the soil is released into the air. Without nitrogen, living organisms would not survive.

Nitrogen is a vital component of cells. It is necessary in the production of chlorophyll, which is used by plants to make their food and energy through the process of photosynthesis.

Q: What is the carbon cycle?
A: The carbon cycle is vital to the food chain and enables ecosystems to survive. Living tissue needs carbon to develop. Every living organism contains carbon. Carbon is also found in the air, water, and minerals. Carbon is attached to oxygen in the atmosphere and is referred to as carbon dioxide. Carbon dioxide is used by plants along with sunlight to produce their own food. The carbon from the carbon dioxide becomes a component of the plant. Carbon dioxide keeps heat in the atmosphere, and without it the earth would be frozen. Plants take carbon dioxide from the air and mix it with water. The plants then use the energy from the sun to turn the mixture into sugars and oxygen. Animals eat the plants containing the sugars. The sugars are broken down by the animals and turned into energy and carbon dioxide. The carbon dioxide is returned to the atmosphere and the cycle continues. When consumers eat plants, the carbon dioxide is passed on as a compound. As these animals breathe, carbon dioxide is released into the air. When plants die, decomposers break down the bodies and release the carbon compounds.

FACT

Interactions that occur within an ecosystem are called *symbiosis*. There are three types of symbiosis: mutualism, parasitism, and commensalism. Mutualism happens when two organisms benefit from their relationship. Parasitism takes place when one organism in a relationship benefits and the other is harmed. Commensalism occurs when one organism in a relationship benefits and the other does not benefit and is not harmed.

Q: What is the oxygen cycle?
A: Every living organism contains some amount of oxygen. Oxygen is a major element found in the atmosphere and is always connected to

other elements. The oceans, rivers, and lakes contain large amounts of oxygen. As water moves through its cycle, oxygen is added. Plants take carbon dioxide and mix it with water. The result of this combination is sugar and oxygen. The plant uses the sugar as food and releases the oxygen into the air. Animals use the oxygen to breathe air and the cycle continues.

Science and Engineering Practices

In learning about ecosystems, your child will use science and engineering practices to better understand the ideas that relate to their energy, interactions, and dynamics. These practices might include:

- Defining a problem and then planning and carrying out investigations about the impact that humans have on ecosystems
- Creating and using a food web model to show how matter and energy transfer throughout an ecosystem
- Analyzing and interpreting data to identify the influences of an increase or decrease in resources on a particular population
- Using mathematics to compare populations within a particular ecosystem
- Constructing explanations about the changes to an ecosystem over a particular period of time
- Engaging in arguments using evidence to discuss the benefits and harm of a new species being introduced to a particular ecosystem
- Constructing and describing a food web of a specific ecosystem, showing energy flow and trophic levels

Next Generation Science Standards Performance Expectations

These performance expectations describe what your child should be able to demonstrate and understand about the specific science unit he is studying in middle school. From these expectations your child's teachers will determine how successfully he understands and can apply the concepts that have been covered.

Discover the Effects of Resources on Organisms

Performance expectation MS.LS2.1 states that students should "analyze and interpret data to provide evidence for the effects of resource availability on organisms and populations of organisms in an ecosystem."

In addition to the idea of resources for plants and their energy transfer and correlation with other beings in the ecosystem, the ecosystem plays an important part in the availability of nutrients for plants.

For example, if you were to look at plants that exist in non-changing climates, like those found near the equator, you see that these plants do not undergo seasonal changes. Palm trees do not change color with the seasons, as they do not have seasons to change with. Due to their environment, palm trees have resources available to them 365 days a year. A palm tree does not need to molt its leaves and hibernate for a cold and dry season like other plants do, because it does not have to undergo such adversities. The same is true for plants like cacti.

FACT

While different organisms require different things to live, all living things need specific things to be able to survive, including food, energy, water, air, space, light, and shelter. Without these things, plants and animals could not survive. Habitats meet these needs for plants and animals, and are homes within an ecosystem.

In areas where climate and air density does change by the season, especially subzero temperatures, plants will molt their leaves and other components that they need to survive. By removing their leaves, a plant reduces the risk of having its insides frozen during the winter. Likewise, in the spring and summer months, when the temperature increases and is temperate, plants have the best possible access to resources, and therefore will be their strongest. It is at this point that plants begin to flower and reproduce, because they are best suited to at that particular time.

Therefore you can conclude that the flow of energy through plants in an ecosystem is dependent on the availability of the resources that they need to survive.

Your child will analyze and interpret information to provide proof of the influence of the availability of resources on organisms in a particular ecosystem. Focus is on cause-and-effect relationships among available resources, individual organism development, and organism populations in ecosystems during periods of both scarcity and abundance.

Predict Patterns of Interactions

According to performance expectation MS.LS2.2, your child should be able to "construct an explanation that predicts patterns of interactions among organisms across multiple ecosystems."

By looking at what you know about plant and animal aspirating relationships, you can apply these same concepts to the ones that exist below the sea. If you understand how humans take in O_2 and expel CO_2, and plants undergo the opposite process, you can then assume that underwater fish and seaweed have a similar relationship. The only difference between the two systems is the medium for transfer of resources. While animals and plants inhale and exhale air, separating the things that they need from it, fish and underwater plants do the same thing within a medium of water.

Your child will construct an explanation that will predict a pattern of interaction among several organisms in a variety of ecosystems. Focus is on predicting patterns of interactions that occur consistently in various ecosystems. Examples might include mutually beneficial, predatory, and competitive interactions.

Describe the Cycling of Matter

Performance expectation MS.LS2.3 states that students should "develop a model to describe the cycling of matter and flow of energy among living and nonliving parts of an ecosystem."

In addition to energy transfer through waste, as in the O_2 and CO_2 exchange discussed in the previous section, there are other ways in which plants and animals cycle energy within a system. Most notably, living things transfer energy through death. When an organism dies, it begins to decompose, thanks to bacteria and molds that feast upon the remnants and rot of the deceased. In turn, the decomposition returns nutrients to the soil in the area in which the plant or animal died. By returning nutrients to the soil, the organism, now deceased, has allowed for other organisms to thrive. If a plant were to be grown in this spot, it would absorb a considerably better amount of resources as compared to dry soil. The life cycle is the perfect way to illustrate how energy flows between the living and the nonliving in an ecosystem.

ESSENTIAL

Decomposers are the last organisms on the food web. They use enzymes to break down organisms that have died. As they are broken down, the nutrients from the dead organisms are returned to the soil and are then used by plants to grow.

Your child will create a model to detail energy flow and matter cycling in both nonliving and living components of ecosystems. Focus is on describing matter conservation and energy flow out of and into a variety of ecosystems and on detailing the limitations of the systems.

Show How Changes in Components Affect Population

According to performance expectation MS.LS2.4, students should "construct an argument supported by empirical evidence that changes to physical or biological components of an ecosystem affect populations."

If you think about how plants act during different seasons, you can imagine how global climate change can affect plants, which in turn can affect humans (as we require them to create oxygen, as well as a food source). Humans must be sure that they do not throw off the natural balance of plants, as it can come back to haunt us in a major way. Additionally, we must make sure that we take good care of the soil of the earth, as there are more threats via contaminants to the ecosystem beyond the air. Chemicals released into the environment though dumping and littering can neuter the once nutrient-rich areas that different organisms require to survive.

We must learn to continue to work in tandem with our ecosystems, as opposed to working against them. We cannot expect plants and other organisms to continue to contribute to the environment if we are slowly killing them off.

ALERT

Species live within a particular ecosystem because they have similar needs and adaptations that are met by the environment. They compete for the resources within the ecosystem and do not necessarily get along. Their primary objective is to survive, and they will get the resources they need to do that.

Your child will use empirical evidence to construct an argument that changes in biological and physical aspects of an ecosystem will influence populations. Focus is on noting patterns in data and making justified inferences about population changes, and on assessing empirical evidence that supports arguments about ecosystem changes.

Assess Design Solutions for Ecosystem and Biodiversity Services

Performance expectation MS.LS2.5 states that students should "evaluate competing design solutions for maintaining biodiversity and ecosystem services."

Your child will discuss the necessity for ecosystem maintenance for the longevity of species, and then consider actual plans for how to accomplish this. In order to come up with solutions for keeping ecosystems healthy through biodiversity, she must understand the current threats to such a status, specifically pests such as disease and invasive species, as well as pollutants that man has brought to nature.

The easiest of these two things to understand and control is pollution. The best way to do this is to use efficient sciences as well as efficient waste disposal. The dumping of solid and liquid waste can be moved away from ecosystems in which they may cause harm. Specifically, waste can be relocated to desolate desert landscapes in which there will be minimal ecosystem damage, considering there is not a significant populace in hot, dry areas.

The other factors that your child must account for, pests and diseases, are something that modern science has allowed us to fully control. For example, we must be fervent in our use of safe chemicals. We must use those that protect plants on the surface, but that do not poison the soil beneath them. We must also be extremely careful about the things that we import, due to the fact that some invasive species can be accidentally transported and pose serious risks to ecosystems. We must attempt to remove the invasive species that can plague our environments.

The reason for all of this conservation is to assure that all of the essential parts of our ecosystem are not strained by other unnatural factors that have been imposed upon them by the very denizens of said environment.

Middle school students will assess competing design solutions for the maintenance of ecosystem and biodiversity services. Examples might include purifying water, recycling nutrients, and preventing the erosion of soil. The design solution limitations may include social, economic, and scientific factors.

Ecosystem Experiment

For this experiment, a question has been provided for you. Work with your child to come up with a hypothesis and then perform the experiment together.

Question

How will water and sunlight affect a biome?

Materials

- 4 clear 2 L plastic bottles
- Scissors
- Ruler
- Small rocks
- Potting soil
- Trowel
- Bean seeds
- Measuring cup
- Water
- Resealable bags (large enough to hold 2 L plastic bottles)
- Permanent marker

Method

1. Cut each of the plastic bottles in half.
2. Place a 2.5 cm layer of small rocks in the bottom of each bottle.
3. Place a 5 cm layer of soil on top of the rocks.
4. Create a finger-width trench in the soil.
5. Place 3 seeds into the trench with a space between each of them.
6. Cover the seeds with soil.
7. Pour 75 mL of water over the soil in one of the bottles. Repeat with the second bottle.
8. Place each bottle into a resealable bag and close the locking zipper.
9. Use your marker to label the amount of water used for the first two bottles.
10. Pour 125 mL of water over the soil of the third bottle. Repeat with the fourth.
11. Place each bottle into a resealable bag and close the locking zipper.
12. Use your marker to label the amount of water used.
13. Place a 75 mL bag and a 125 mL bag in a sunny area.
14. Place the other 75 mL and 125 mL bags in a darker area.
15. Leave the biomes for one week.
16. Check the biomes daily and record your observations.

Consider Testing . . .

- How did the sunlight affect the growth of the seeds?
- How did the water affect the growth of the seeds?
- Which seeds grew the most?
- Which seeds grew the least?
- What would happen if you introduced earthworms into the biome?

Let's Review—Checklist

As your child is learning about organisms and how they interact, here are some key points you should know in order to help with his studies:

- Living organisms rely on their interactions with biotic and abiotic factors in order to survive in an environment.

- Access to resources that are limited can affect the size of the population and the growth of organisms.
- Resources that are limited can create competition between organisms within an ecosystem.
- The relationships between organisms within an ecosystem can be competitive, mutually beneficial, or predatory.
- Energy and matter move through an ecosystem between consumers, decomposers, and producers.
- Energy is needed for survival, and much of it is produced through photosynthesis.
- Food webs model the relationships of organisms and how matter and energy move through an ecosystem.
- Consumers within a food web eat animals and plants.
- Decomposers within a food web break down dead material and release the nutrients into the soil.
- Producers within a food web create their own food.
- The cycle of matter moves between air, living organisms, and soil in ecosystems.
- Energy and matter are continuously recycled through ecosystems.
- An ecosystem can be impacted if the biotic or abiotic factors within it are changed.
- New species that are introduced into an ecosystem can upset its state of balance.
- Biodiversity involves the amount of species variety in ecosystems on the earth.
- Ecosystems can be affected by human activity.

CHAPTER 13

Heredity—Inheritance and Variation of Traits

How do traits get passed on from generation to generation? How do individuals who are related have different traits? Heredity is the reason that offspring are similar to the parents. It refers to the biological actions that take place through which traits are passed from generation to generation through genes. Genes contain the necessary information needed to make the proteins responsible for the traits of every living organism. Genes are contained within chromosomes, which are found in every cell. Sometimes these genes develop mutations that can affect the physical traits of an individual. The development and ability of an individual to function is influenced by the connections between genes and the environment.

What Should My Child Already Understand?

Your child should understand that some of the similarities between parents and children are inherited physical traits and others are learned behaviors. She should also know that:

- Living organisms of the same kind may have many similar traits because they are passed on from parents to offspring.
- Some organisms develop characteristics because of the interactions within the environment in which they live.

FACT

Chromosomes are found in all types of cells within an organism, not just the sex cells or blood cells. When cells divide, the new cell that is created contains the same number of chromosomes as the original cell.

She should also understand the significant role that technology plays in society. It is able to manipulate materials with far more efficiency than humans. Many changes that take place in the world are necessary for survival, including changes to communication, food, protection, shelter, and transportation, as well as the ability to learn and express new ideas. Advances in technology have led to development in genetic research and engineering. These developments have enabled scientists to manipulate DNA, in order to find cures for illnesses. DNA changes are also used to modify animals and plant food sources.

Disciplinary Core Ideas

The following concepts have been established by the Next Generation Science Standards as some of the important points of understanding in studying heredity. Following are some of the topics your child will learn about and discuss in school.

Inheritance of Traits

How are traits between generations related? Genes control a particular protein that influence the traits of an individual. Genes are found in chromosomes within cells. Every chromosome pair has two forms of many specific genes. Every distinct gene regulates the creation of particular proteins that then influence the characteristics of an individual.

ESSENTIAL

Organisms that reproduce sexually pass an entire set of DNA from the mother and an entire set of DNA from the father to the offspring. Every cell in the offspring contains DNA from both the mother and the father.

Modifications to genes are referred to as mutations. Mutations to genes can lead to alterations in proteins that can influence the functions and structures of an organism and result in a change in its traits. Alterations of inherited traits between parents and their offspring result from genetic differences that are caused by an inherited subset of chromosomes.

Variation of Traits

Why do individuals within the same species look and behave the same? Through sexual reproduction, each of the parents supplies one half of the genes that the offspring acquires, which leads to a variation between the offspring and its parents. Offspring have two of each chromosome and two alleles of each gene, each of them acquired from the particular parent. The two alleles are a result of a parent's traits, which is why the offspring resembles the parents.

ALERT

All of the cells within an organism contain identical sets of DNA molecules, each with identical genetic information. For example, the DNA molecules that are found in the leaves of a plant are the same as the DNA molecules that are in the flower of that plant.

Mutations can cause genetic information to be changed. Mutations can have beneficial, harmful, or neutral effects on an organism's proteins or traits. Mutation could lead to a malformed system or appendage on an organism, or an appendage or system that would give the organism a better chance of survival over others.

Key Heredity Terms

These terms are important to a good understanding of heredity:

- Allele—A variant form of gene
- Amino Acid—A compound that is necessary for building proteins
- Cell—Basic structural unit of living organisms
- Characteristics—Specific qualities of living organisms
- Chromosome—The component of the cell that carries genes
- Deoxyribonucleic Acid (DNA)—The molecule that holds and carries genetic information
- Diversity—A variation within living organisms
- Dominant Allele—An allele that produces the same phenotype regardless of its paired allele
- Fertilization—The joining of female and male gamete cells
- Gamete Cells—Reproduction cells
- Gene—A DNA segment that contains code for a particular trait
- Genetic Engineering—The process of artificially adding DNA to an organism
- Genetics—The study of genes, heredity, and genetic variations
- Genome—The complete set of DNA for an organism
- Genotype—The genetic composition of a particular individual
- Heredity—The process of transmitting characteristics from parents to their offspring
- Heterozygous—A genotype with two different alleles for one trait
- Homozygous—A genotype with two of the same alleles for one trait
- Meiosis—Cell division that creates gametes
- Mitosis—The stage of cell division when the nucleus divides, and two cells are produced with the same number and type of chromosomes as the initial cell

- Nucleotides—Four complex molecules that create a DNA molecule: adenine, cytosine, guanine, and thymine
- Nucleus—The cell component that has genetic information contained within it.
- Ova—Female gamete cells
- Protein Synthesis—The process of producing proteins
- Recessive Allele—An allele that will not be expressed if it is present with a dominant allele
- Replication—DNA duplication that takes place before the completion of cell division
- Ribosomes—Particles in the cytoplasm where amino acids come together to produce protein
- Sperm—Male gamete cells
- Trait—A characteristic of an organism that is passed from parents to offspring
- Variation—Variant forms of traits
- Zygote—The fusion of male and female gametes, e.g., a fertilized egg

Key Heredity Concepts

Heredity is the transmission of genetic traits from one generation to the next. By studying heredity, your child learns why some traits are passed on and some are not.

Heredity Q&A

Q: What is heredity?
A: Heredity is the passing of traits from parents to offspring. Our traits are contained within our genes. We have thousands of genes that contain our DNA and are found in our chromosomes. Humans have two sets of 23 chromosomes, making 46 in total, in each of our cells. When parents reproduce, they pass one complete set to their offspring. This takes place when the sperm cell joins with the egg cell to form a unicellular zygote. The zygote cell will divide into more cells until it develops into a baby. The chromosomes that are passed to offspring are contributed in a random sequence.

Q: What is a trait?

A: A trait is an observable characteristic in an organism. Traits are passed from parents to offspring. There are physical and behavioral traits. Physical traits determine the characteristics of an organism's physical form. Behavioral traits determine the characteristic of how an organism acts. Your traits are defined by the instruction codes in your genes. The set of genetic information of each trait is referred to as an allele. Each person has two alleles for each trait. When there are two of the same alleles for a specific trait, it is referred to as a *homozygous genotype*. When there are two different alleles for a specific trait, it is referred to as a *heterozygous genotype*. The heterozygous genotype will have a dominant trait and a recessive trait. It is the dominant trait that becomes the expressed trait. The alleles of a person are determined by their parents, one set from the mother, and one set from the father. Each offspring of a set of parents receives a different combination of alleles.

Q: What is DNA?

A: The nucleus of every cell contains instructions for growing and living. The cell is able to fulfill its role within an organism based on these instructions. The instructions are contained within a DNA molecule. DNA stands for deoxyribonucleic acid. The DNA is the blueprint for the development of that cell. A strand of DNA contains a sequence of the four nucleotides: guanine, thymine, adenine, and cytosine. The nucleotides are formed into sequences. These sequences of nucleotides become the genes that instruct your cells to produce the proteins needed to perform specific functions.

Q: What are nucleotides?

A: Nucleotides are the chemical structure of DNA and have three components: a phosphate group, a base with nitrogen, and a five-carbon sugar also referred to as deoxyribose. The nitrogen base has four possible sequences that include adenine, guanine, thymine, and cytosine.

Q: What are genes?

A: Genes are the instructions that tell your cells to build the proteins you need to function. Genes contain your DNA.

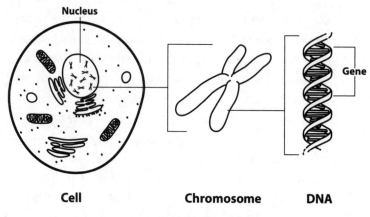

Genes broken out of cell

Q: What are proteins?

A: Proteins make living organisms function. Humans contain millions of cells that all have a particular job to do. Each of these cells contains thousands of different types of proteins that come together to make the cell function properly. Cells use the DNA code in their genes to make the proteins they need. When a cell needs a specific type of protein, the nucleus produces an RNA message molecule and sends it into the cytoplasm. Inside the cytoplasm, the ribosomes decode the instructions and produce the correct type of protein. The new protein moves to the locations within the cell where it is needed and begins to work.

Q: Why do organisms build proteins?

A: Proteins are needed by the body to build muscles, transport oxygen, control chemical reactions, and perform life's functions. Proteins are composed of amino acid units. DNA holds the instructions needed for placing the amino acids into a particular order, which is necessary for the creation of proteins. Each human cell contains about twenty-two thousand genes. Every cell has the same genes but not the same proteins. The type of protein in a cell is based on the function of the cell.

Q: What are chromosomes?

A: Chromosomes are the small units in which DNA is contained.

Q: Who was Gregor Mendel?

A: Gregor Mendel is considered to be the father of genetics. He experimented with plants to determine which ones produced offspring with traits that were the same as those of the parent plant. Through his experiments he discovered the law of segregation.

FACT

Gregor Mendel formulated the law of segregation, the law of independent assortment, and the law of dominance while studying pea plant reproduction in the mid-1800s. These laws are still relevant today.

Q: What is the law of segregation?

A: The law of segregation states that there are two factors that regulate a particular characteristic, one of which is dominant over the other, and these factors separate and are passed on to different gametes when parents reproduce.

Q: What is genetic code?

A: The sequences of the four bases of the nucleotide create the genetic code in cells. Since chromosomes hold millions of nucleotides, the possible sequence combinations of these bases are vast.

Q: What is DNA replication?

A: Each time new cells are created in your body, your DNA makes a copy of itself. The DNA in these new cells must be the same as all of your other cells or they could potentially fail. The DNA replication process must be accurate so that the new cells are formed properly with the correct genetic information. DNA replication takes place in the cell cycle's S phase before the cell is divided or mitosis occurs.

Q: What is a Punnett square?

A: A Punnett square is a tool that uses the laws of probability to predict the offspring of two parents. Punnett squares are created using the factors of each parent and placing them correctly on a specialized grid.

A Punnett square is a diagram model that predicts the results of a specific breeding analysis. It gets its name from Reginald C. Punnett who developed the tool. Biologists use the model to find out the probability of an offspring being born with a specific genetic trait. The Punnett Square is an arrangement that shows all of the possible combinations that could be transferred to an offspring from the traits of the mother and the father.

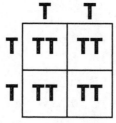

Two dominant tall parents

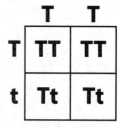

One dominant tall and one mixed hybrid parent

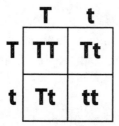

Two mixed hybrid parents

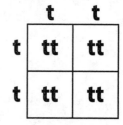

Two recessive short parents

Q: What is a mutation?

A: DNA replication must be accurate for cells to perform as they should. When the replication process is not accurate and a base is placed incorrectly in a sequence, a permanent change takes place. This change is called a mutation. A mutation in a single nucleotide would have very little effect on an organism. A mutation of a protein could affect the performance of the protein, which could significantly affect an organism.

Q: What are chromosomal mutations?

A: Mutations that take place within chromosomes are called chromosomal mutations. These mutations can potentially affect many of the genes in an organism. Types of chromosomal mutations include the deletion, duplication, inversion, insertion, and translocation of a DNA segment.

Q: What are the possible causes of mutations?

A: Mutations do not typically occur because of replication errors. They can happen unintentionally or they can be caused by chemicals in the environment.

Q: What are genotypes and phenotypes?

A: Genotypes are the combinations of alleles for a specific gene that an individual has. There are four types of genotypes: homozygous, heterozygous, homozygous dominant, and homozygous recessive. Homozygous genotypes have two of the same alleles. Heterozygous genotypes have one dominant and one recessive allele. Homozygous dominant genotypes have two dominant alleles. Homozygous recessive genotypes have two recessive alleles. Phenotypes refer to the traits that can be observed. They are the traits that are formed from the genotype information. Polygenic inheritance takes place when more than one gene controls a particular trait.

Science and Engineering Practices

In learning about heredity, your child will use science and engineering practices to better understand the ideas that relate to inheritance and variation of traits. These practices might include:

- Knowing and applying concepts that explain how living organisms function and adapt to their environment.
- Explaining how cells are the building units of living organisms and describing what cells need to survive.

- Comparing the characteristics of living organisms produced from one parent to those produced from two.
- Defining potential problems with genetically engineered materials.
- Using models to develop and test hypotheses involving gene behavior.
- Planning and carrying out investigations of the genes that are passed from plants to their offspring.
- Analyzing and interpreting data from his investigations of Mendelian genetics.
- Using mathematics to determine the ratios of dominant and recessive traits in various conditions.
- Constructing explanations about the cause of some mutations in humans.
- Engaging in argument using evidence to discuss the benefits and challenges of genetic testing.
- Obtaining, evaluating, and communicating information about the location of genetic information within a cell and its transfer in various organisms.
- Using a model as evidence to explain inheritance patterns that take place in offspring from sexual reproduction.

Next Generation Science Standards Performance Expectations

These performance expectations describe what your child should be able to demonstrate and understand about the specific science unit he is studying in middle school. From these expectations your child's teachers will determine how successfully he understands and can apply the concepts that have been covered.

Show How Changes in Genes Affect Proteins

Performance expectation MS.LS3.1 states that students should "develop and use a model to describe why structural changes to genes (mutations) located on chromosomes may affect proteins and may result in harmful, beneficial, or neutral effects to the structure and function of the organism."

Your child will take a look at things that can non-intentionally anchor to and alter DNA. Usually, these mutations brought on by chemical induction are negative, and more often than not, this negative mutation results in cancer. The chemicals that cause this sort of mutation are referred to as carcinogens, and there has yet to be a case of positive mutation as a result of interaction with these materials. Humans must be careful of things like these, such as lead, which is the reason that lead piping, paint, and petroleum are so dangerous.

FACT

There are many different kinds of protein molecules that are produced within an organism's cells. The actions of these protein molecules can influence the behaviors and physical characteristics of the organism.

Your child will create and utilize a model to describe the reason that structural changes in genes on chromosomes may influence proteins and may lead to beneficial, harmful, or neutral results in the function and structure of an organism. Focus is on the concept that changes in genes may lead to the creation of different proteins.

Describe the Differences in Reproduction Types

According to performance expectation MS.LS3.2, your child should be able to "develop and use a model to describe why asexual reproduction results in offspring with identical genetic information and sexual reproduction results in offspring with genetic variation."

Asexual organisms do not need to find a mate to reproduce; they split their own DNA to create an offspring. Because of this, there are extremely small amounts of mutation, and therefore these organisms do not tend to show any evolutionary progression.

ESSENTIAL

Many different species reproduce asexually, meaning that there is no joining of two sex cells. When organisms reproduce asexually, the parent passes on its entire DNA to its offspring.

It is by asexual function that the cells of the human body reproduce. We can see through human cell reproduction, like that of skin cells, that asexual reproduction has little variation in DNA, especially compared to those who reproduce sexually (require the genetic information of two individuals). This can be shown by the rates of cancer found between the two populations. While human beings tend to have a considerably high cancer rate within its population of 7 billion, skin cells, which reproduce millions of times daily, do not have this same considerably high rate, as they do not mutate genetic information nearly as much.

Students in middle school will create and utilize a model to describe the reason that asexual reproduction leads to offspring with genetic information that is identical, and that sexual reproduction leads to offspring with genetic information with a variation. Focus is on using models including illustrations, Punnett squares, and simulations to detail the cause-and-effect relationship of the transmission of genes between parents and offspring that result in a genetic variation.

ALERT

Genes are not traits but rather are chemical sequences of nucleotides. Organisms use nucleotides to make DNA and RNA. Every DNA molecule has genetic information encoded within it.

Heredity Experiment

For this experiment, a question has been provided for you. Work with your child to come up with a hypothesis and then perform the experiment together.

Question

Can you see DNA?

Materials

- 5 mL rubbing alcohol
- Room temperature water

- 2 clear 500 mL plastic containers
- 10 mL dish soap
- 2 mL salt
- 1 whole strawberry
- 2 L zip-top bag
- 30 cm × 30 cm cheesecloth
- Tweezers

Method

1. Place the rubbing alcohol in the freezer for 5 minutes.
2. Pour 90 mL of water into a container.
3. Pour the dish soap into the water.
4. Add the salt to the soap and water solution.
5. Place the strawberry in the zip-top bag.
6. Place 20 mL of the solution into the bag with the strawberry.
7. Reseal the bag and mash the strawberry into the solution.
8. Place the cheesecloth over the second container.
9. Open the zip-top bag and pour the mixture through the cheesecloth and into the container.
10. Squeeze the excess liquid through the cheesecloth, and then place the remaining strawberry material into the garbage.
11. Add the rubbing alcohol to the strawberry liquid.
12. Use your tweezers to remove the white fibrous strands from the liquid.
13. What do you see?

Consider Testing . . .

- What happens when you do not freeze the rubbing alcohol?
- What happens when you use a different fruit or vegetable?
- What happens when you leave the strands in the liquid for a period of time?

Let's Review—Checklist

In order to help your child with her studies on heredity, keep these facts in mind:

- Cell chromosomes contain genes.
- Cells divide to form new cells for development and repair.
- Every pair of chromosomes has two variants of every gene.
- All genes affect an individual's traits.
- Traits can be changed through mutations that can affect the function and structure of a particular organism.
- Egg and sperm cells are specialized cells.
- Reproduction of organisms can occur sexually or asexually.
- During sexual reproduction, genetic information is passed from the joined egg and sperm cells to the offspring.
- Offspring from sexual reproduction receive a set of genetic information from each parent.
- Sexual reproduction passes on many variations of inherited traits.
- Genetic code is contained in DNA.
- The same genetic information is contained in every cell of a living organism.
- Each cell in an organism contains the same genetic information.
- Offspring from asexual reproduction have genetic information identical to their parent.

CHAPTER 14

Biological Evolution—Unity and Diversity

With all of the different kinds of animals, plants, and micro-organisms on earth, it seems improbable that they could be similar in any way. The study of evolution helps in explaining both how various species are similar and how they are different. Through the use of fossil records, genetic analyses, and technology advancements, relationships among organisms can be explored.

What Should My Child Already Understand?

By the end of grade five, your child understands that many kinds of living organisms can be sorted into a variety of groups using different attributes, for example size, shape, color, body parts, and movement. Within a particular ecosystem, some organisms are able to survive and thrive, and others are unable to survive and die off. Individual organisms can have similar characteristic differences. These differences can enable these individuals to better reproduce and survive. Fossils give proof of organisms that lived long ago and they can be compared to organisms living today to find similarities and differences.

FACT

The conditions of the earth's environment, including temperature and precipitation, can change over time. These changes can happen gradually or abruptly. Regardless of how they happen, these changes can cause alterations to the environment itself, such as expanded deserts, smaller glaciers, and higher sea levels.

Disciplinary Core Ideas

The following concepts have been established by the Next Generation Science Standards as some of the important points of understanding in studying biological evolution. Following are some of the topics your child will learn about and discuss in school.

Evidence of Common Ancestry and Diversity

What evidence is there to show the relationships between different types of species? A fossil record refers to fossil collection and its organization in chronological order. A fossil record establishes the existence, variation, extinction, and alterations of many forms of life and the environments in which they lived throughout the history of the earth. A fossil record and correlations of the similarities among organism anatomies make it possible to infer the lines of descent through the process of evolution. Comparisons of the development of embryos of various species can show similarities and relationships that might not be obvious in completely formed anatomical structures.

Natural Selection

How do changes in genes among living organisms influence how they are able to reproduce and survive? Natural selection results in the preponderance of specific traits in a particular population and the suppression of other traits. Through artificial selection, humans are able to affect specific traits of organisms through selective breeding. It is possible to choose specific traits of a parent that are determined by genes that are transmitted to the offspring. Natural and artificial selection are caused by specific traits providing some individuals advantages to survival and reproduction, which leads to a preponderance of particular traits found in a population.

Adaptation

Over generations, the process of adaptation through natural selection leads to alterations in the traits of species in response to changes in the conditions of the environment. Particular traits that promote reproduction and survival in new environmental conditions become more prevalent. Traits that do not promote reproduction and survival do not become more prevalent. This is how the distribution of traits in a particular population changes over periods of time.

Biodiversity and Humans

Why do individual organisms within the same species look and behave differently? Biological evolution explains the similarities and differences within a species and from one species to another. Evolution is an ongoing process that takes place as natural selection gradually influences and changes genetic traits over many generations. The traits that are passed on from one generation to the next provide the best possible advantages for meeting environmental challenges. Over many generations, the genetic changes that occur through evolution and natural selection lead not only to changes in a particular species but the development of completely new species as well.

Key Evolution Terms

These terms are important to a strong understanding of evolution:

- Adaptation—A trait that enables an organism to reproduce and survive within its environment
- Diversity—The variety and number of a particular species living in a particular ecosystem
- Evolution—The process of change within a species that takes place gradually over generations
- Evolve—To change gradually over generations
- Extinction—The disappearance of a particular species
- Fitness—The ability of a species to reproduce and survive
- Fossil—The preserved remains or trace of an organism that was alive long ago
- Fossil Record—The record of the existence of living organisms through the evidence provided by fossils
- Gene—A basic unit of hereditary information that regulates the traits passed from parents to their offspring
- Genetic Adaptation—A change to genetic code that enables the offspring of parents to better reproduce and survive in their environment
- Inherit—To get genetic characteristics from parents and previous generations
- Migrate—To move from one location to another and back in order to survive and reproduce
- Mutate—To change the state of a genetic structure that causes a new trait in the offspring of parents
- Natural Selection—A process where organisms evolve, developing new traits, in order to better survive and reproduce in a particular environment
- Offspring—The products of reproduction of a species
- Population—A group of organisms of the same species living together in the same area
- Species—A group of similar organisms that is able to reproduce to create fertile offspring
- Variation—A difference in a characteristic existing within a particular population

Key Evolution Concepts

Evolution explains biodiversity. It explains the similarities and differences among species, the changes that take place within populations, and how new organisms are created.

Evolution Q&A

Q: What is Darwin's theory of evolution?

A: Charles Darwin was an influential scientist who was intrigued by the diverse forms of life on planet Earth. He investigated to find out why some living organisms are different, why some are similar, and why there are so many diverse kinds. He studied plants and animals around the world over a twenty-year period and recorded his observations of them. Darwin developed "the theory of evolution by natural selection," and by evolution he was referring to change. His theory explains why evolution takes place. He discovered that plants and animals develop certain traits over a period of time due to the different conditions within their environments.

Q: What is natural selection?

A: Natural selection refers to the changes in the inherited genetic traits of a particular population that take place over a period of time. Inherited traits are characteristics that are passed from parents to their offspring. These inherited genetic traits are affected by your genes, which are passed from parents to offspring over generations. The ability of an organism to develop the necessary characteristics that allow it to reproduce and survive is explained by natural selection.

Q: What are adaptations?

A: Every living organism needs certain characteristics to survive. Being able to survive requires building shelter, getting food to eat, and finding a mate to reproduce. The traits that enable an organism to survive are referred to as *adaptations*. Some adaptations are more beneficial than others. Many adaptations make it possible for organisms to live in their physical environment.

Natural selection takes place when organisms within a particular species develop a variation of their inherited genetic traits. This variation makes natural selection possible. Some individuals will have advantages of reproduction and survival over others within their species, making it more probable that these individuals will produce more offspring.

Q: Why are there so many different species on earth?
A: The conditions within environments change over periods of time, which affects the organisms living within them. These organisms must adapt to the changes in order to survive. Diversity in a species makes it possible for some of its organisms to adapt and live within the changed environment.

Q: What is common ancestry?
A: While two different species may appear to have different characteristics, it is possible for them to have similar internal structures. These similarities provide evidence that they originated from a common ancestor during a period long ago and then evolved over time to be the organisms they are today. Evidence of common ancestry can also be noted in the growth structures of organisms.

ALERT

Plants and animals did not come from different ancestors. Every plant and animal came from one common ancestor. There are similarities between all organisms even if they are not visible or evident.

Q: What are vestigial structures?
A: Vestigial structure refers to the parts of a body whose use has become lost through the process of evolution. These body parts imply that the structure was used at one point but that over time its purpose became changed or voided. For instance, penguins have wings but they do not fly; instead, their wings are used for swimming.

Q: Why are similarities in embryo structures important?
A: An embryo is the initial stage of growth in a plant or animal. This stage takes place before the birth or hatching of an organism. Many embryo structures in different species appear to be similar. These sim-

ilarities provide evidence of some type of common ancestry at some point in history.

Q: What is molecular evidence?

A: Molecule studies provide more evidence of evolution and common ancestry. The use of molecular clocks enables scientists to determine the relationship between the two species by calculating the differences in their amino acid and DNA sequences. The greater the difference in the sequences, the farther apart the relationship. The smaller the difference in the sequences, the closer the relationship.

Q: What are mutations?

A: Mutations refer to changes in genes that happen randomly. Some mutations have negative effects and some have positive effects. If the mutation increases the probability of an individual's survival, it is positive. If the mutation decreases the probability of an individual's survival, it is negative.

Science and Engineering Practices

In learning about biological evolution, your child will use science and engineering practices to better understand the ideas that relate to unity and diversity. These practices might include:

- Asking and answering questions that research the factors involved in natural selection
- Using models to build a geological timeline
- Planning and implementing investigations that identify the role of variations on natural selection
- Analyzing and interpreting data to explore animal classification patterns
- Using mathematics to create a precise timescale model depicting geological time
- Developing explanations involving organisms and their relationships with the environment-based fossil records
- Using evidence to explain and predict the evolution of various animals
- Obtaining, evaluating, and communicating information to argue with evidence about the intervention of humans on animal extinction

- Creating a concept map model to show how adaptations, biodiversity, environment, evolution, fossil records, geological time, and natural selection are connected
- Creating an evolutionary tree model showing the evolution of certain animals using fossil records and DNA information

Next Generation Science Standards Performance Expectations

These performance expectations describe what your child should be able to demonstrate and understand about the specific science unit he is studying in middle school. From these expectations your child's teachers will determine how successfully he understands and can apply the concepts that have been covered.

Explore Fossils for Patterns

Performance expectation MS.LS4.1 states that students should "analyze and interpret data for patterns in the fossil record that document the existence, diversity, extinction, and change of life forms throughout the history of life on earth under the assumption that natural laws operate today as in the past."

Evolution through the natural selection of genetic traits is the engine that has driven the advancement of life forms on our planet since the very beginning of cellular life on earth. One way that your child can observe that this is a concrete fact is through fossil records. By extracting fossils from the earth, we can analyze ancient DNA of animals and their relation to animals today. We can then use carbon dating to find the approximate (within an accurate time frame) age of the organism, and then we can see at what stage in the evolutionary process this organism was at its point in life, relative to its existence on the planet.

For example, we can take the ancient remains of early human beings, date the time in which it lived, and then compare it to modern humans. This is how we have discovered the ancient chain of humans, which includes the well-known *Homo erectus* and *Homo sapien*. While there is still much mystery surrounding the chain of early humans, these findings show how today's human has advanced from the stick-wielding caveman of the ancient eras.

Your child will analyze and interpret information for patterns in fossil records that establish the existence of the diversification, extinction, and changes in organisms throughout history with the inference that laws of nature work today as they did in past times. Focus is on recognizing patterns of change in the complexity of specific organisms' anatomical structure, as well as the chronological organization of the appearance of fossils in layers of rock.

FACT

There are two types of fossils: fossilized bodies and fossilized traces. Fossilized bodies can include the remains of an organism as well as mold and cast fossils, which create a negative impression of an organism. Trace fossils show the activity of an organism and include things like footprints and nests.

Research Evolutionary Relationships

According to performance expectation MS.LS4.2, your child should be able to "apply scientific ideas to construct an explanation for the anatomical similarities and differences among modern organisms and between modern and fossil organisms to infer evolutionary relationships."

When we conceptualize the concept of life on earth and evolution, we must turn to the fact that life was created from an unexplainable spark in a nutrient-rich ooze, which allowed the first unicellular organisms to form and reproduce, evolving into the life that we see today. This was a long and trying process for earthly beings, spanning millions of years. From this idea of a single being, which gave way to the evolution and creation of all life on earth from its life and reproduction forward, we must realize that all life on earth, then, has a common ancestor. During the process of evolution, the branching off of species due to mutations is common. This is the way that today, human beings exist alongside primates, our closest cousins. Human beings have an ancient common ancestor, which during the evolutionary process, branched off to the common ape and the common human.

In this same way, we have the different canines and felines of the earth. Ancient common ancestors of cats and dogs branched from the genealogy of the more advanced and aggressive wolves and lions to the more docile house-pet dogs and cats that currently live with you today.

Your child will apply scientific concepts to build an explanation for the similarities and differences in the anatomy of modern organisms, and between fossil and modern organisms. Through the explanation, he will make inferences about evolutionary relationships. Focus is on explaining evolutionary relationships in organisms with regards to their similarities and differences in the appearance of their anatomical structures.

Analyze Data to Find Similarities in Organisms

Performance expectation MS.LS4.3 states that students should "analyze displays of pictorial data to compare patterns of similarities in the embryological development across multiple species to identify relationships not evident in the fully formed anatomy."

While we cannot actually physically see or simulate the common ancestor to all living beings, there is a way to test this theory. In addition to fossil evidence, the main thing that we can focus on regarding common ancestry is the formation of multicellular organisms. The embryo of all sexually reproducing animals on planet Earth looks the same. By looking at picture records, we see that the embryo of an offspring looks like a small bean with protruding digits and head attached. This is evidence of a common ancestor, as before birth, all organisms on planet Earth look the same. From humans, to fish, to whales, to penguins, and anything in between, we all have the same embryos. This is evidence, then, that all beings came from a common ancestor, and then evolution has caused the branching off of different organisms from a single base map of cells that we call the embryo.

Middle school students will display graphic information to compare the patterns of similarities in the development of embryos in a variety of species to identify particular relationships that are not distinct in the fully developed anatomy. Focus is on making inferences about general patterns of relationships among embryos of various organisms by making comparisons of the macroscopic appearance of illustrations and pictures.

Investigate How Some Mutations Lead to Survival

According to performance expectation MS.LS4.4, your child will be able to "construct an explanation based on evidence that describes how genetic variations of traits in a population increase some individuals' probability of surviving and reproducing in a specific environment."

Thanks to this effect of evolving from a base map of cells, we see the ease of organic evolution within an organism. This evolution has caused different traits to be adapted by different types of animals. This is because throughout the course of history, different animals have assumed different forms with different abilities that are considered more desirable to mates and/or will give them a greater chance of survival in their environment.

ESSENTIAL

Individuals within a species can have different physical features today than they might have had in past generations. Changes can happen over generations because traits that enable survival are passed on from one generation to the next, and traits that are unnecessary for survival are not.

For example, the mutation of lungs from the first land-born species of animal had the best possible traits for survival, considering that the land was not inhabited by any other animal on the planet. This meant that this organism had no natural predators on land and an abundance of food to eat in the form of plants, which had existed on land for a longer period of time.

We can also look at the evolution of humans regarding traits, where human beings have changed greatly since our last ancestral level. Humans over time have become taller, wider, stronger, and smarter. One of the most prevalent bits of evidence regarding human evolution is our creation of technology. While over the last 100 years humans have not changed very much physically, we have changed in the way in which we are able to analyze data and adapt tools to our environment.

Your child will use evidence to develop an explanation describing the beneficial effects of genetic trait variations in survival and reproduction in a particular environment. Focus is on using basic probability and proportional reasoning in building the explanation.

Explore the Role of Technology in Evolution

Performance expectation MS.LS4.5 states that students will "gather and synthesize information about the technologies that have changed the way humans influence the inheritance of desired traits in organisms."

All animals on the planet exist for the very purpose to pass down their genetic information in an attempt to continue their ecological footprint beyond their own physical life. Reproduction is not a choice, but a goal. It is the reason that all beings on earth grow to reach a level of maturity in which they can reproduce, and it is also the reason that beings have this ability at such a young age. We live to quickly and efficiently pass down our genetic code to the next generation so that they may continue our own "legacy."

In this way, we can identify the specific ways that beings prepare themselves for mating. Some animals perform a dance, and others have physical characteristics that are attractive to the opposite sex of that species. Plants begin special processes in which they release their DNA in specific ways so that it may be transferred to other plants.

If a plant or animal does not have the sufficient means to attract a mate to reproduce, then they will not do so, and their genetics were not fit enough for reproduction. This is the basis for the theory of evolution and the survival of the fittest.

Your child will collect and incorporate information about forms of technology that have altered the way humans affect the transmission of desired characteristics in organisms. Focus is on synthesizing data from reliable sources about the impact of humans on genetic results in artificial selection, and on the effects these types of technology have on society and scientific discovery.

Investigate Natural Selection

Performance expectation MS.LS4.6 reads: "use mathematical representations to support explanations of how natural selection may lead to increases and decreases of specific traits in populations over time."

We can only predict how the world will change over time as organisms react to the environment around them. Due to the mass of human beings on the planet, around 7 billion, coupled with the effects that stem from the last bout of human technological evolution in the last 200 years, we can see that the rest of the ecosystems of the earth will likely undergo considerable changes. For instance, we will likely see an increase in the levels of scavenger organisms throughout the globe as humans continue to pollute the planet with trash that actually has a considerable nutritional value, or resources that can be derived from our trash, a system that we may begin to see emerging in plant life.

Regarding plant life, we will more than likely see an increase in the amount of plants that can harness the power of our pollutants, as these resources are becoming the most abundant in our environments. However, we must make sure that we curtail our pollution (as we can never truly eliminate it all) before too much life is killed off before it has the chance to adapt to the rapidly changing environments we are creating for it.

ESSENTIAL

If a change in an environment occurs, the organisms with traits that are suited for the change will have a better chance of surviving and reproducing. Organisms cannot deliberately develop these traits overnight in order to be able to survive.

Middle school students will utilize mathematical representations to justify explanations of the impact of natural selection on decreases and increases in specific characteristics over a period of time. Focus is on utilizing mathematical models, proportional reasoning, and probability to justify explanations of patterns in changes to populations over periods of time.

Evolution Experiment

For this experiment, a question has been provided for you. Work with your child to come up with a hypothesis and then perform the experiment together.

Question

How do recessive alleles become lost through generations?

Materials

- Permanent marker
- 3 sandwich-sized plastic bags
- 20 yellow jelly beans
- 20 purple jelly beans
- 1 small paper bag

Method

1. Using the permanent marker, print FF on the first plastic bag. Print Ff on the second plastic bag. Print ff on the third plastic bag.
2. The jelly beans represent birds. The yellow jelly beans represent birds with the allele for feathers: (F). The purple jelly beans represent birds with the allele for no feathers: (f). The small paper bag in which the jelly beans are combined represents the tree where the birds build their nests to reproduce.
3. Place the 20 yellow and 20 purple beans into the small paper bag and combine them.
4. Select 2 jelly beans without looking.
5. If you select one yellow and one purple jelly bean, place them in the bag marked Ff.
6. If you select two yellow jelly beans, place them in the bag marked FF.
7. If you select two purple jelly beans, place them in the bag marked ff and put them aside because these birds will not survive without feathers.
8. Continue selecting jelly beans two at a time until you have removed all of them from the paper bag.
9. Place the FF and Ff jelly beans back into the small paper bag and combine them again to produce the next generation.
10. Repeat steps until the no feather allele has been lost through the generations.

Consider Testing . . .

- What happens if you use larger allele samples?
- What might happen to the birds that reproduced offspring of the birds with and without feathers?
- Since birds come and go from actual habitats, how could this be recreated?

Let's Review—Checklist

In order to help your child as she is studying biology, keep the following important points in mind:

- Biological evolution accounts for the diversity of species developed through gradual processes over many generations

- Fossils give us evidence of the diverse organisms that at one time lived on earth but are now extinct
- Thousands of layers of sedimentary rock give us evidence of earth's history and the forms of life that lived on it throughout time
- The most recent layers of sedimentary rock contain remains that are more closely related to species that currently exist on earth
- Genetic variations among individual organisms within a population give them advantages for survival and reproduction
- These genetic variations are referred to as the natural selection process
- A species is able to change to meet changes in the conditions of an environment through natural selection adaptations that take place over generations
- Biodiversity refers to the wide range of life forms that exist on earth and that have developed adaptations to their environmental conditions
- A species becomes extinct when it is unable to adapt to changes in its environment
- Each living organism has a set code that specifies its genetic traits
- Scientists use external and internal structures to classify organisms
- A species refers to a group of organisms that are able to mate and reproduce fertile offspring
- The functions of a particular population within an ecosystem can be used for its classification
- The internal structures can be used to determine similarities and relationships among groups of organisms
- Organisms with similar survival needs compete for resources within environments
- The development and survival of organisms are based on the physical conditions of their environment
- Artificial selective breeding makes it possible for people to regulate specific traits of certain plants and animals
- Through the process of selective breeding, small differences between generations can develop, resulting in significant differences between ancestors and descendents

CHAPTER 15

Earth's Place in the Universe

How can the universe be explained, and where does the earth fit into it? The universe spans both time and space. The earth is a very small component of the universe that evolved over a long period of time. By observing conditions of the universe, it is possible to determine its structures and processes. It is important to understand these phenomena in order to better understand the processes, structures, and systems of the earth.

What Should My Child Already Understand?

By the time your child begins middle school, he should have some understanding about the earth and its movements. For example, the earth rotates on an axis, and this movement produces daytime and nighttime. He should also know:

- Star patterns in the sky are constant and are visible only at certain times of the year.
- The sun is actually a star.
- There are different sizes of stars, but from a distance they all appear to be small points of light.
- Several planets orbit the sun, including the earth.
- The moon rotates around the earth.
- The force of gravity on the earth pulls objects toward its center.

Your child should also be able to identify the seasons and the hemispheres and have an understanding of longitude and latitude.

ESSENTIAL

The solar system includes more than the sun, the planets, and the moon. It includes the sun and everything that orbits it, including eight planets and their satellites, dwarf planets, asteroids, comets, and meteoroids. It was formed more than four and a half billion years ago and is a part of the Milky Way.

Disciplinary Core Ideas

The following concepts have been established by the Next Generation Science Standards as some of the important points of understanding in studying the earth's place in the universe. Following are some of the topics your child will learn about and discuss in school.

The Universe and Its Stars

How can the universe be described and how can stars be explained? While the universe is vast space, it is possible to describe and explain it by breaking it down into its components. Within the universe are planets, stars, and galaxies. Planet Earth and its solar system are found in the Milky Way. The Milky Way is one galaxy among billions of others in the universe. By studying the components of the universe, students come to understand and are able to describe and predict the patterns of the moon, stars, and sun.

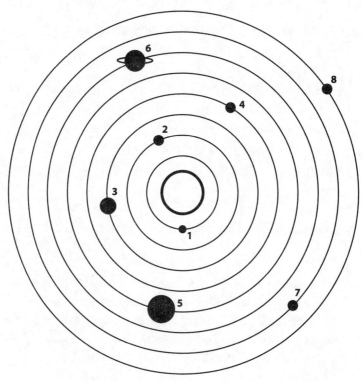

1. Mercury; 2. Venus; 3. Earth; 4. Mars; 5. Jupiter;
6. Saturn; 7. Uranus; 8. Neptune

Earth and the Solar System

How does the movement of the earth within the solar system cause predictable patterns within systems? There are many varied objects within the solar system that are kept together through the force of gravity. Models of the solar system can be used to help your child explain and predict seasons, lunar phases, and eclipses. A model of the eclipses of the moon and the sun explains how the earth's axis became fixed in a particular direction over a short period of time but is tilted in relation to its orbit of the sun. The seasons occur because of the tilt in the axis and are the result of variances in sunlight intensity on different parts of the earth during different times of the year. The solar system is made up of the sun and various objects, including asteroids, planets, and their moons. The solar system is kept together and orbits the sun through the force of gravity. The solar system seems to have been created from a disk of gas and dust that was pulled together by a gravitational force.

FACT

The sun is actually an enormous star that is made up of hydrogen and helium. The energy that the sun produces is nuclear fusion. While the surface temperature of the sun is about five thousand degrees Celsius, the temperature within the sun can reach fifteen million degrees Celsius.

The History of Planet Earth

How can the events of the earth's history be dated and reconstructed? Fossil record and rock strata can be utilized as proof to correlate major historical occurrences through the history of the earth. Rock strata provide a geologic timescale that offers a means of organizing the history of the earth. Fossil record and rock strata analyses give only the relative dates of historical occurrences rather than an absolute scale. New ocean sea floor is generated at ridges and old sea floor is destroyed at trenches through the continual processes of tectonics.

ALERT

In 2006 the term "dwarf planet" was formulated by scientists. A dwarf planet is an object in the solar system that is larger than comets and asteroids but not as large as other planets. This new definition changed how Pluto was characterized. No longer considered a planet, Pluto is now recognized as a dwarf planet.

Key Earth's Place Terms

These terms are important to learning about the earth and its place in the universe:

- Crescent—A phase of the moon when less than half of it seems illuminated
- Earth's Axis—An imaginary line that goes through the center of the earth connecting the poles, and around which the earth rotates
- Eclipse—The passing of a moon or planet through the shadow of another planet or moon
- Equator—An imaginary line of latitude at 0 degrees that runs perpendicular to the earth's axis
- First Quarter—The phase of the moon when it is waxing and half of it appears illuminated
- Full Moon—Moon phase in which all of the moon appears illuminated
- Gibbous—Moon phase in which more than half of the moon appears illuminated
- Gravity—The attracting force between all objects
- High Tide—The highest point that a rising tide reaches
- Low Tide—The lowest point that a falling tide reaches
- Lunar Eclipse—An eclipse that occurs when the moon passes through a portion of the shadow of the earth
- New Moon—The phase of the moon when none of it appears illuminated
- North Pole—The most northern point of the earth located at the northern end of the axis of the earth
- Northern Hemisphere—The half portion of the earth that is located north of the equator
- Orbit—The path of travel of a planet or moon around another planet or moon
- Revolve—To move along a circular path
- Rotate—To turn around an axis
- Season—A division of the year that lasts three months and is based on changes in the weather
- Solar Eclipse—An eclipse when the shadow of the moon moves over a section of the earth
- Solar Energy—Energy generated by the sun

- South Pole—The most southern point of the earth located at the southern end of the axis of the earth
- Southern Hemisphere—The half portion of the earth that is located south of the equator
- Third Quarter—A phase of the moon when it is waning and half of it appears illuminated
- Tidal Bulge—A swelling of water created by a pull from the sun and the gravity of the moon
- Tides—The regular fall and rise of the surface of the ocean created by the force of gravity from the sun and the moon
- Waning—Shrinking in size
- Waxing—Growing in size

Key Earth's Place Concepts

It is important to understand the universe and its many components in order to better understand the processes, structures, and systems of the earth.

Universe Q&A

Q: How is the universe defined?

A: The universe includes the dust, galaxies, gases, and star systems along with the energy and matter that existed throughout history, currently exists, and will exist throughout the future. It is made up of all time and space.

Q: What makes up the solar system?

A: The solar system includes the sun, the planets revolving around it, asteroids, comets, and moons.

Q: How are the movements of the objects within the solar system related?

A: The orbit of the earth is almost circular. The movements of most of the objects in the solar system are regular and can be predicted. The movements of these objects can be used to explain days, years, moon phases, eclipses, tides, and comet and meteor showers. The rotation and revolution of the earth can be used to explain the movement of some of the objects in the solar system. The length of the day as twenty-four hours is a result of the rotation of the earth. The locations of the rising and setting of the sun and moon are the result of the rotation of the earth. The length of a year as 365.25 days is the result of the revolution of the earth. The seasons on earth are the result of it revolving around the sun and the tilt of its axis.

Q: Where are we in relation to the solar system?
A: The earth, sun, and other planets are found inside the Milky Way galaxy. Earth is located about twenty-six thousand light years away from the galaxy's center. Earth orbits the sun. The sun and solar system orbit the center of the Milky Way. One orbit around the center of the Milky Way takes around two hundred and fifty million years.

Q: How did the earth come to be?
A: At the beginning of its time, the earth was an extremely hot planet that had no water and no atmosphere. This environment made it impossible for living organisms to exist on it. The collision of the materials in space generated heat on planet Earth. The heat melted the materials on the earth. The gravitational pull on the earth forced all of the denser material to the center of the planet. The less dense materials rose to the earth's surface and created an atmosphere and water.

Q: How was the moon formed?
A: A great deal of space debris was located in the solar system when it was young. Asteroids moving about collided with planets, including the earth. The energy from the collision melted a great deal of the planet. Material from an asteroid and from the earth was forced into orbit and over time it developed into the moon.

Q: How do fossils help us learn about the history of the earth?
A: Some of the history of the earth can be determined through the discovery of fossils and the information they provide. Fossils provide information about significant events, living organisms, climates, and environments. Most fossils are found in sedimentary rock and can be

used to learn about the environments, ecosystems, and climates of the past. The concept that all of the continents were once joined is supported by their current land forms and correlating fossil records.

Q: What are index fossils?

A: Index fossils are used to determine the age of layers of rock. These fossils provide the remains of organisms that existed in a large area, over a short time period. Trilobite fossils are a type of index fossil. Trilobites lived in a specific time period, making it possible to identify the age of the rocks in which their fossils are found.

Q: How do stars form and develop?

A: The life cycle of a star is much like that of a living organism. Stars are born, grow, change, and eventually die. Stars are created from clouds of dust and gas, which are referred to as nebulae. As stars use their hydrogen, they fuse helium atoms into other heavier atoms like carbon.

Q: What is a galaxy?

A: A galaxy is an enormous group of stars containing millions to billions of stars. There are three different types of galaxies based on their shapes: elliptical, irregular, and spiral.

Q: What is the Milky Way?

A: The Milky Way is a galaxy within our solar system in which the earth is situated. Each star that can be seen at night belongs to the Milky Way. It contains billions of stars and a vast amount of dust and gas. Its appearance seems different from other galaxies because the perspective from the earth shows the interior of the galaxy. The Milky Way has spiral arms, a central bulge, and a disk. The distance across the disk is about one hundred thousand light years, and its thickness is about three thousand light years. The majority of the dust, gas, stars, and clusters are found in the disk. Based on its shape, it is identified as a spiral galaxy. There is rotational movement demonstrated by the velocity of the gas and the stars within the Milky Way. The dust, gases, and color are found in most other spiral galaxies. According to astronomers, a vast black hole exists in the center of the Milky Way.

Q: What is the geologic timescale?
A: The geologic timescale is a timeline model that separates the history of the earth into periods that include Precambrian, Paleozoic, Mesozoic, and Cenozoic.

Q: What is the law of superposition?
A: The law of superposition states that deeper layers of rock are typically older than layers of rock that are nearer to the earth's surface.

Q: What is relative age?
A: Relative age refers to the comparison of the age of a particular area of rock and the age of the rocks that are nearby.

Q: How do maps help us better understand the earth?
A: Maps can be created and used as symbolical representations of the surface of the earth. Topographic maps showing contour lines and points of elevation can be created and used to represent landforms. Weather maps can be used to show patterns of isolines, isobars, and isotherms.

Science and Engineering Practices

In learning about the earth's place, your child will use science and engineering practices to better understand the ideas that relate to the universe. These practices might include:

- Knowing and applying concepts that explain how the universe is structured and the earth's place within it
- Simulating, analyzing, and explaining the impact of the force of gravity on the solar system
- Asking and answering questions about the seasons on the earth
- Developing a scale model that identifies the connections between the earth, the sun, and the moon
- Planning and carrying out investigations involving the tilt of the earth's axis and its impact on light intensity

- Analyzing and interpreting data to explain the changes to the length of the day based on the time of the year and the location on the planet
- Using mathematics to calculate the rate at which the earth rotates around the sun
- Constructing explanations of tide patterns and their relationship to the moon
- Explaining the connections between extreme tides and the moon phases
- Engaging in arguments that debate misconceptions about movement within the solar system
- Obtaining explanations about the seasons, moon phases, and eclipses
- Evaluating the validity and challenges of models
- Communicating information through presentations
- Analyzing data about a particular planet and using the information to make predictions about days, months, years, and seasons
- Creating models and building explanations about the characteristics of a particular planet
- Constructing a concept map that communicates the main ideas and important details about the earth and its place in the universe

Next Generation Science Standards Performance Expectations

These performance expectations describe what your child should be able to demonstrate and understand about the specific science unit he is studying in middle school. From these expectations your child's teachers will determine how successfully he understands and can apply the concepts that have been covered.

Use Models to Show Patterns in the Galaxy

Performance expectation MS.ESS1.1 states that students will "develop and use a model of the earth-sun-moon system to describe the cyclic patterns of lunar phases, eclipses of the sun and moon, and seasons."

When you think of the solar system, you may think of the major planets that orbit the sun, and the natural satellites (moons) that orbit these planets.

But how do these structures affect the natural bodies in motion around the sun and around the planets? How does spatial position change climates on the surfaces that man inhabits? In order to understand this, you can look closely at the cycles our own planet experiences during its orbit around the sun, and the effects of the moon as well.

A lunar eclipse happens when the earth moves between the sun and the moon. This causes a shadow on the moon. A solar eclipse occurs when the moon moves between the sun and the earth. This causes a shadow on the surface of the earth.

As the earth orbits and rotates around the sun, we experience days, as well as seasons. The earth's rotation in relation to the sun is what allows light to be shed on each side of the planet approximately every twenty-four hours. Because the earth is not resting perpendicular to the sun, different areas of the planet experience different lengths of sunlight throughout the year. This is evidenced by how the north and south poles of the earth experience six months of sunlight and then six months of darkness. Due to the orientation of the earth in reference to the sun, we have what we call the time of day.

Furthermore, the earth's distance from the sun, as opposed to its orientation, is what creates the seasons. Each rotation of the earth around the sun brings you a little close to the sun, and then pushes you out a little farther back. As the earth becomes closer to the sun, you experience the hotter seasons, like spring and summer. As the earth moves away from the sun, you experience the colder fall and winter.

The orientation of the earth can determine the seasons, in a sense, for certain areas of the planet. For areas near the equator, the center line of the planet, the distance to the sun is much closer than northern and southern areas at all times of the year. Therefore, these areas that are always closest to the sun are generally hot year-round, or are at least much hotter than any other region on the planet at all times.

Middle school students will learn all this information through developing and utilizing a model of the system of the earth, sun, and moon to detail the seasons, eclipses of the moon and the sun, and cyclic patterns of lunar phases. Examples might be conceptual, graphical, and physical.

Explore Gravity

According to performance expectation MS.ESS1.2, your child will "develop and use a model to describe the role of gravity in the motions within galaxies and the solar system."

Why is our planet constantly rotating around the sun? Why is our moon constantly rotating about us? In order to explain this, we must look to gravity. The size of objects in our universe dictates their relation with other objects due to the concept of gravity. As objects increase in mass, they increase in gravitational pull. Since our sun is the most massive object in our solar system, all of the other planets are slave to its energy. However, our planet, along with the others in our solar system, exist in harmony with the sun, as the current orbit of all planets allows us to orbit the sun as opposed to being sucked directly into its gravitational pull.

In the same way, the moon orbits the earth. Our moon does not crash into the earth, nor do we into it, but it does exhibit gravitational forces toward the earth, such as controlling the tides. As the moon orbits around the earth, its gravitational pull changes the orientation of the tidal water levels in our seas. This is the reason why the seas rise and fall throughout the day.

ALERT

Without the moon, there would still be tides in the ocean. Those tides would be less powerful, but they would still occur. The sun also influences tides. While the sun is much farther away than the moon, it is also much larger and exerts a great deal of pull on all of the planets, including the earth.

Another way to demonstrate lunar gravity is by the fact that humans have landed upon the moon. The gravitational force of a body in space is dependent on its mass, and because the moon is so much smaller than the earth, it has a smaller mass. Therefore, the gravity on the moon is much less than that of the gravity on the earth. This is the reason why video records of astronauts on the moon show them leaping to superhuman heights with ease.

If the gravity of the moon were to be any stronger, there is the potential for the catastrophic failure of the gravitational relationship between the earth and it, so we are lucky to be living in a balanced solar system.

Your child will create and utilize a model to detail the part gravity plays in movement within the solar system and galaxies. Focus is on the force of gravity that pulls the Milky Way and the solar system together and governs the orbital motions in them. Model examples might include computer visualizations or mathematical proportions.

Use Models to Examine the Universe

Performance expectation MS.ESS1.3 states that students should be able to "analyze and interpret data to determine scale properties of objects in the solar system."

Our solar system is but a tiny speck in the grand scheme of our galaxy, and an even more miniscule dot in the potentially endless universe. At the center of all galaxies is a black hole. This black hole will eventually consume and destroy our entire galaxy. However, this will not happen for billions of years, but it does show how small we truly are in the grand scheme of things.

FACT

The Milky Way is a galaxy within the universe. It got its name from the milky appearance it creates in the night sky. It began forming about twelve billion years ago and is a member of a group of fifty galaxies called the Local Group. The solar system is a part of the Milky Way. The center of the Milky Way has a massive black hole.

Much like the end of the galaxy through black hole destruction is the end of solar systems through the dying of stars. As our sun continues through its life cycle, it will grow in size and strength. First it will become too hot for planet habitability, then it will engulf entire planets at a time. Scientists suggest that Venus, our sister planet, had a climate similar to that of Earth, but as the sun progressed through its cycle, this climate was destroyed by extreme heat.

We must turn to the scale and similarities of our planet in reference to the other planets and systems in our universe to predict how our planet, sun, solar system, galaxy, and universe will play out over the course of time.

Your child will analyze and interpret information to determine the scale properties of solar system objects. Focus is on data analysis from spacecraft and instruments located on the earth to determine the differences and similarities among objects in the solar system. Scale properties examples include the layers of an object, the features of a surface, and orbital radius. Data examples might include illustrations, models, photos, and statistics.

Examine the History of Earth

According to performance expectation MS.ESS1.4, your child will "construct a scientific explanation based on evidence from rock strata for how the geologic time scale is used to organize earth's 4.6-billion-year-old history."

When you discuss the earth in reference to the rest of the planets in our solar system, galaxy, and so on, one of the most important factors you must look at is time. How long does the earth have left? How long have we been on the earth? But most importantly, how old is the earth itself?

Current estimates put the earth at 4.6 billion years of age. But how do we know this? Generally speaking, the most common means of dating things on earth is through the use of carbon dating. This provides a generally accurate estimate of the age of most things on the planet.

FACT

A light year is not a unit of time but rather a unit of distance. It measures how far light travels in one year, which is about ten trillion kilometers. The distance across the Milky Way galaxy is about one hundred and fifty thousand light years.

Expanding on this is documenting what state the earth and its inhabitants were in over the course of its history. This is done by dating the sediment samples in the earth. However, due to the estimation, it is extremely difficult to link two different pieces of earthly history together with this method. Instead, geologists take a look at the layers of the earth, and their formation, to date the periods of the earth's history, and subsequently, the goings on of organisms of that time.

For example, by dating a layer of sediment, we can then trace through the history of that time period by analyzing what has been found within that layer of sediment, whether it be nutrients, mineral deposits, or fossil findings. In this way, the earth can be dated much like a tree. By looking at the earth's "rings" of sediment, we can see just how old the earth is, and what happened on the earth at that age. Such a concept can be visualized as well. By looking at cross sections of sediment, we can see that there is discoloration due to different types of minerals in the sediment, suggesting a difference in the environment of the earth at that time in that location. This phenomena can be observed at natural wonders such as the Grand Canyon, and at the cliffs near the shores of eastern Canada and the United States.

Your child will build a scientific explanation established on proof from rock strata for the use of geologic timescale in organizing the comprehensive history of planet Earth. Focus is on how the analysis of fossils contained in rock formations is the basis to determine the time periods of major historic events on the earth. Major event examples might include the Ice Age, *Homo sapien* fossils, and the earliest evidence of the existence of life.

Soil Experiment

For this experiment, a question has been provided for you. Work with your child to come up with a hypothesis and then perform the experiment together.

Question

How does soil vary in different locations?

Materials

- 5 (250 mL) samples of soil from various depths at different locations
- 5 clear 1 L containers with lids
- Room temperature water

Method

1. Place the soil from one particular location into a container. Repeat with the remaining samples.

2. Pour water over the soil in each container until the containers are almost ¾ full.
3. Secure the lid to the container and shake the materials until they are combined.
4. Allow the containers to sit for 24 hours.
5. Observe the results each hour.

Consider Testing . . .

- What happens if you change the temperature of the water?
- What happens if you change the amount of water?
- What happens if you change the amount of soil?

Let's Review—Checklist

As your child explores the earth and the universe, keep these key points in mind:

- You can observe, describe, and make predictions about the patterns in the movements of the earth, sun, moon, and stars
- The seasons have an impact on the length of the day and the sun's height in the sky
- The earth's revolution around the sun determines the length of the year and the seasons
- The orbit of the earth around the sun influences the intensity of the energy that reaches the earth's surface and as a result, the seasons
- The appearance of the moon changes regularly following a repeated pattern
- You are able to predict future moon phases based on the lunar cycle
- The moon does not generate light but it does reflect it
- The moon phases include new, first quarter, gibbous, last quarter, crescent, and full
- The moon's orbit around the earth causes the phases of the moon
- Waxing and waning refer to the portions of the moon that are visible
- A full moon and a new moon coincide with extreme tides
- The rotation of the earth and the force of gravity cause low and high tides

CHAPTER 16

Earth's Systems

How and why has the earth changed? The surface of the earth is composed of several complicated systems that interact, including the atmosphere, biosphere, geosphere, and hydrosphere. The processes of the earth that take place are caused by the flow of energy and the cycling of matter throughout these systems. Weather and climate are affected by these systems, as is the water cycle. The continual interactions of processes and systems create constant change. By studying Earth's systems, students will develop a better understanding of the science behind weather, climate, and natural disasters, and they will be able to connect natural weather events with the Earth's systems.

What Should My Child Already Understand?

Your child will have a basic understanding of the earth and its changes. He will understand that some changes happen quickly and others take so long to occur that they cannot be observed. These changes can take place in several ways. They can be constant and regular or spontaneous and irregular. For example, a rock starts out as individual minerals. As these minerals come together, they form rock. Over time the effects of weather on the rock cause it to break down into small particles. These tiny particles come together with the remains of plants and animals to make soil. This process takes many, many years and countless changes take place within it over time.

FACT

The sunlight feels warmer around the middle the day than it does earlier in the morning and later in the day because that is when the sun is at its highest point in the sky. It is colder during the winter at a particular spot than it is in the summer not because the sunlight has farther to travel but because the sunlight reaches that location at a smaller angle.

Disciplinary Core Ideas

The following concepts have been established by the Next Generation Science Standards as some of the important points of understanding in studying the earth's systems. Following are some of the topics your child will learn about and discuss in school.

Earth Materials and Systems

What are the major systems on planet Earth and how can their interactions be described? Among and within the systems of the earth there is a flow of energy and cycle of matter, which includes the interior of the earth and the sun as principal sources of energy. One of the results of these processes is plate tectonics (see the following section).

All of the processes of the earth occur because of energy flow and matter cycling. The flow of energy originates from the hot interior of the earth and the sun. Energy flow and matter cycling generate physical and chemical alterations in the living organisms and materials on the earth. The interactions of the systems of the planet range from global to microscopic, and function over billions of years to milliseconds.

Plate Tectonics and Large-Scale System Interactions

What causes continental movement, volcanoes, and earthquakes? The movement of rocks on the surface of the earth is explained through the process of plate tectonics. The evidence of plate tectonic movement is displayed through maps. Investigations of fossils and rocks provide the evidence needed to create maps of ancient patterns of water and ancient landforms. The collision and spreading movement of the plates of the earth over large distances is evident through these maps.

ALERT

The earth has between twelve and fifteen tectonic plates that are made from rock. They are visible in some areas where there is no water or soil covering them. These plates can have a thickness of almost one hundred kilometers. The edges of each of these plates are touching all of the surrounding plates.

The Role of Water in Earth's Surfaces Processes

What is the water cycle and how does it affect the earth and other earth systems? Sunlight and gravity propel cycles of water among oceans, landforms, and the atmosphere. Variations in water temperatures and the density of sea water drive the interconnected currents of the oceans. Weathering, erosion, and changes in landforms can be the result of water movement.

Transpiration, evaporation, condensation, crystallization, and precipitation allow water to cycle continually among atmosphere, ocean, and land. Local weather patterns and climate are determined by complex patterns of change and movement of water. Winds, currents, ocean temperatures, and landforms determine these movements and changes in water. The movement of water underground and on land results in erosion and weathering, which changes features of the land and creates formations underground.

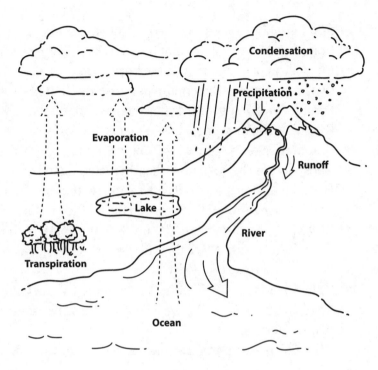

Stages of the water cycle

Weather and Climate

How are weather and climate similar and different, and how are they regulated? Interactions among the atmosphere, the ocean, ice, living things, and landforms influence climate and weather. The altitude, latitude, and geography of these interactions affect atmospheric and oceanic flow patterns. The complexity of these patterns results in probabilistic predictions of weather. The ocean greatly impacts weather and climate through its absorption of the sun's energy and its global release of that energy through ocean currents.

Key Earth's Systems Terms

Understanding these terms will help in learning about the earth's systems:

- Altitude—The height of an object above the surface of the earth
- Atmosphere—The mass of gases around the earth
- Climate—The weather of a particular region over a long period

- Condensation—The process of water vapors changing into a liquid
- Convergent—Two plates that have moved together
- Crystallization—The process of becoming crystals
- Cycles of Matter—The continual transformation of matter
- Divergent—Two plates that have moved apart
- Erosion—The movement of sediments through ice, gravity, water, or wind
- Evaporation—The process of a liquid changing into a gas
- Geosphere—The solid part of earth including the crust and outer mantle
- Humidity—The amount of water vapor within the atmosphere
- Hydrosphere—All of the water on the surface of the earth
- Latitude—The distance to the north or the south of the equator
- Ocean Currents—A continuous flow of water near the surface of the ocean that is caused by wind
- Plate Boundaries—The boundaries where two tectonic plates interact
- Precipitation—The process where a substance settles from a solution that is saturated
- Rock Cycle—The process through which rocks form, break down, and reform
- Temperature—The heat intensity of an object
- Transpiration—The process where a plant absorbs water as a liquid through its roots and releases it as a vapor through its leaves
- Water Cycle—The circulation of water among the atmosphere, the oceans, and land
- Water Vapor—The state of water as a gas
- Weather—The conditions of the atmosphere at a particular location and time
- Weathering—The process of breaking rock into smaller pieces

ESSENTIAL

There are three types of rocks: igneous, sedimentary, and metamorphic. Igneous rock is formed when magma from inside the earth cools and becomes solid. Sedimentary rock is formed in layers by sediment deposits, and is usually found near oceans and lakes. Metamorphic rock is formed through heat and pressure. When heat and pressure are exerted on sedimentary and igneous rock, they become metamorphic rock.

Key Earth's Systems Concepts

The earth's systems influence changes to the planet, and these changes affect all organisms living on the earth.

Earth's Systems Q&A

Q: What is a mineral?

A: Minerals can be found everywhere. There are over 4,000 different types of minerals in the earth's crust. Minerals have specific characteristics. They must be produced naturally, and be solid, inorganic, and crystalline. They must also contain specific chemicals. Minerals are identified by their physical properties including luster, color, cleavage, streak, fracture, density, hardness, and odor. When minerals are refined, they lose their mineral definition because they become substances that are no longer crystalline. Substances are either organic or inorganic. Inorganic substances have structures that are not made from living organisms. Organic substances contain carbon and were created by the carbohydrates, oil, and proteins from living organisms.

Q: What is the chemical composition of the earth?

A: Most of the earth's crust comprises eight different elements that include aluminum, calcium, iron, magnesium, oxygen, potassium, silicon, and sodium. Some minerals come from only one substance, but most of the minerals have a particular composition of chemical compounds.

Q: What are tectonic plates?

A: The earth's land is constantly moving at a pace that is too slow to see. The outermost part of the earth is the lithosphere, and it moves about six inches each year. The lithosphere is composed of the crust and upper mantle. The sections of the lithosphere that move are referred to as tectonic plates. These plates vary in size from small to extremely large. The earth is covered by eight major plates and several other minor plates, each with a thickness of about sixty-two miles. The two main types of plates are continental and oceanic.

Q: What are tectonic plate boundaries?

A: The boundaries between the plates show the most evidence of movement. The three boundaries are convergent, divergent, and transform. Convergent boundaries take place when two plates are pushed together. When the plates collide, the movement of one plate under another can cause volcanic and earthquake activity as well as mountain formation. Divergent boundaries occur when two plates are forced apart. When the plates divide, the movement causes a space that is called a rift. Magma fills the rift by pushing up from beneath the earth to fill the space. The cooled magma creates new landforms. Transform boundaries happen when one plate slides past another plate. These locations are referred to as faults. Many earthquakes occur at fault locations.

Q: What is the plate tectonic theory?

A: Folds and faults in the rock layers of the earth's surface imply that there was movement of the crust in the past. The theory of plate tectonics explains the ability of lithosphere plates to float on molten mantle sections. These plates move apart or together. When they collide, they can cause earthquakes, volcanic activity, and mountain formation. The tectonic plates form the lithosphere of the earth. Under the lithosphere is the asthenosphere, which is composed of molten rock. This area is continually hot due to the heat from the earth's center. The energy from the center of the earth melts rock and changes it from a solid to a liquid form. Convection within the mantle of the earth forces the plates to move. The tectonic plates float over the molten rock, moving slowly. Movement of the continents and plates is referred to as continental drift. Scientists have studied the movement of tectonic plates for a long time. They have found evidence that the continents of today were once a larger supercontinent called Pangea. The shapes of the current continents fit together much like a puzzle. Scientists also studied fossil records and the types of rocks on the different continents and discovered that the remains and rocks were similar. The plants, animals, and rocks had been together on one continent, but over time the land was divided.

Q: What is weathering?

A: Weathering refers to the process that turns rock into sediments. Sediments are small pieces. Weathering disintegrates rock, breaking it into smaller pieces. The process of erosion then moves smaller pieces away from the rock. Weathering takes place over long periods of time. Through weathering, sharp mountain peaks become rounded and hills become flatlands.

Q: What is the source of the earth's energy?

A: Most of the energy on the earth comes from the sun. The internal heat within the planet is also a major source of energy. Geothermal and nuclear are other energy sources. There are various forms of energy that include chemical, electrical, heat, light, mechanical, nuclear, and sound. Electromagnetic energy has different forms, each with different wavelengths. Electromagnetic energy includes gamma rays, infrared heat, light, microwaves, ultraviolet waves, and x-rays. Most daily activities involve energy transformation.

Q: What energy resources are available?

A: An energy resource can be renewable or nonrenewable. Renewable energy sources do not run out because they are naturally replaced. Nonrenewable energy sources are used up and cannot be replaced. Renewable energy includes solar, water, and wind. These resources are abundant, fairly simple to produce, and are able to be replaced. Nonrenewable energy includes coal, natural gas, and oil. These resources take a long time to produce and cannot be replaced.

Q: What is the atmosphere?

A: Most of the atmosphere is found in a thin shell surrounding the earth. The atmosphere is divided into layers and contains carbon dioxide, oxygen, and water vapor. Most weather takes place in the atmosphere's lowest layer. Substances can penetrate the atmosphere either naturally or due to human activity and can influence climate, living organisms, and the weather. These substances include volcanic dust, greenhouse gases, and methane.

Q: What is weather?

A: Weather includes air pressure, air temperature, humidity, cloud cover, precipitation, wind direction, and wind speed. All of these aspects of weather occur in the lower level of the atmosphere. Weather refers to the conditions of the atmosphere at a particular location and time. The energy from the sun affects all of the aspects of weather. When air has little movement over a large area, it develops into masses that are influenced by the temperature and humidity conditions from that location. Humidity, temperature, and pressure of an air mass influence weather in a particular location. Air mass movements affect local weather conditions. Prevailing winds and upper air currents cause air masses to move. Boundaries between air masses are referred to as fronts. Precipitation is probable in the boundary areas. Systems with high pressure bring good weather. Systems with low pressure bring unstable weather. High and low systems move from west to east. Blizzards, hurricanes, ice storms, tornadoes, and thunderstorms are examples of hazardous weather.

Q: What is climate?

A: Climate refers to predictable weather patterns in a specific area over long periods of time. Climate includes air temperature, humidity, precipitation types and levels, as well as wind direction and speed. Climate in a particular area is consistent and changes slowly.

Q: What is the water cycle?

A: The water cycle process moves through the atmosphere, lithosphere, and hydrosphere. The sun regulates the water cycle, giving water the necessary energy to evaporate. Water is stored in the oceans. Through evaporation, water transforms from a liquid to a gas and becomes a water vapor. The water from the oceans and lakes evaporates into vapors that rise in the atmosphere where they stay until the process of condensation turns them into a liquid. The drops of water are formed into clouds, which move about under the force of the wind. When the droplets in clouds collide, they fall out of the sky as a form of precipitation. Precipitation includes rain, snow, hail, and sleet. The water can return to the lakes and oceans or fall onto the land.

When water falls as snow, it melts over time and becomes a liquid that flows into rivers, lakes, and oceans. Eventually the water is evaporated again and returns to the atmosphere where the cycle continues. Plants also influence the water cycle. They take water into their roots from the soil. They use the water in photosynthesis. Through photosynthesis the water becomes a vapor that is released through their leaves. The release of water vapor from plants is referred to as transpiration.

Q: What is the Coriolis effect?

A: The earth's rotation causes objects in the northern hemisphere to deflect to the right and objects in the southern hemisphere to deflect to the left. This effect forces the wind to move right or left depending on the hemisphere. The Coriolis effect gets its name from the French engineer Gustave Gaspard Coriolis who studied the effects of supplementary forces.

Q: What are the phases of the moon?

A: The orbit of the moon around planet Earth makes it seem like the shape of the moon is changing. The moon appears to start off as non-existent and then grow from small to full over several days. These changes in the appearance of the moon are called phases. The phases are created by the way in which the sun and moon become aligned. The lunar phase refers to the amount of the moon that can be seen, which changes every day. The moon does not generate energy or light. It reflects the light from the sun. The part of the moon that is facing the sun reflects the light and appears to be lit. The part of the moon that does not face the sun does not reflect the light and is dark. The moon phases are based on the moon's position as it relates to the earth and the sun. The phases of the moon begin with new moon and cycle to full moon over a period of twenty-nine and a half days. The eight phases of the moon are: new, waxing crescent, first quarter, waxing gibbous, waning gibbous, last quarter, waning crescent, and full.

Q: How does the moon affect the tides?

A: Tides refer to the increase and decrease in the ocean levels and are caused by the rotation of the earth and the force of gravity from the moon and the sun. As the moon orbits the earth and the sun's position changes, the tides rise and fall. This cycle of tide change takes place once or twice each day. The moon has the greatest effect on tides. The moon's gravitational pull causes high tide on the part of the earth that is the closest to it and low tide on the part of the earth that is the farthest from it.

Science and Engineering Practices

In learning about the earth, your child will use science and engineering practices to better understand the ideas that relate to its systems. These practices might include:

- Knowing and applying concepts to describe the resources of the earth.
- Analyzing and explaining the forces and processes that affect the landforms of the earth.
- Describing the interactions among the atmosphere, the earth, living organisms, and the oceans.
- Asking and answering questions about the benefits and dangers of living near areas that experience earthquake or volcanic activity.
- Developing a model of the layers of the earth.
- Planning and carrying out an investigation that uses rock properties to determine an unknown substance.
- Analyzing and interpreting data to explain the patterns and history of natural hazards in a particular region and to predict future events.
- Constructing explanations for the effects of earthquakes on structures and designing solutions for safer buildings.
- Using representations of plate movement to calculate future movement.
- Engaging in arguments using evidence to support or refute plate movement theories.
- Obtaining information about fossils, rocks, and minerals.
- Evaluating the advantages of studying historic geological events and communicating the information through a presentation.

Next Generation Science Standards Performance Expectations

These performance expectations describe what your child should be able to demonstrate and understand about the specific science unit he is studying in middle school. From these expectations your child's teachers will determine how successfully he understands and can apply the concepts that have been covered.

Examine the Flow of Earth's Energy

Performance expectation MS.ESS2.1 states that students will "develop a model to describe the cycling of earth's materials and the flow of energy that drives this process."

The weather systems on the earth do not simply operate for fun; they have a distinct purpose. The way that weather works on our planet is to keep deposits of resources in balance to ensure a healthy planet. For example, rain works in a process of evaporation, condensation, and precipitation. This occurs for a reason. By the process of the water cycle, the earth removes deposits of standing water that would serve to break down the nutrients of a certain geographical area, and transport it to another area on the planet.

ESSENTIAL

Wind and water can wear away at the surface of the earth, moving small amounts of rock material from one place to another. This is referred to as weathering and erosion. Over long periods of time, mountains can develop rounded peaks and valleys can become filled. These changes can drastically change the appearance of a landscape.

Additional to this is how the earth attempts to keep environments well nourished with resources. As the water is removed from an area before it can cause harm, small amounts of nutritional sediments are absorbed into the water, which is then evaporated into the air. As the mineral water condenses and precipitates in another area, the earth has transferred resources from one location to the other. In this way, we must be careful in what we put into our waters, and what may seep into them, as all chemicals absorbed into the water will eventually be transferred elsewhere.

Middle school students will develop a model to detail the flow of energy driven by the cycling of the materials of the earth. Focus is on several processes, including weathering, sedimentation, melting, deformation, and crystallization, and the impact of these actions on rock and mineral formation.

Investigate Geoscience

According to performance expectation MS.ESS2.2, your child should be able to "construct an explanation based on evidence for how geoscience processes have changed earth's surface at varying time and spatial scales."

Many people visualize the earth as just one giant lifeless rock. What they fail to think about is the fact that our planet is alive and extremely powerful. Aside from the massive storms that we experience each year across the globe, there are also immense forces beneath our feet that not only dictate the state of the earth, but also how it was formed.

FACT

The earth is made of several spheres: the lithosphere, the hydrosphere, the biosphere, and the atmosphere. The lithosphere includes all of the rock material of the earth. The hydrosphere includes all of the water on the earth. The biosphere includes all of the living organisms on the earth. The atmosphere is the blanket of gases that surrounds the planet.

The earth's rocky outer surface hides deep within it a dense concentration of molten rock and metal. You can see evidence of this through volcanic action. Volcanoes are pipelines that directly release the hot gases and liquid overflow of the core of our planet. Much like a living, breathing entity, the earth must aspirate in order to stay functional. Due to the fact that the surface we live on is not static, the earth has the opportunity to move beneath us—and move rapidly. This is what is known as an earthquake, which occurs during the collision of tectonic plates. Although we usually cannot feel or see it, the earth's surface is moving constantly.

Your child will build an explanation supported by evidence of the influence of geoscience processes on changes to the surface of the earth at varying spatial scales and times. Focus is on changes in the earth's surface due to a variety of processes, including slow plate movement and landslides. Students will also focus on the natural geoscience processes such as volcanoes and earthquakes and their resulting catastrophes. Geoscience process examples might include weathering and local geographic features.

Explore Plate Movement

Performance expectation MS.ESS2.3 states that students will "analyze and interpret data on the distribution of fossils and rocks, continental shapes, and seafloor structures to provide evidence of the past plate motion."

The earth has not always looked the way that it does today. In the beginning of its life, our planet was covered with nothing but water. Thanks to the formation of volcanoes, the earth's crust began to poke its head out from under the water. After millions of years of the growth and spewing of rock and metal from these vents, the earth's plates began to collide. This effect of growth and collision led to the creation of one giant landmass known as Pangea. Pangea was the compilation of all continents and landmasses that currently exist on the earth today (with the exception of a few altered due to catastrophe). It is on Pangea that the first bouts of early life were created.

Over time, massive earthquakes and tectonic shifts separated Pangea into the world we know today. This separation led to the creation of the earth's continents.

ESSENTIAL

As each continent shifted into its own climate and ecosystem, the early humans had to adapt to the new environment. For example, those on the African continents as well as in those areas near the equator grew darker skin in order to adapt to the hot and constant sun. Inhabitants of northern areas grew to be lighter skinned and more burly, dealing with the intense cold of winters. Those in more chemically dense and high-wind areas grew to have smaller eyelids in order to protect their vision.

The main evidence supporting Pangea (besides the fact that human beings have been found on all continents of the planet), is that fossil evidence of ancient beings, specifically dinosaurs, have been found on all of these continents. Specifically, these dinosaur fossils come from animals that are not best suited for the climate of the immediate area where they were found, while fossils of the same animal are found in areas where they would be expected. Obviously these animals were not capable of singlehandedly crossing oceans, nor would they be born in ecosystems that did not benefit them. Therefore, all of these fossils originated from dinosaurs that lived in a similar area under a similar climate, and it is the earth itself that moved their remains across the globe.

Middle school students will analyze and interpret information involving fossil and rock distribution, continental forms, and structures on the sea floor to provide proof of plate movement. Data examples might include fossils and rocks found on various continents, continent shapes, and structures in the ocean.

Investigate the Water Cycle

According to performance expectation MS.ESS2.4, your child will "develop a model to describe the cycling of water through earth's systems driven by energy from the sun and the force of gravity."

To understand the water cycle, you must be familiar with the concepts of evaporation, condensation, and precipitation.

Evaporation is the natural process of water becoming aerated and rising into the sky. Water characteristically does this at all temperatures above freezing, but the rate of evaporation increases as temperature rises. So when more heat is applied to liquid water, the faster it will evaporate into the air. In nature, this happens as the sun beats down waves of heat onto bodies of water. The only time that the sun is not in contact with water is at night, when minimal evaporation occurs, and during the day when there are clouds blocking the sunlight. When clouds are dense enough to block sunlight from heating up and evaporating water, this is the environment's natural way of avoiding supersaturating (too much water in the air). Due to the fact that clouds with high water content are the only devices that hinder evaporation, the earth does not allow too much water to be evaporated into the sky.

Condensation is the process in which the gaseous water in the air becomes liquid again, so that it may fall back down to earth. High up in the clouds where this process occurs, the temperature is much lower than that on the surface of the earth, so the condensation of water molecules in the air begin as ice crystals, or what we know as snowflakes. These flakes are materialized out of the air due to specks of mineral dust in the clouds agitating the water enough to become solid again. Once enough water has solidified, the cloud can no longer withstand holding all of the crystals, and so they are dumped back down to earth.

FACT

Water is made of hydrogen and oxygen. Its formula is H_2O. The water cycle includes condensation, infiltration, runoff, evaporation, precipitation, and transpiration. Throughout the water cycle, no new water is produced. Water is a nonrenewable resource.

Precipitation can come in many different forms. Although water forms in crystals in the sky, the form that the crystals may have taken by the time that they hit the ground may have drastically changed. The form of precipitation is a function of heat, wind, and volume of precipitate. In rapid condensation and precipitation, we may see large clumps of ice come together as hail, which fall too fast to be affected by the heat of the environment, and stay ice for the duration of their fall. Other times, the crystals may only slightly melt, and begin to clump together with other falling crystals, forming heavy "sleet." Then in a normal scenario during a warm season, there will simply be rain. Temperature is the largest factor during cold months, as different air pressures and temperatures will determine the type of snow that will fall.

ALERT

Clouds are not vessels that hold water to make rain. When the temperature of the air cools, water droplets are formed from water vapors, and rain falls from the clouds. If the droplets are not heavy enough to fall, there will be no rain.

Your child will construct a model to detail the drive of the sun's energy and the force of gravity on the cycling of water through the systems of the earth. Focus is on the changes in water states as it travels through paths of the hydrologic cycle.

Explore Weather

Performance expectation MS.ESS2.5 states that students will "collect data to provide evidence for how the motions and complex interactions of air masses results in changes in weather conditions."

Much like the blood vessels in the body, the clouds in the sky, as a function of air pressure, move water around the world. What causes all this motion is air pressure. Air pressure is a function of all of the factors in our atmosphere: temperature, atmospheric pressure, humidity, and precipitation. As water is absorbed into the air, it causes the air to be more humid. Humidity is the measurement of the ratio of air to water particles in the air. The more humid it is, the more dense the air is, and therefore, the higher the pressure exerted on the atmosphere around you. This humidity is what makes the air around you feel thicker or thinner, as well as hotter or colder. Though the air temperature may stay the same, the amount of water particles interacting with your body due to high humidity can make it seem much hotter than it actually is.

Our planet is constantly trying to maintain a state of equilibrium. To be in equilibrium, the planet will force high-pressure areas to low-pressure ones and vice versa. This changing in air pressures leads to high winds and powerful storms as nature attempts to release all of the pent-up energy stored within its high-pressure systems. In this way, as a high-pressure system rolls into an area and disperses a storm, it is likely for cold weather to follow, as a considerable amount of energy has exited the system.

Your child will gather information to provide proof of the influence of motions and complex air mass interactions on weather condition changes. Focus is on air flow from high-pressure regions to low-pressure areas, which causes weather to change suddenly. Students will also focus on the use of probabilistic ranges in predicting weather. Data examples might include diagrams, weather maps, and visualizations.

Investigating How Earth's Rotation Can Induce Wild Weather

According to performance expectation MS.ESS2.6, your child will "develop and use a model to describe how unequal heating and rotation of the earth cause patterns of atmospheric and oceanic circulation that determine regional climates."

The earth's orientation in reference to the sun plays a very large and important role in the climates and air masses of certain regions of the earth. Those areas that are closer to the sun will be hotter, and those farther away will be colder. However, these inequalities can have massive implications on the world's ecosystems. Due to the earth's rotation, the aquatic masses of our planet are affected in the same way that the air is. The closer to the sun, the warmer the waters, but also the more sunlight that is available for evaporation, the more evaporation there will be.

In this way, tropical climates are prime candidates for super-massive storm systems that can wreak havoc on land and sea. For centuries humanity has documented massive monsoons, typhoons, and hurricanes. These massive storms are created by the fast evaporation of water from the seas into the air, along with fast-moving winds due to ever-changing pressures, thanks to the evaporation of the sea. As these waters and air masses churn from the high winds, pressures, and temperatures, they create extremely powerful supersystems.

While these storms are extremely dangerous for the regions in which they are created, they can also be hazardous for the immediate areas as well. Depending on size, temperature, and pressure of the storm, its location, and surrounding locations, these fast-moving and powerful storms can find their way moving latitudinally, with their end destinations varying from several miles from their area of birth, all the way up near the northern pole, slightly past northeastern Canada and Russia.

ALERT

These storms are completely natural and cannot be controlled by human hands. They are simply the cause of the earth's global ecosystem and how it expels the great amounts of pressure built up over periods of time, however long.

Your child will develop and utilize a model to detail how the earth's rotation along with uneven heating lead to patterns of oceanic and atmospheric circulation that drive climates in different regions. Focus is on pattern differences due to altitude, latitude, and geography. Atmospheric circulation focus is on latitudinal banding driven by sunlight, the Coriolis effect, and prevailing wind systems. Ocean circulation focus is on heat transfer from the global ocean convection cycle. Model examples might include maps, globes, diagrams, and digital representations.

Earth's Systems Experiment

For this experiment, a question has been provided for you. Work with your child to come up with a hypothesis and then perform the experiment together.

Question

How do changes in temperature affect water and rain?

Materials

- Small glass bowl
- Large glass bowl
- Water
- Plastic wrap
- Tape

Method

1. Place the small bowl inside the large bowl.
2. Pour water into the large bowl but do not allow it to get into the small bowl.
3. Cover the large bowl with plastic wrap and secure it in place with tape.
4. Place the large bowl on a sunny windowsill and allow it to sit for several days.
5. Observe the results each morning and evening.

Consider Testing . . .

- What happens when you don't heat the water?
- What happens when you replace the water with fresh ice?

Let's Review—Checklist

While your child is learning about the earth's systems, keep these points in mind:

- Energy transformation affects matter cycling.
- The three layers of the earth are the core, the mantle, and the crust.
- The upper mantle and the crust form tectonic plates.
- The outer layer of the earth is made of twelve to fifteen large and many small tectonic plates that move slowly.
- Tectonic plates are situated on the hot molten layer of the earth.
- The tectonic plates interact through creating convergent, divergent, and transform boundaries.
- Magma is contained within the earth and affects the tectonic plates, earthquakes, volcanoes, and mountains.
- Some changes to the earth take place over short periods and some changes occur over long periods.
- Rocks can be formed through cooling or accumulation, or through changes from heat and pressure.
- The process of changes in rock is referred to as the rock cycle.
- Weathering can change the surface of the earth.
- Weathering can be caused by wind and water.
- Sedimentary rock provides evidence of the history of the changes to the earth.
- The deeper the layers of sedimentary rock, the older the history that can be observed.
- Geologic time is separated into eons, eras, and periods.
- The history of the earth can be divided into Precambrian, Paleozoic, Mesozoic, and Cenozoic.
- Geological conditions affect evolution.

CHAPTER 17

Earth and Human Activity

How do the interactions between humans and the processes of the earth affect one another? Humans need the atmosphere, land, oceans, and the biosphere to supply resources such as air, animals, energy, minerals, plants, soil, and water. Without these resources, they would not survive. Some of the resources are renewable and some are not. Studying the impact of human activity on planet Earth will help students better understand both the positive and negative effects of human activity and will give them the opportunity to consider how humans can better influence the earth in the future.

What Should My Child Already Understand?

Your child should understand that machines can run on the energy generated from moving water and air, and from the energy that comes from the sun. Currently, people get their energy and fuel from natural resources. For example, they cook food and warm the space within buildings by burning fuels such as coal, natural gas, oil, and wood. They also use electricity for energy. Using these resources affects the environment. Some of these resources are renewable and can be replaced. Other resources are not renewable and cannot be replaced. People are working toward conserving resources and reducing pollution by using less fuel.

FACT

Flow resources are natural resources that have to be used where they are located and when they are available. These resources include wind, water, and sunlight.

Industry, agriculture, and daily living affect the air, atmosphere, landforms, vegetation, and water. People are attempting to work together to decrease the negative effects of human activity on the environment. Every living organism will experience the effects of a continued increase in the average global temperature.

Disciplinary Core Ideas

The following concepts have been established by the Next Generation Science Standards as some of the important points of understanding in studying the earth and human activity. Following are some of the topics your child will learn about and discuss in school.

Natural Resources

Why do people need the earth's resources and how do they use them? Humans need the atmosphere, biosphere, land, and ocean for resources. Many of these resources, such as fresh water and minerals, are nonrenewable. Many resources are not evenly distributed over the earth because of geologic processes that have occurred in the past.

Natural Hazards

What are natural hazards and how do they affect humans? We can predict possible locations of future hazard events through an understanding of geologic forces and the mapping of historical natural hazards in a specific region.

Human Impacts on Earth's Systems

How has the earth been changed by humans? Human activity has significantly changed the biosphere and resulted in some damage. Natural habitats have been destroyed and extinctions of species have occurred due to human activity. Also, the increases in per-person consumption of natural resources by humans have led to negative effects on planet Earth. The impact of human activity on the earth can be reduced through engineered activities and technological advances.

The negative impact of human activity can be decreased through awareness and efforts in protecting the planet. These efforts can include using more renewable energy, cutting down on waste, being more energy efficient, and staying aware of the state of the environment.

Global Climate Change

How are the effects on climate by human activity predicted? Global warming is influenced by human activity that includes the burning of fossil fuels and the release of greenhouse gases. Decisions to decrease the effects of global warming are predicated on understanding the science of climate, the capabilities of engineering, and the dynamics of society.

Human activity has also had a negative impact on the ozone layer. Overuse of chlorofluorocarbons has created a hole in the ozone layer. The ozone layer protects the earth from the dangerous ultraviolet rays of the sun. These rays can cause harmful health issues. While the ozone problem is serious, it does not significantly affect climate change.

Key Earth and Human Activity Terms

These terms are relevant to learning about the earth and human activity:

- Atmosphere—The mass of gases that surrounds the earth
- Biosphere—The regions of the earth where organisms live, including the surface, the atmosphere, and the hydrosphere
- Climate—The conditions of weather that occur in a particular region over a long duration
- Climate Change—A change in the patterns of climate of the earth caused by an increase in the surface temperature
- Consumption—The use of materials
- Deforestation—The cutting down and burning of forests to create clear land
- Erosion—The process in which the earth's surface is worn away
- Fossil Fuel—A natural fuel produced from the remains of living organisms
- Global Warming—A rise in the average global temperature of the surface of the earth caused by an increase in the release of gases into the atmosphere
- Greenhouse Effect—Containment of heat from the sun in the lower atmosphere caused by an increase of gases
- Greenhouse Gases—Gases within the atmosphere that influence the greenhouse effect
- Human Impact—The positive and negative effects of human activity on the systems of the earth
- Natural Habitat—A region in the natural environment where organisms live
- Natural Hazard—A naturally occurring event that causes harm to people
- Natural Resources—Naturally occurring materials such as water, wood, and minerals that people use
- Nonrenewable—Naturally occurring materials that are consumed more quickly than they are replenished
- Ozone Layer—A layer within the stratosphere that absorbs most of the ultraviolet rays from the sun
- Pollution—The release of substances into the environment that cause harmful effects

- Renewable—Naturally occurring materials that are able to replenish themselves
- Stratosphere—The second layer of the atmosphere of the earth

ESSENTIAL

Many natural hazards are the result of weather. Some of them can be predicted; others cannot. Predicting natural hazards through technology and informing communities of potentially dangerous weather events can save many people from harm. The types of natural hazards that occur depend on the geographic location and the climate conditions.

Key Earth and Human Activity Concepts

Human activity has greatly influenced planet Earth, both positively and negatively.

Earth and Human Activity Q&A

Q: What are natural resources?

A: Natural resources are materials that occur naturally and that people use. Natural resources that are renewable can be replaced. Renewable resources are naturally occurring materials that replenish themselves naturally over a period of time. These resources include solar, water, wind, and wood energy. Nonrenewable resources cannot be replaced. Nonrenewable resources are naturally occurring materials that are consumed more quickly by people than they can be replenished. These resources include coal, natural gas, and oil. When these resources run out, there will be none left. The value of resources increases based on how much is available and how easily it can be extracted.

Q: What are natural hazards?

A: Natural hazards are also a component of the natural world. A natural hazard is a naturally occurring event that has a significant effect on the people living in the area. Earthquakes, floods, severe weather, tornadoes, and volcanoes are examples of natural hazards. Some natural hazards occur because of the effects on the environment produced by human activity.

Q: What causes earthquakes?

A: There are several signs that indicate the potential for an earthquake. These include smaller quakes, ground tilting, and fluctuations in water levels. Many earthquakes happen near volcanoes. The magma below the earth's crust pushes upward and exerts pressure on the nearby rock. This pressure causes the ground to shake.

In being able to predict an earthquake, scientists need to be able to tell when, where, and at what strength the event will take place. Scientists are not yet able to provide all of that information with enough accuracy. The location of an earthquake would be the simplest aspect to forecast. Scientists use plate boundary information to determine the region where an earthquake might happen. The time when an earthquake might take place is more difficult to forecast. Since the stress that creates an earthquake is constant, the events should take place regularly, but this is not the case.

Q: What causes volcanoes?

A: Volcanoes are caused by magma rising from the upper mantle and lower crust to the earth's surface. Gas builds up in the magma and causes it to explode out of the earth. Volcanic activity and eruptions are also difficult to predict. There are signs of potential activity, but the time of the event cannot be forecast. When a volcano erupts, there are many abrupt changes to the surrounding environment. Scientists attempt to predict the eruption of a particular volcano through its historical information about past eruptions.

Q: What causes tornadoes?

A: Severe thunderstorms involve strong winds that can produce tornadoes. Tornadoes are strong rotating winds that form a funnel-shaped cloud. As the cloud moves, the power of its strong winds destroys objects in its path. The more intense the winds of a tornado, the greater the damage they can cause.

Q: What is the impact of human activity on the systems of the earth?

A: Human activity can positively and negatively impact the systems of the earth. Examples of the negative effects of people include deforestation, erosion, and pollution. Deforestation occurs when forests are cut down or burned in order to make space for buildings. Erosion takes place when the earth's surface becomes worn down. Human activities, including deforestation, lead to erosion. There are many types of pollution, including air, land, and water pollution. The release of dangerous substances into the air has a significant effect on the air and atmosphere. These pollutants create holes in the ozone layer. Harmful gases are trapped in the atmosphere, causing a rise in the average global temperature of the earth's surface. Pollution can lead to damage to the life cycles of living organisms and global warming. By becoming more aware, burning less fuels, and using fewer nonrenewable resources, people can have a more positive impact on the systems of the earth.

Q: What is global climate change?

A: Air pollution causes many environmental problems, including global climate change. As people burn fossil fuels, more carbon dioxide gases are released into the atmosphere, which in turn creates a greenhouse effect. This effect increases the temperature of the surface of the earth.

Q: What is the greenhouse effect?

A: The greenhouse effect takes place when the heat of the sun is radiated back to the earth by gases in the atmosphere. Without this effect, the heat from the sun would move into space and the temperature of the surface of the earth would be too cold for living organisms.

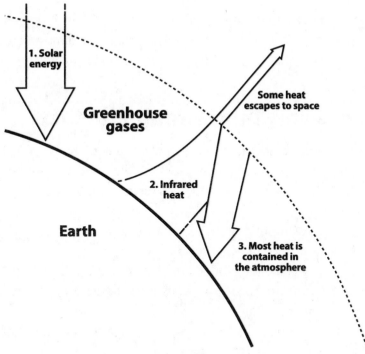

Greenhouse effect on the earth

Q: What is global warming?

A: Global warming refers to the rise in temperature of the surface of the earth that has recently occurred. Over the last century, there has been a significant increase in the temperature. Carbon dioxide in the atmosphere greatly affects global warming, causing an increase in the greenhouse effect. There is more carbon dioxide in the atmosphere due to an increase in fossil-fuel burning.

Q: What are the effects of climate change?

A: The changes in climate temperature have resulted in drought conditions, heat waves, rising sea levels, flooding, and increased precipitation in particular regions. These results affect the people, animals, plants, microorganisms, and ecosystems living in these regions.

Q: What can people do about climate change?

A: People can reduce global change through reductions in energy use. A decrease in energy use would reduce the amount of carbon dioxide that is released into the atmosphere. A decrease in the levels of carbon dioxide being released into the atmosphere would also be beneficial. This could be accomplished by planting new forests.

Science and Engineering Practices

In learning about the earth and its interactions, your child will use science and engineering practices to better understand the ideas that relate to human activity. These practices might include:

- Knowing and applying information and ideas to describe the earth's processes and features
- Evaluating the biodegradability of natural resources
- Asking and answering questions about how the transfer of energy drives matter cycling
- Developing and using models to learn more about how fossil fuels and natural gases are formed
- Planning and carrying out an investigation that shows how heat is transferred
- Analyzing and interpreting data to show the consequences of energy distribution and transformation on the environment
- Using mathematics to determine how much carbon dioxide is released from fuel burning
- Designing an instrument that functions using energy forms such as wind and solar
- Engaging in argument with evidence support to discuss the benefits and challenges of using different sources of energy
- Obtaining, evaluating, and communicating information that describes how energy can only be transformed and not created or destroyed
- Asking and answering questions about changes in the temperature of the earth and its effects on the water cycle
- Developing and using models to show how gases keep the energy of the sun in the atmosphere
- Planning and carrying out investigations to find out whether air masses take up space

- Analyzing and interpreting data to show how a rise in the amount of greenhouse gases affects the surface temperature of the earth
- Using mathematics to analyze patterns as evidence in debates relating global warming to greenhouse gases
- Designing an instrument to collect weather information
- Obtaining, evaluating, and communicating information that shows how solar radiation travels to the earth

Next Generation Science Standards Performance Expectations

These performance expectations describe what your child should be able to demonstrate and understand about the specific science unit he is studying in middle school. From these expectations your child's teachers will determine how successfully he understands and can apply the concepts that have been covered.

Explore the Distribution of Natural Resources

Performance expectation MS.ESS3.1 states the students will "construct a scientific explanation based on evidence for how the uneven distributions of earth's mineral, energy, and groundwater resources are the result of past and current geoscience processes."

There are some regions of the earth where there is not an even distribution of minerals and resources, most specifically of these being water. Some of these happenings are natural, and others are the result of man's hand.

The lack of water in certain areas in the modern world is referred to as drought. Certain areas can be starved for water, which in turn can damage the ecosystem around it by starving plants and animals of the essentials for life. Because of massive human consumption in the modern age, this process can happen far more often than it used to. Structures such as dams and other such water controllers in our ecosystems can be the culprit, as vast amounts of water do not flow freely throughout the earth's natural systems.

This does not mean that these things cannot happen naturally as well. For example, deserts and dry lowlands, like those seen in India and Africa, have a miniscule amount of rainfall every year relative to the precipitation of the rest of the planet. The difference, however, is that this uneven distribution exists because of the environments that exist. The climates and ecosystems of these areas do not receive considerable rainwater because they do not need it. The organisms in these areas have adapted to the environment that does not provide them great resources. The issue lies with the uneven distribution in areas that do not have hearty inhabitants and can be greatly affected by a lack of resources. These areas are at great risk if there were ever to be a shortage of water. The earth replenishes these resources in a natural way, but consuming them unnaturally and quickly in these areas will increase the chances for shortages. Even though our global society has ways to combat the adverse effects of these shortages, humans should try their best not to throw off the balance of the earth's natural processes.

Middle school students will construct a scientific explanation supported by evidence for the unequal distribution of minerals, groundwater, and energy and the effects of past and present geoscience processes. Focus is on the limitations of these resources and the changes in their distributions due to human activity. Uneven distribution examples might include petroleum, metal ores, and soil.

Forecast Natural Hazards

According to performance expectation MS.ESS3.2, your child should be able to "analyze and interpret data on natural hazards to forecast future catastrophic events and inform the development of technologies to mitigate their effects."

How can the dangerous concoctions of pressure and temperature that cause natural hazards be controlled? Humans have been able to devise ways to control the various natural disasters on the earth. This has been a practice tested and hypothesized on for decades, most notably being the High-Frequency Active Auroral Research Program (HAARP) experimental facility created to analyze our atmosphere in order to create a means of controlling it. We as a society have created ways to induce rain and pull harmful pollutants from our skies. So we must now hypothesize ways to mitigate the effects of other powerful systems on the earth.

For example, the eruption of a volcano in our modern era would be catastrophic. People often flock toward volcanoes to reap the benefits of a warm and highly mineralized ecosystem. What they do not tend to focus on, however, is the fact that in any moment, the volcano could erupt and wipe out all civilization near it, as is what happened to the volcanic city of Pompeii. In an instant, the entire region was wiped out by hot ash and flowing magma, not to mention the powerful and poisonous gases that engulfed the area. Due to high wind travel, if any major volcano were to erupt on earth, like the one located in Yellowstone National Park, the ash cloud created could black out over half of the United States.

FACT

The climate of the earth has changed throughout history due to natural factors. The intensity of the sun, volcanic activity, and the position of the continents have all played a part in natural climate changes through history.

With modern science, however, humanity could devise ways to avoid this sort of catastrophe. As previously stated, weather machines are capable of firing high concentrations of pressurized air and water into our atmosphere, inducing rain. We must think, then, that in order to avoid a blackout by ash, we could use this machine to soak up the ash from the sky and cause it to rain down to earth, ending the blackout that it would cause. This same machine could be used to create pressure systems that could deter the formation of powerful storms, or at least create a pressure barrier that could stop and hold the storms from hitting land, thus allowing the storms to expel themselves safely over the seas where minimal damage would occur.

Students will analyze and interpret information on natural hazards in order to predict future catastrophes and reduce their effects. Focus is on how some phenomena are preceded by natural hazards that allow for reliable forecasts while others are not and cannot be reliably predicted. Natural hazard examples might include earthquakes, volcanoes, tsunamis, and severe weather. Data examples might include magnitudes, locations, and natural hazard frequency. Technology examples might include satellites and reservoirs.

Explore How to Minimize Human Impact

Performance expectation MS.ESS3.3 states that students should "apply scientific principles to design a method for monitoring and minimizing a human impact on the environment."

Much work needs to be done on reducing the human footprint from the earth, as it is obvious that we have already created adverse effects on the environment. This can be done in several ways, all of which include the reduction of our consumption—most notably, our consumption of land. While the human population on the earth is growing exponentially, we must not consider this a good thing. Our planet only has so many natural resources. The more humans we have, the more we consume. In this way, the more we grow, the more we deplete.

Water is one of the most important, if not the most important, resource on the earth. All living things require water to live, and as human population grows, so does our consumption of water. As we begin to overconsume, we begin to cause droughts and starve other areas of the planet of water. Doing this enough can destroy our way of life. An example of this can be seen in the 2011–2015 California drought, which has killed off fields worth of crops due to lack of water, reducing the amount of specific food available across the country. This also drives up prices, which can change, and potentially destroy, industry and economies. By cutting down on the human consumption of resources like water, we can reduce the effects of droughts.

Your child will apply principles of science to design a process for examining and reducing the impact of human activity on the environment. Design process examples might include monitoring human impact on the environment and evaluating the types of solutions that might be effective. Human impact examples might include land and water usage and pollution.

Investigate How Human Consumption Impacts the Earth

According to performance expectation MS.ESS3.4, students should be able to "construct an argument supported by evidence for how increases in human population and per-capita consumption of natural resources impact earth's systems."

The number of humans on our planet causes several problems. Due to each person having certain needs to be met, certain amounts of resources must be allotted to each human in the overall picture of humanity. The smaller the number of people, the smaller the number of resources that must be distributed, or at least the more resources that are available to those who do not have access to necessities as easily as those in modernized countries do.

ALERT

The other thing that is proportional to human beings on our planet is the amount of pollution we produce. Each person living on this planet creates a significant amount of solid, liquid, and aerated waste each year, which contributes to global pollution as a whole.

Your child will develop an argument supported by proof for the impact of a human population increase and the consumption of natural resources on the systems of the earth. Evidence examples might include human population databases and rates of natural resource consumption. Impact examples might include changes in the composition, structure, and appearance of the systems of the earth along with the rates of these changes.

Investigate Climate Change

Performance expectation ESS3.5 states that students should "ask questions to clarify evidence of the factors that have caused the rise in global temperatures over the past century."

There are a great number of global climate phenomena that have been caused by the hand of man, most notably being major changes in climate since the dawn of the industrial revolution. Due to the increase in human technologies over the last 200 years, we have seen a great deal of pollution enter the earth's atmosphere. From natural volcanic burn-off, to the greenhouse gases emitted by the burning of fossil fuels, to the mass collection of methane released into the air due to factory farming, the earth is being plunged into dangerous territory by the hand of man.

The most notable of these is the collection of methane. Methane is the number one greenhouse gas present in our atmosphere, and this is due to the concentration of animals that we cluster in order to efficiently factory farm. The waste from all of these animals collects into the highest concentration of dangerous chemicals on the planet, which far surpasses the emissions of all of the combustion engines on the earth combined.

FACT

Global warming refers to the increase in the average surface temperature of the earth. This has been caused by burning fossil fuels that produce carbon dioxide. Deforestation and land erosion has also affected carbon dioxide amounts in the atmosphere.

However, one cannot overlook the emissions from the burning of fossil fuels, which has occurred for over 200 years, starting with the first coal-burning engines at the dawn of the modern age. These emissions travel into the sky and break down our layer of protective ozone gases, which shield the earth from direct heat that comes from the sun. The more ozone that is depleted, the higher the temperatures of our air and seas.

Your child will investigate how natural processes and human activity have influenced gradual and sudden changes in global temperatures as well as greenhouse gas and carbon dioxide concentrations in the atmosphere throughout the past century.

Earth and Human Activity Experiment

For this experiment, a question has been provided for you. Work with your child to come up with a hypothesis and then perform the experiment together.

Question

How does an area's covering affect its air temperature?

Materials

- 2 small thermometers
- 2 large glass jars

- Clear tape
- 1 large jar lid
- 2 pieces white paper
- Timer

Method

1. Place a small thermometer into both of the jars and secure them in place with tape.
2. Secure the lid on one of the jars.
3. Place 2 pieces of white paper along a windowsill that receives direct sunlight.
4. Place each jar on one of the pieces of paper.
5. Observe and record the temperatures of each thermometer and any changes occurring in the jars every 10 minutes for 1 hour.

Consider Testing . . .

- What happens if you add an enclosed jar with water in it?
- What happens when you place the jars in a darker area?
- What happens when you add ice to the small jar?

Let's Review—Checklist

In order to help your child while she is learning about the earth and human activity, keep these points in mind:

- Energy has a connection to electricity, heat, light, mechanical motion, and sound.
- There are several ways that energy is transferred.
- The movement of heat is predictable. It moves from objects with more heat to objects with less heat.
- There is a transfer of energy in and out of a system during many chemical changes.
- The law of conservation of energy states that energy can only be changed into a different form; it cannot be destroyed or created.
- Energy as heat is a product of energy transformation.

- Energy acquisition, transformation, and distribution affect the environment.
- Carbon dioxide is released into the atmosphere through fuel burning.
- Chemical energy is transformed into thermal energy through fuel burning.
- The transportation of energy is easier with some forms than others.
- Several energy sources produce electrical energy. Electrical energy is transformed into many other forms.
- Solar energy is a renewable resource.
- Various regions around the globe have different energy resources in varying amounts.
- The sun produces a majority of the energy that people use.
- People need the atmosphere, biosphere, landforms, and oceans to get resources including minerals and water.
- There is not an even distribution of natural resources throughout the earth.
- People are developing new technologies to better utilize natural resources.
- Natural hazards usually take place following particular phenomena. By understanding the phenomena, some predictions can be made about the events. By mapping historical natural hazards and relating the information to geological forces, the probability and location of these events can be better predicted.
- Human activity has significantly affected the biosphere, creating negative effects. Humans must work toward developing technology and making environmentally conscious decisions to change these effects.
- The increase in the mean surface temperature of the earth has been caused by the release of greenhouse gases. These gases are released through fossil-fuel burning.
- Humans can reduce the negative effects of climate changes by becoming more aware of climate and developing technology that will solve these issues.

CHAPTER 18

Engineering Design

How are engineers able to use design applications to solve problems? The process of design is the engineering foundation for solving problems. It involves defining a problem, developing and using a model, investigating, analyzing and interpreting data, applying mathematics, and determining the effective solution options. These practices integrate a depth of understanding regarding standards and limitations, analysis of models, and accommodations and maximizations of solution possibilities.

What Should My Child Already Understand?

In terms of engineering, your middle-schooler should already know certain facts, including:

- The solution possibilities are defined by the materials and resources that are available when working toward solving a problem.
- Success is based on the chosen aspects of the solution.
- Solution choices are compared by their ability to meet the chosen aspects and by how well they take into account the materials and resources needed.
- A problem should be researched through several formats before the development of a solution begins.
- Solutions are effectively generated through brainstorming with others.
- Solution testing involves an investigation of performance levels over a range of conditions that determine areas for improvement.
- Communication with others is a significant component of the solution process in order to share ideas and improve designs.
- Testing of several solutions is necessary in order to identify which component best solves the problem while meeting its criteria and constraints.

FACT

The word "engineer" originates from the Latin word *ingeniare*, which means to design or devise. It is also associated with the meaning cleverness. There are several branches of engineering, including aerospace, biomedical, chemical, civil, computer, electrical, environmental, forensic, genetic, mechanical, military, nuclear, reverse, software, and structural.

Disciplinary Core Ideas

The following concepts have been established by the Next Generation Science Standards as some of the important points of understanding in studying engineering design. The following are some of the engineering concepts your child will be learning and discussing in school.

Defining and Delimiting Engineering Problems

What is a solution design and why is it necessary to include criteria and constraints? The more precisely a design task's criteria and constraints can be defined, the more likely it is that the designed solution will be successful. Specification of constraints includes consideration of scientific principles and other relevant knowledge that is likely to limit possible solutions.

ESSENTIAL

The engineering process is iterative, which means that it is a continual system. Engineers work continually, designing and redesigning, until the optimal solution to the problem has been formulated.

Developing Possible Solutions

What steps are involved in the design solution process? A solution must be tested and altered based on the results of the tests so that it can be improved. Solutions are evaluated using systematic processes that determine how well the solution met the criteria and limitations of a particular problem. Components of different solutions can be joined to build a solution that is better than the ones that were created before it. Models are crucial for testing a solution.

ALERT

The words model and prototype are sometimes used in place of each other, but they are not the same. A *model* demonstrates or explains how a solution will function and what it will look like. A *prototype* is used by engineers to test various features of a solution before the final design is completed.

Optimizing the Design Solution

How are different solutions to a particular problem compared and improved? While one design might not function at an optimal level through all tests, determining the characteristics of the design that worked the best in every test can offer helpful information for redesigning the solution. Design solution testing is an iterative process. The iterative process of testing designs for the best solutions makes it possible to continually change the design until it has been refined into the optimal solution.

Key Engineering Design Terms

These terms are important to a solid understanding of engineering and technology:

- Analyze—To divide something into its components to examine
- Clarify—To make something less confusing or easier to understand
- Collaborate—To work together with another person on a project
- Constraints—Limitations or restrictions
- Construct—To build; to create
- Control—Constant and unchanged
- Criteria—A standard for testing something
- Critique—Assessment or evaluation
- Data—Information
- Dependent Variable—The variable in an experiment that is being tested
- Design—A plan to show the function and properties of a solution
- Develop—To become more advanced
- Engineering Process—A sequence of steps that are followed to design a solution to a problem
- Evidence—Facts that prove something is true
- Hypothesis—A proposed explanation for an observation
- Identify—To establish or verify
- Independent Variable—The variable in an experiment that is designed to change
- Infer—To make a conclusion based on evidence
- Interpret—To provide the meaning of something
- Investigation—A systematic examination of facts
- Model—A three-dimensional representation of a structure or phenomenon
- Observation—The process of watching something to gain information
- Qualitative Observation—The process of using the senses to gain information

- Quantitative Observation—The use of instruments to measure results and gain information
- Scientific Law—The description of a phenomenon that is consistently observed under specific conditions
- Scientific Method—A sequence of steps that is followed in order to test a hypothesis
- Scientific Theory—An explanation of a phenomenon in the natural world that has been well-proven through the scientific method
- Solution—A means of resolving a problem
- Variables—The aspects in an experiment that change

Key Engineering Design Concepts

Engineering design is a continual process that is used to develop the best solutions to problems.

Engineering Q&A

Q: What is the scientific method?

A: The scientific method involves a sequence of steps that are used to answer scientific questions. The same steps are not always followed throughout every experiment. The steps that are used are based on the complexity of the question. Experiments that are designed to answer scientific questions should include only one variable in order to produce reliable results. The steps of the scientific method are:

- Make an observation
- Ask a question based on the observation
- Conduct research about the question
- Form a hypothesis
- Design and perform an experiment to test the hypothesis
- Collect and analyze data from the experiment
- Make conclusions from the results and determine if they support the hypothesis
- Communicate the results and conclusions of the experiment

Q: How is an experiment designed?

A: In order to perform an experiment that provides reliable results, scientists follow a sequence of steps. The steps in designing an experiment are:

1. State the scientific question to be answered.
2. Determine how the independent variable might affect the dependent variable.
3. Conduct background research on the topic and describe how this information might influence the experiment.
4. Form a hypothesis describing what will happen and why using the background research information.
5. State how the independent variable will affect the dependent variable and why.
6. List all materials needed for the experiment.
7. List the step-by-step instructions for performing the experiment.
8. Note the independent variable, dependent variable, and control variables.
9. Note what will be measured to determine whether there was an effect by the independent variable.
10. List any safety concerns.
11. Perform the experiment.
12. Record all observations through notes, photographs, and videos.
13. Collect the data.
14. Create diagrams, graphs, and data tables.
15. Analyze the data.
16. Draw a conclusion from the data.
17. Determine if the results support the hypothesis.
18. Communicate the results and conclusion of the experiment with others.

Q: What is a hypothesis?

A: A hypothesis refers to a proposed explanation for a particular observation. A hypothesis should be written as an expression so that it can be tested with evidence, be proven to be supported or not supported, and provide results that can be measured.

Q: What are variables?

A: Scientists and engineers look for cause-and-effect relationships in performing experiments and designing solutions. In order to produce reliable results, they change a quantity of an experiment or design and observe for predictable effects of the change. The changes can be any aspect or condition, and are referred to as variables. There are three types of variables: control, dependent, and independent. Control variables are quantities that remain the same. Dependent variables are quantities that change as a result of the independent variables. Independent variables are the quantities that are changed. Most experiments have only one independent variable. The value of each variable in an experiment should be measureable.

Q: What is the engineering process?

A: The engineering process is a sequence of steps that engineers use to design a solution to a problem. The solution usually involves the development of a product that performs a specific task. The same steps are not always followed in sequential order throughout every design process. The design process is iterative, and there are continual changes made to create the best possible solution to a problem.

The steps of the engineering process include:

1. **State the problem:** List the problem that requires a solution.
2. **Generate ideas:** Conduct background research about the problem. List the requirements and the limiting factors of the problem.
3. **Select a solution:** List all of the possible solutions to the problem. Choose the best two solutions to use and debate the two solution choices with others. Select the solution that best solves the problem.
4. **Build the item:** Design and build a prototype.
5. **Evaluate:** Test the prototype and judge how it performs.
6. **Present results:** And if necessary, refine the design based on the test results.

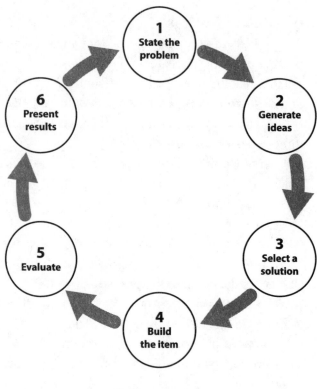

Design process

Q: How do the scientific method and the engineering design process differ?

A: The scientific method is used to answer scientific questions by performing experiments and making observations. The engineering process is used to solve problems by designing solutions that meet specific criteria and constraints.

Q: How do scientists and engineers communicate their observations, results, and solutions?

A: Scientists and engineers must communicate their results and solutions in order to be effective and productive in their fields. One means of communication is through journals. Results and solutions can be published in scientific and engineering journals to allow peers to review the work. Another means of communication is through presentations at conferences and universities. Presentations enable scientists and engineers to speak to groups of their peers and answer questions directly. A third means of communication is through the media, including newspapers, magazines, and Internet articles and blogs.

Science and Engineering Practices

In learning about engineering, your child will use science and engineering practices to better understand the ideas that relate to design. These practices might include:

- Defining a solution for a problem that might involve developing an instrument, tool, or process that meets several criteria and constraints.
- Constructing a model to develop a data set that tests design solutions using inputs and outputs.
- Analyzing and interpreting data to identify all of the similarities and the differences in the results of the design test.
- Evaluating competing solutions on the basis of developed criteria.

Next Generation Science Standards Performance Expectations

These performance expectations describe what your child should be able to demonstrate and understand about the specific science unit he is studying in middle school. From these expectations your child's teachers will determine how successfully he understands and can apply the concepts that have been covered.

Solve a Design Problem

Performance expectation MS.ETS1.1 states that students should "define the criteria and constraints of a design problem with sufficient precision to ensure a successful solution, taking into account relevant scientific principles and potential impacts on people and the natural environment that may limit possible solutions."

When creating a design problem that you can test, you must take into account all relevant factors about said problems, as well as all realistic assets regarding the outcome you are trying to achieve. To make relevant designs in order to come up with concrete solutions to real-world problems, you must be extremely realistic with the materials that you use in two ways: Are they truly relevant, and are they truly realistic?

FACT

There are many similarities between scientists and engineers. Scientists have an inclination for discovering new knowledge, and engineers tend to apply the knowledge that is learned to designing solutions.

For example, if you are to create an experiment to monitor the amount of human consumption of water and how varying the numbers of humans in an environment can change water levels, you must think about realistic numbers for this sort of experiment. Obviously, you cannot use an entire civilization to test this theory, but you also cannot use a small number of people, say four. Both of these groups would not yield truly specific results.

ESSENTIAL

When engineers begin their search to solve a problem, they develop several possible solutions and not one single design. All of these potential solutions are tested to determine how well they solve the problem.

Your child will detail the foundations and limitations of a design problem with competent correctness to develop a successful solution, considering pertinent principles of science and potential effects on people and the environment that may restrict solution possibilities.

Evaluate Design Solutions

According to performance expectation MS.ETS1.2, your child will "evaluate competing design solutions using a systematic process to determine how well they meet the criteria and constraints of the problem."

It is important as a scientist to evaluate and critique the findings and experimentation of others. By doing this, scientists can find a way to perfect an experiment. By critiquing and tweaking, scientists can further an experiment in order to create a more perfected outcome.

For example, companies have begun to create vehicles that cut down on the amount of carbon emissions. Searching for alternative power sources to run vehicles will cut down on the amount of greenhouse gases that are emitted into the air. There have been several concepts that have emerged in the last ten years, and all of these concepts seek to fix these issues. However, different concepts have worked at different efficiencies and have only worked so much at certain levels. By critiquing these, one can eliminate the factors that would not be very helpful, and help promote the ideas that do work in order to be perfected.

For example, three concepts to decrease emissions by using less petroleum in engines have come in the form of the hybrid car, the electric car, and the hydrogen-powered car. The hybrid car used a petroleum engine as well as battery-powered motors. However, the batteries in these vehicles could not realistically handle the amount of flow between the engines and the motors (engines=mechanical, motors=electrical), and so the car would mainly revert to the engine, making the electric component moot.

So the next step in this process was the electric car, which used only batteries, and is a viable option for vehicles without emissions. The car runs on no fuel and has considerable mileage on batteries that last due to minimal mechanical confusion. However, in order to power these cars, one must use electricity, which is created in several ways in order to be applied to the car for charging, many of which include pollutant-heavy power generation from plants (natural generation is far outweighed by mechanical). Therefore, the electric car was better, but still not perfect for controlling emissions.

Then came a car that ran on hydrogen. Hydrogen-powered cars run on chemical reactions based upon the most abundant element in our universe, hydrogen. This chemical process has no emissions, and therefore it is a good solution to our problem. Contrarily, it is the most expensive. So now, we as scientists must critique this working idea in order to make it more affordable so that we can get it into the hands of the masses.

In this way, you can see how the process of scientific critique through the required criteria can improve and perfect an idea.

Your child will assess competing design solutions utilizing a logical process to determine the effectiveness of the designs in meeting the problem criteria and limitations.

Analyze Data to Create a New Solution

Performance expectation MS.ETS1.3 states that students should be able to "analyze data from tests to determine similarities and differences among several design solutions to identify the best characteristics of each that can be combined into a new solution to better meet the criteria for success."

Even if an idea is not particularly good or perfect, the critique must analyze the good and the bad of the idea. This is especially the case when you are critiquing two ideas that seek to solve the same problem. When critiquing, you can generally take the better of two ideas and combine both worlds to make the best end product possible. By promoting the good and eliminating the bad, you can create the best possible solution to a product. For example, the inventions of both Thomas Edison and Nikola Tesla, the fathers of modern electricity, both (at one point) worked in tandem to eliminate the issue of creative conflicts, and find the best possible power solution to their problem. Thanks to these two, you are able to use both AC and DC power in tandem to power your electronics.

Your child will analyze information from tests to conclude the differences and similarities among different design solutions to determine the best traits of each that can be joined into a new solution to better satisfy the basis for success.

Develop a Model

According to performance expectation MS.ETS1.4, your child will "develop a model to generate data for iterative testing and modification of a proposed object, tool, or process such that an optimal design can be achieved."

When creating a design, the most important thing that you must focus on is creating reliable data from your tests. Therefore, the most important thing to do is to create an input and output model for everything that you plan to test. Creating a spreadsheet that analyzes all input and output variables will produce the most concrete results. There is no point in attempting to solve a problem if your figures do not reflect actual data. This would be neither beneficial, nor honest.

ALERT

> It is vital to communicate the results of an investigation and the features of a design solution so that all of the data involved in the analysis can be understood.

By creating a model of what you input to your designs, you can more accurately pinpoint any sort of problems with designs, as your hypothesis should not only be based in ideology but also in numbers. If your expectations are off, you can refer back to your data model to see what must be tweaked, changed, removed, or added. This use of organization for your designs will ensure the most optimal product.

Your child will create a model to generate information for continual assessment and changes of a prospective tool, object, or procedure in order that the best design might be developed.

Engineering Design Experiment

For this experiment, a question has been provided for you. Work with your child to come up with a hypothesis and then perform the experiment together.

Question

How many pennies can a paper bridge hold?

Materials

- 2 books
- Ruler
- 1 piece of paper
- 100 pennies

Method

1. Place the two books 20 cm apart.
2. Lay the paper to create a bridge between the books without attaching it to the books or any other supporting materials.
3. Place as many pennies as possible anywhere on the freestanding part of the bridge. Observe and record your results as you add more pennies to the bridge.

Consider Testing . . .

- What happens if you fold the paper?
- What happens when you change the placement of the pennies?

Let's Review—Checklist

As your child is learning about engineering practices, keep these important points in mind:

- When more precise criteria and constraints are used in the design of a solution, there is a greater likelihood of a successful solution.
- Defining specific constraints involves considering the scientific principles and knowledge that are relevant to the problem and that might limit the solution options.
- Solutions require testing and modifications based on results to be effectively improved.
- The evaluation of solution possibilities involves a systematic process that considers criteria and constraints.
- Components of different solution options can be united to build the best possible solution.
- Solution development is most effective through the communication of explanations with others.
- Models are vital for solution testing.
- Computers are an effective tool in creating, using, and analyzing system simulations.
- Simulations are effective tools in predicting the results of a solution under a variety of conditions and for improving models.

- Solution design comparisons involve testing and recording of results to determine which solution is most effective.
- The continual process of testing the best solution options and modifying them based on test outcomes results in developing the optimal solution design.
- When the optimal solution has been determined, it is crucial to communicate and explain the development, including the conditions, criteria, and constraints, with others.

CHAPTER 19

Science Fair Projects

A science fair is an event in which students of the sciences can apply their knowledge as well as practice their understanding of the scientific method and engineering practices. The science fair allows for all contestants to make observations, form hypotheses, and test experiments in order to come up with a solution to a problem they have identified. Contestants are judged based on how they execute their scientific processes, and how significant their findings on their subjects are. However, the science fair isn't created simply for competition; instead, it is created for the advancement of science.

Helping Your Child Choose a Project

The science fair is an extremely useful and meaningful collaboration of scientists of all ages. With the common goal of problem solving through research, the science fair can create some great results from bright minds. The idea of all like-minded scientists coming together to complete tasks and find solutions using the scientific method with implemented engineering practices is a great way to derive a lot of new information from questions these minds have asked themselves.

The different projects are not created to one-up the others. Instead, all projects are created to be the most in-depth scientific process that they can be. Each project will attempt to uncover the most information possible. While there can be winners, there is no loser, so long as a discovery is made.

When choosing a science fair project, your child must look to uncover an issue that has yet to be uncovered. Simply repeating past projects and experiments is not so much science as it is showmanship. The goal is to make a discovery, even if it is not particularly "exciting." When deciding, make sure your child understands that her project must be honest and true. Plagiarizing other people's work is not only morally wrong, but it serves no scientific purpose, as no discovery will be made. However, if she can further expand upon someone's previous work in order to learn more information, then there is nothing wrong with this.

ALERT

A science fair project does not have to include expensive materials and equipment to be successful, nor does the display have to present extravagant images. Most experiments can be completed at home on a very small budget. While the appearance of the display is important, it is not the key aspect of the project.

While the classic baking-soda volcano is an exciting experiment to watch, it simply contributes nothing to knowledge or the derivation of knowledge from an experiment. Stay away from experiments that are simply interesting to look at, and look deeper into problems that have yet to be solved.

Also make sure your child is being realistic about the experiment she wishes to undertake. The traditional science fair is not meant to include experiments that observe the populace of the world or completely change general aspects of human life. Make sure she keeps her project relative so that it can be the most effective.

Your child should also exercise caution with her experiment. If her experiment is dangerous to herself or those who would view her findings, proceed in a controlled environment with professionals who can help her. She should always be as safe as possible when she is trying to collect data.

After your child has determined her topic, make sure she follows the scientific method to the best of her ability. If her topic contains areas that can't be represented by different stages of this method, such as an experiment that cannot be accurately testable, she should move on and find another topic.

ESSENTIAL

Your child should choose a topic that interests her. Don't let her wait until the last minute. The best way to find a successful topic is for her to think about the science fair months before the competition. She should write down science questions she would like to answer, then as the fair gets closer on the calendar, she can decide on the one that best suits her.

Forming a Hypothesis

When forming her hypothesis about her topic and/or observation, make sure that she makes the most educated guess possible. By forming a more educated approximation of what she thinks her results may be, she will be able to more precisely tailor her experiment to receive relatable data. However, she should not be so specific as to try to sway the results of the experiment toward her desired expectations. If her hypothesis is incorrect, there is absolutely nothing wrong. So long as knowledge was gained from the experiment and meaningful data was collected, her hypothesis is simply an afterthought. The results are what matter, not what she thinks or hopes they may be.

Designing Experiments and Recording Results

When designing an experiment, make sure that your child organizes all of her data. Whether she has fifteen variables or five, she should keep tabs of every single piece of input and output data. The more data that she has, the more specific she can be about each aspect of her experiment.

ESSENTIAL

Organizing data is especially helpful later on down the road of the project if your child is ever confused about result data that she has. If there is an issue with her findings, she can better pinpoint where the problem lies if she collects specific data about each thing that goes on.

Experiment and Collect Data

Make sure your child accurately logs each of the processes that occur during her experiment. For instance, if she is burning a material in an attempt to find the final temperature or composition, she should not simply record the final composition and temperature. During combustion, she should record how long the combustion took, what colors that it burned, if there was a smoke emitted, the color of said smoke, and so on. This same ideology can be applied to any experiment. She should simply make sure to record every single finding that she makes. This can potentially open up the door for new information and findings, or other experiments to take place after her initial experiments, based upon her findings. Being specific about science allows us to expand on it more thoroughly.

ESSENTIAL

Take time to work the entire process. The project should take more than an afternoon to complete. Multiple tests and designs require time and opportunity, so be sure your child starts the process early.

As she interprets her results, make sure that she does not draw conclusions until she has fully analyzed all data that she found. By jumping to conclusions, she can come up with incorrect results. Just because the majority of data points toward a certain outcome, it does not mean the outcome is completely assured. Make sure she completely analyzes all of her data no matter how specific and linear previous data is pointing. This is important in two ways. If her data begins to sway away from a trend, then she may have to expand further upon her experiment, as obviously there is something investigable about that set of data that she derived away from the trend. Additionally, the sway of her trend may come from inaccurate testing or recording of data. If she has results that sway away from the trend, make sure she tests her experiment a couple more times to ensure she has correct data around that series of responses.

FACT

Your child should choose innovative science questions. If the question has been used or the project has been done before, have her look for another idea. If that is not possible, make sure she adds personal connections to the concept.

When your child is experimenting with her variables, it is important to make sure that she has concrete and accurate data. Therefore, it would make sense for her to repeat her experiment many times. The more times she experiments, the more data she can receive. By taking the average of all of the data she collects from several runs of the same experiment, she gets the most accurate results, and therefore the most concrete answer.

Draw Conclusions

After collecting all of her data, the next step for your child is to draw conclusions from what she has found. As she does this, make sure that the conclusions are drawn directly from the data, and not what she thinks or hypothesizes the data might represent. She should not be afraid to repeat experiments, or create more if need be. When she does come to a conclusion, it must be completely a result of the data that she has collected. This must show in the report that she'll create to accompany the project. If this is not the case, then there are holes in her project.

Your child should be completely sure of all of the things that she has inputted into her project, as inconsistencies as well as lapses in reputable data can hinder her discoveries greatly. If she is looking to solve a problem through a science fair project, she should have the best possible solution based upon the mathematics of the situation, and not what she thinks might be the solution.

ALERT

A science fair is not about following a procedure or a demonstration. It's about testing an idea or design. The project or design should include distinct variables and provide results or solutions.

Share the Results

After your child has come to concrete conclusions through her data, her next step in the scientific process is to share her results. In the setting of a science fair, this is done by presenting her project to the other experimenters. This sharing of information is essentially the basis behind the concept of a science fair. However, should she find substantial results, help her find a way to submit her findings to the scientific community as a whole.

Projects That Make a Difference

It is logical to base science fair projects upon pressing scientific issues that we as humans face. The scientific method required in the science fair is akin to the practices of engineers. The overall goal is to solve a problem. To solve a problem you must first find a real issue, as opposed to simply coming up with filler that one could experiment with.

For example, a science fair project could be conducted where the observation on human waste could be tested over several variables in order to see how the placement of waste can affect the surrounding environment. This experiment could utilize variable simulated environments for testing, such as a sand box to replicate a desert, a pond to replicate an underwater environment, or an icebox to replicate an arctic environment. Your child could then record the data of how different levels of pollution affected each of these areas over time. The change in composition of the sediment and surrounding areas of the simulation environments would indicate the effect of the pollution on these environments. She could then conclude which environments are affected the most by certain conditions with regard to pollution.

Science Fair Project Stages

A science fair project typically takes a few weeks to complete. In order to perform a reliable experiment that will produce valuable results, it is important to follow through the process properly over a period of time. Rushing through a project to finish in a day will not only cause your child some stress, it will most likely produce fairly mediocre results. It's important to follow through the process, step-by-step, in order to have the best learning experience possible.

Your child should:

- Pick a topic for his project. Make sure it is a topic that interests him. He might want to discuss the idea with you and then submit his topic to his teacher.
- Write down the purpose of his experiment in a question format. He should state what he is trying to discover through his project.
- Do some research on his topic. Visit the library for journals and periodicals. Search online for information about his topic. Be sure to keep notes of every resource he uses for his project. He will need this information for his bibliography.
- Form his hypothesis. Think about what he thinks will occur during his experiment based on his research and his background knowledge on his topic.
- Plan how he will complete his project. How is he going to test the hypothesis he formed? What experiment will he conduct? What equipment will he need? What variables will he use? How will he measure the results of his experiment? Where is he going to keep all of his project notes?
- Gather all of the materials he will need. Determine a place where he will keep all of his materials. Choose a spot where all of the materials can be stored safely for the length of time it will take to prepare his project, complete his experiments, analyze his data, and create a display board to present.
- Design and conduct his experiment. He will collect more reliable data if he conducts his experiment more than once. When he has collected all of the data, he can average the results. As he is working through his experiment, he should use his senses to observe all of the results. Record the results in his project notebook. Be sure to add the date and time to

every note he includes. All of his measurements should be clearly written, using the correct units of measure.

- Draw his conclusions from the experiment. What new information did he learn from his experiments? Did his results support his hypothesis? Keep in mind that if his results do not support his hypothesis, that doesn't make his hypothesis wrong. It means that his hypothesis was not proven.
- Create his charts, graphs, and illustrations from the data he collected and recorded. Make sure these components are neat, colorful, and easy to read. Each of these parts should have a title and be labeled correctly.
- Organize his display. Get his board and decide where he will place all of his information.
- Prepare his oral presentation and practice delivering it. He will need to be able to talk freely about his hypothesis, his experiment, his results, his conclusion, and the connection to the real world.

Science Project Safety Tips

Safety is a main concern for any science fair project. Most projects involve little risk but there are some pieces of equipment and some procedures that can lead to potential safety problems. The list below provides some guidelines on what safety issues to check for when your child is completing his science fair project.

- Science fair projects should never involve the use of animals, drugs, explosives, or firearms. They should not break any local, state, or federal laws.
- When using the Internet for research or any other aspect of her project, your child should never provide personal information to anyone that she does not know personally. Make sure the sites she visits are acceptable to you and her teachers.
- Her display board and all of its components must meet all of the requirements of the science fair. Her teacher will provide her with a list of the requirements.
- She should wash her hands before she begins her experiment and after she has completed it.

- Your child should not eat while she is conducting her experiment. She could accidentally contaminate her materials, and this could affect her results.
- She should keep her experiment workspace neat.
- If she is conducting an experiment that could potentially cause an injury to her eyes, she needs to put on protective eyewear.
- She should not inhale, taste, or touch any chemicals.
- Your child should be respectful to all forms of life. Animals cannot be used in experiments. She should also not conduct an experiment that could potentially harm a person.
- An adult should supervise her experiment, particularly if there are dangerous aspects of the experiment, including the use of sharp tools or electricity.
- She should properly dispose of all waste from her experiment.

Science Fair Project Reports

Your child's project should include a written summary of everything that he did in working through his activities. The report is a way to communicate his experiment and the new information he learned to others. His report should be between five and twenty-five pages long. This is his opportunity to share all of the aspects of his project with his peers, teachers, and judges. Once he has completed his report, he should be sure to reread, revise, and edit all of his text, and to reread and recheck his grammar, spelling, and calculations.

The Format of the Report

Your child's report should be typed and bound in an appropriate binder. The text of his report should be typed using Times New Roman font, in a 12-point size, and in a double-spaced format with 1-inch margins. Some other important aspects of your child's report are:

- All sections, illustrations, photographs, tables, and charts should have a title and labels or captions where necessary.
- His report should have a title page. It should be placed at the beginning of his report and should include his project title, his name, class, grade, and date of submission.

- A table of contents should follow his title page. It should provide a list of the components of his project along with the corresponding pages on which they can be found in his report.
- A statement of purpose should be included after his table of contents. It is written in the form of a question and communicates the purpose of his project.
- His hypothesis should follow the statement of purpose. It communicates his thoughts on the potential results of his experiment.
- His research is included after his hypothesis. This section of his report provides all of the background information that he gathered about his project. All of the articles, books, and Internet resources that he used to collect information should be summarized here. All of the text that is included here should be written in his own words.
- The materials he used in his experiment should be listed in a section after his research. The materials and their quantities should be included in the list.
- The procedure he followed in conducting his experiment comes after his list of materials. The procedure is listed in a step-by-step format, using a numbered sequence.
- The observations and results of his experiment follow the procedure section. In this part of the report, he communicates what he learned from the experiment. He also includes all of the charts, graphs, illustrations, and photographs of his observations and results.
- His conclusion follows his observations and results. This section explains whether his hypothesis was supported or not. If his results did not support his hypothesis, that doesn't make the hypothesis wrong. It means the results did not support or prove the hypothesis that he formed. His conclusion also explains why the results occurred and how the experiment and results connect to the real world.
- His reference page is found at the end of his report. It should include an alphabetical list of all of the resources he used throughout his project.

Science Fair Oral Presentations

Many students become nervous about presenting their projects to a large group of people or to a judge. Try to remind your child that the audience is curious about what he has learned and is looking forward to hearing about his findings. He should do his best to smile and enjoy the experience. When his turn comes to present his project, he should be prepared. For the presentation, he should:

- Dress confidently, speak clearly, and look at the audience.
- Introduce himself and his project.
- Explain why he chose this topic.
- State the purpose of his experiment and the hypothesis he formed.
- Tell the audience about all of the new information he learned through his research.
- Explain how he designed his experiment, the materials he used, and the steps he followed.
- Describe his observations and results, pointing out all of the visual organizers he created to show his results.
- Explain the conclusions he came to based on his results and whether or not his hypothesis was supported.

The oral presentation component of a science fair project is an important part of the process. This is when he is able to communicate all of the aspects of his hypothesis, experiment, observations, results, and conclusions. In a science fair competition, this is the part that sets one competitor apart from the next. Students who are able to confidently express their project earn higher scores in this area, and in turn, higher scores overall. A successful presentation is essential in a science fair competition.

Appendix A: Resources

Bill Nye's Climate Lab
Chabot Space and Science Center
Simulations and Digital Activities

www.chabotspace.org/bill-nye-climate-lab.htm

Bozeman Science
Paul Anderson
Video Lesson

*www.bozemanscience.com/
next-generation-science-standards*

CELLS *alive!*
Jim Sullivan
Videos, Simulations, and Digital Activities

www.cellsalive.com

Chemistry 4 Kids
Andrew Rader Studios
Videos, Animations, and Digital Activities

www.chem4kids.com

www.cosmos4kids.com

www.biology4kids.com

www.physics4kids.com

CK-12.org
CK-12 Foundation
Videos, Animations, and Digital Activities

www.ck12.org/ngss

Common Core State Standards
Common Core State Standards Initiative
Common Core Outline

www.corestandards.org

Drag-and-Drop Genetics: ZeroBio.com
E. Kimmel
Simulation

www.zerobio.com/drag_gr11/mono.htm

E-Learning for Kids
Digital Activity

www.e-learningforkids.org/science/grade/6

Edheads
Edheads.com
Simulations and Digital Activities

www.edheads.org/index.shtml

Evolution
Bioman Biology
Simulations and Digital Activities

*www.biomanbio.com/GamesandLabs/EvoClassGames/
evolution.html*

Evolution Lab
Biology in Motion
Digital Activities

http://biologyinmotion.com/evol/index.html

Exploring Nature Educational Resource
Sheri Amsel
Cell Information

www.exploringnature.org

Genetics Web Lab Directory
Education Development Center
Digital Activities

www2.edc.org/weblabs/WebLabDirectory1.html

Georgia Virtual Learning
Georgia Department of Education
Videos, Animations, and Digital Activities

*www.gavirtuallearning.org/Resources/MSResources/
MSShared/SharedMSScience6thGrade.aspx*

*www.gavirtuallearning.org/Resources/MSResources/
MSShared/SharedMSScience7thGrade.aspx*

*www.gavirtuallearning.org/Resources/
SharedMSScience8th.aspx*

Google Science Fair
Projects and Ideas

www.googlesciencefair.com/en

Interactive Sites for Education
Karen Ogen
Digital Activities

http://interactivesites.weebly.com/science.html

LearningScience.org
Videos, Simulations, and Digital Activities

www.learningscience.org/index.htm

NeoK12.com
Videos, Simulations, and Digital Activities

www.neok12.com

Next Generation Evidence Statements
Achieve.org
Performance Evidence Outline

www.nextgenscience.org/
middle-school-evidence-statements

Next Generation Science Standards
Achieve.org
Program Outline

www.nextgenscience.org

PhET Interactive Simulations
University of Colorado Boulder
Simulation

http://phet.colorado.edu/en/simulations/category/
by-level/middle-school

The Physics Classroom
Tom Henderson
Simulation

www.physicsclassroom.com

Science Buddies
ScienceBuddies.org
Projects and Ideas

www.sciencebuddies.org

Science Fair Projects and Experiments
Julian's Science Fair
Projects and Ideas

www.juliantrubin.com/fairprojects.html

A Student's Guide to Global Climate Change
United States Environmental Protection Agency
Simulations and Digital Activities

http://epa.gov/climatechange/kids

Study Jams
Scholastic.com
Videos, Animations, and Digital Activities

http://studyjams.scholastic.com/studyjams/jams/science/
index.htm

Understanding Geologic Time
Berkeley.edu
Simulations and Digital Activities

www.ucmp.berkeley.edu/education/explorations/tours/
geotime/gtpage1.html

Virtual Lab Punnett Squares
McGraw-Hill Education
Simulations and Digital Activities

www.mhhe.com/biosci/genbio/virtual_labs/BL_05/
BL_05.html

Weather, Climate, Atmosphere
Center for Science Education
Simulations and Digital Activities

http://scied.ucar.edu/
games-sims-weather-climate-atmosphere

What Judges Want in a Science Fair Project
Leon County Schools
Video

www.youtube.com/watch?v=9dO4Gumhs18

Appendix B: Bibliography

Academy for Academic Excellence

www.lewiscenter.org/AAE/Departments/Science/ Teaching-the-Next-Generations-Science/index.html

Berkeley.edu

www.ucmp.berkeley.edu/education/explorations/tours/ geotime/gtpage1.html

Biology in Motion

http://biologyinmotion.com/evol/index.html

Bozeman Science

www.bozemanscience.com/ next-generation-science-standards

California Energy Commission

http://energyquest.ca.gov/story/index.html

Cellsalive.com

www.cellsalive.com

Center for Science Education

http://scied.ucar.edu/ games-sims-weather-climate-atmosphere

Chabot Space and Science Center

www.billsclimatelab.org/labdash.html

Chem4Kids

www.chem4kids.com

Chicago Public Schools: Science Content Framework, Elementary (K-8)

http://inquiryteaching.weebly.com/ uploads/1/0/3/3/10332398/final_cps_science_content_ framework_elementary_5-9_copy.pdf

CK-12 Foundation

www.ck12.org/ngss

Common Core State Standards

www.corestandards.org

e-Learning for Kids

www.e-learningforkids.org/science

EcoKids

www.ecokids.ca

Edheads

www.edheads.org/activities/weather/index.shtml

Education Development Center

www2.edc.org/weblabs/WebLabDirectory1.html

Energy Star Kids

www.energystar.gov/index.cfm?c=kids.kids_index

ExploringNature.org

www.exploringnature.org/db/detail. php?dbID=93&detID=3555

A Framework for K-12 Science Education: Practices, Crosscutting Concepts, and Core Ideas

www.nap.edu/openbook.php?record_id=13165

Georgia Virtual Learning Center

www.gavirtuallearning.org/Resources/ SharedPhysicalScience.aspx

Interactive Sites for Education

http://interactivesites.weebly.com

Learningscience.org

www.learningscience.org

McGraw-Hill Education

www.mhhe.com/biosci/genbio/virtual_labs/BL_05/ BL_05.html

National Science Teachers Association
http://ngss.nsta.org

Neo K-12
www.neok12.com

Next Generation Science Standards
www.nextgenscience.org

Pbs.org
www.pbs.org/wgbh/evolution/students/index.html

PhET
http://phet.colorado.edu

The Physics Classroom
www.physicsclassroom.com

Scholastic
www.scholastic.com

Science Museum
www.sciencemuseum.org.uk/online_science/games.aspx

Science Unleashed
www.scienceunleashed.ie/Games/States of Matter.swf

United States Environmental Protection Agency
http://epa.gov/climatechange/kids

Zerobio.com
www.zerobio.com/drag_gr11/mono.htm

Index

Abiotic factors, 166, 167–68
Acceleration, 96, 98, 99, 100, 110, 114
Achieve reform group, 19, 21
Active transport, 143, 151
Adaptation
    in ecosystems, 166, 176
    evolution and, 197, 199–200
    genetic, 187, 198
    molecules to organisms and, 143, 157
    mutations and, 157, 204–5
Adenine, 184, 185
Age, relative, 218
Alleles
    defined, 182
    dominant, 183
    evolution experiment, 207–8
    genotypes, phenotypes and, 189
    heterozygous genotypes and, 183, 185
    homozygous genotypes and, 183, 185
    recessive, 184, 207–8
    trait variations and, 183
Altitude, 120, 229, 244
Amino acids, 183, 186, 201
Amoeba, defined, 143
Amplitude, of waves, 129, 130, 131, 134–35
Analyze, defined, 266
Arguments, writing, 39–40
Asexual reproduction, 141, 142, 143, 144, 191–92
Astronomy. See Earth, place in universe; Moon; Solar system
Atmosphere. See also Carbon dioxide; Weather and climate
    defined, 229, 233, 249
    global climate change/warming and, 248, 249, 252–54, 259–60
    impact of human activity on, 252
    origins of, 216
    other "spheres" and, 238
    oxygen cycle and, 171–72
    water cycle and, 228–29, 230, 234–35
Atomic mass, defined, 75, 78

Atomic number, defined, 75, 78, 79
Atoms. See also Chemical reactions
    charge of, 78
    chemical reactions and, 83. See also Mixtures, chemical
    defined, 75, 76–77
    developing models to describe, 86
    elements, compounds, molecules, mixtures and, 84
    key atomic concepts, 76–79
    key atomic terms, 75–76
    mass of, 75, 78
    molecules and, 79
    NGSS performance expectations, 86–90
    predicting changes in particles, 88–89
Author, determining purpose of, 53–54
Axis, of earth, 214

Bacteria, 147, 156, 166, 170, 175
Biodiversity services, assessing design solutions, 176–77
Biological evolution, 195–209. See also Diversity; Fossils; Mutations
    about: overview of, 195
    adaptation and, 197, 199–200
    analyzing data to find organism similarities, 204
    biodiversity and humans, 197
    common ancestry, diversity and, 196–97, 200, 201
    Darwin's theory of, 199
    defined, 198
    disciplinary core ideas, 196–97
    embryo structure similarities and, 200–201
    experiment, 207–8
    exploring fossils for patterns, 202–3
    extinction and, 196, 198, 201, 202, 203, 248
    fitness and, 198
    key concepts, 199–201
    key terms, 198
    molecular evidence of, 201

    natural selection and, 197, 198, 199, 200, 202, 206–7
    NGSS performance expectations, 202–7
    researching evolutionary relationships, 203–4
    science and engineering practices, 201–2
    technology role in, 205–6
    vestigial structures and, 200
    what child should already understand, 196
Biomes, 168, 177–78
Biosphere, 238, 247, 249
Bonds. See also Chemical reactions
    chemical, defined, 80
    formation of new substances, 84
    ions and, 80
Book overview, 10–11
Brain, proving reaction to stimuli forms memories, 159–60

Carbon cycle, 171
Carbon dioxide
    carbon cycle and, 171
    global climate change/warming and, 252, 253–54, 260
    photosynthesis and, 117–18, 142, 145, 158, 166
Carnivores, 165, 166
Carrier proteins, 143
Cause and effect, 63–64
Cause and effect text, 53
Cells. See also Nucleus, cellular
    about: overview of, 140
    active transport, 143, 151
    centrioles, 143
    chloroplasts, 143, 148, 149, 166
    cycle, 152
    cytoplasm, 143, 147–48, 149, 150, 186
    cytosol, 150
    defined, 143, 147–48, 183
    endoplasmic reticulum, 144, 148, 149
    eukaryotic, 144, 147–48, 150, 152
    exocytosis of, 144

Cells—*continued*
exploring how function, 154–55
facilitated transport, 144
Golgi complex (apparatus), 144, 148, 149
homeostasis, 144, 151
investigating proof of, 153–54
lysosomes, 144, 148, 149
membrane, 143, 147, 148, 149, 150–51
mitochondria, 145, 148, 149
multicellular organisms, 141–42, 145, 154–55, 204
nucleolus, 145, 150
organelles, 145, 148–49. *See also specific organelles*
osmosis between, 145
parts of, 148–49
passive transport, 145, 151
plasma membrane, 145, 148, 150
prokaryotic, 145, 147–48, 158
ribosomes, 145, 148, 149, 150, 186
showing body is composed of, 155–56
structure and functions, 141–42
transport explanation and methods, 150–51
types of, 147–48
unicellular organisms, 141, 143, 146, 147, 154, 203
vacuoles, 146, 148, 149
wall, 143, 149, 155
Cell theory, 143, 147
Cellular respiration, 118
Centigrams, 37
Centiliters, 37
Centimeters, measuring with, 36, 37
Centrioles, 143
Centripetal force, 96
Chemical, defined, 80, 81
Chemical bonding, defined, 80
Chemical change, defined, 71
Chemical composition of Earth, 231
Chemical energy, 89, 114, 116, 117, 262
Chemical formulas, defined, 80, 81
Chemical numbers, use of, 81
Chemical property, defined, 71, 74
Chemical reactions. *See also* Atoms; Mixtures, chemical

about: overview of, 70
analyzing and interpreting data on properties before and after, 87
atomic structure and, 83
atoms, elements, compounds, molecules, mixtures and, 84
bonding defined, 80
clues indicating occurrence of, 83
defined, 70, 80, 83
determining, 87
energy role in, 84
formation of new substances, 84
importance of understanding, 84
key concepts, 81–85
key terms, 80
key terms related to matter and, 71–72
law of conservation of mass and, 80, 82, 89
NGSS performance expectations, 86–90
outcomes of, 83
portraying conservation of mass, 89
precipitates and, 87, 89, 120, 122
predicting changes in particles, 88–89
products, 80
slowing down, 84
speeding up, 83
testing thermal energy, 89–90
Chemical symbols, use of, 81
Chlorophyll, 118, 143, 171
Chloroplasts, 143, 149, 158, 166
Chromatin, 143
Chromosomal mutations, 189, 190–91
Chromosomes, 143, 150, 180, 181, 182, 183, 184, 187
Chronological text, 53
Clarify, defined, 266
Climate. *See* Weather and climate
Collaborate, defined, 266
Colliding objects, 102–3, 112
Colloids, 81, 82
Common Core English language arts standards. *See also* Writing
college, career and, 16, 17
defined, 14–15

importance of, 19
increasing levels of complexity, 16
key shifts for, 16–18
nonfiction texts and, 16, 17–18
reading lists and, 17
reasons for focusing on, 19
text evidence importance, 16–17
uniformity between states, 17
vocabulary spotlight, 16
Common Core mathematics standards
defined, 15–16
importance of, 19
key shifts for, 18–19
major focus of, 18
middle school emphasis, 18–19
reasons for focusing on, 19
uniformity between states, 18
wide-ranging content of, 18
Common Core standards
about: overview of, 10
defined, 13–14
importance of, 14
Communicating information, 43, 62, 286–88. *See also* Writing
Comparing and contrasting information, 55
Comparing and contrasting text written in style of, 53
Compounds, atoms, elements, molecules, mixtures and, 84
Compounds, defined, 80
Compression, wave, 129, 132, 133, 136
Computational thinking, using, 60
Concave lenses, 129
Concept maps, 32–33
Concepts, key. *See specific topics*
Condensation, change of states and, 71, 73, 74–75, 88
Condensation, water cycle and, 228, 229, 230, 234–35, 237, 241
Conservation of energy, law of, 113, 114, 116, 119
Conservation of mass, law of, 80, 82, 89
Constraints, defined, 266
Construct, defined, 266
Consumers, 164, 165, 166, 169, 170, 171

Consumption, human, 248, 249, 255, 258–59
Control, defined, 266
Convergent plates, 230, 232
Convex lenses, 129
Coriolis effect, 235, 244
Crests, of waves, 129, 130, 131, 135
Criteria, defined, 266
Critique, defined, 266
Crosscutting concepts, 23, 63–67
Crystallization, 228, 230, 238
Cytoplasm, 143, 147–48, 149, 150, 186
Cytosine, 184, 185
Cytosol, 150

Darwin, Charles, 199
Data, analyzing and interpreting, 59–60
Data, defined, 266
Decameters, 37
Decigrams, 37
Deciliters, 37
Decimeters, 37
Decomposers, 164, 165, 166, 169, 170
Deforestation, 249, 252, 260
Dekagrams, 37
Dekaliters, 37
Density, defined, 71, 73
Density, importance of, 73–74
Deoxyribonucleic acid. See DNA
Dependent variable, defined, 266
Design, defined, 266
Design process, engineering, 270
Develop, defined, 266
Diffusion, 151
Digitized signals, 127, 128, 133, 136–37
Disciplinary core ideas
    about, 23–24, 67
    biological evolution, 196–97
    Earth and human activity, 247–48
    Earth's place in universe, 211–13
    Earth's systems, 227–29
    ecosystems, 163–65
    energy, 113–14
    engineering design, 264–66
    force and motion, 94–96
    heredity, 181–83
    matter and its interactions, 69–70
    molecules to organisms, 141–42

waves and their applications, 127–28
Displacement, 72, 97
Distance
    displacement and, 97
    measuring, 35–36
    speed/velocity and, 97–98. See also Speed; Velocity
Divergent plates, 230, 232
Diversity
    biodiversity and humans, 197
    biodiversity in ecosystem, 165, 176–77
    defined, 183, 198
    evidence of common ancestry and, 196–97
    evolution and, 199, 200, 202, 203
    in species, 200
DNA (deoxyribonucleic acid), 183, 185. See also Chromosomes
    defined/functions of, 144, 148, 185
    in fossils, 202
    genes and, 186, 192
    genetic code and, 144
    genetic engineering and, 183
    genome and, 183
    location of, 147, 186
    molecular evidence and of evolution and, 201
    mutations, 188–89
    nucleotides in, 184, 185, 187, 188, 192
    protein sequences and, 186, 190–91
    replication, 184, 187
    reproduction types and, 191–92
    traits passed along with (heredity), 182, 184
    what child should already understand, 181
Dominant allele, 183
Dwarf planets, 213

Earth, human activity and, 246–62
    about: overview of, 246; review checklist, 261–62
    disciplinary core ideas, 247–48
    experiment, 260–61
    exploring minimizing human impact, 258

exploring natural resource distribution, 255–56
forecasting natural hazards, 256–57
global climate change/warming and, 248, 249, 252–54, 259–60
greenhouse effect/gases and, 248, 249, 252–53, 259–60, 273
human consumption and, 248, 249, 255, 258–59
impact of human activity, 249, 252–53
impacts on Earth's systems, 248
key concepts, 250–54
natural hazards and, 247, 249, 250, 251, 256–57
natural resources and, 117, 247, 250
NGSS performance expectations, 255–60
science and engineering practices, 254–55
what child should already understand, 247
Earth, place in universe, 210–25. See also Moon; Solar system
    about: overview of, 210; review checklist, 225
    disciplinary core ideas, 211–13
    exploring gravity, 221–22. See also Gravity/gravitational force
    history of Earth and, 213, 216, 223–24. See also Fossils
    key concepts, 215–18
    key terms, 214–15
    maps helping understand, 218
    models to examine universe, 222–23
    models to show galactic patterns, 219–21
    NGSS performance expectations, 219–24
    science and engineering practices, 218–19
    seasons and. See Seasons
    soil experiment, 224–25
    universe, stars and, 211–12, 215
    what child should already understand, 211

Earth, systems of, 226–45. *See also* Atmosphere; Weather and climate
about: overview of, 226; review checklist, 245
chemical composition of Earth, 231
disciplinary core ideas, 227–29
energy flow examination, 237–38
energy source, 233
experiment, 244–45
geoscience investigation, 238–39
impacts on. *See* Earth, human activity and
key concepts, 231–36
key terms, 229–30
materials and systems, 227–28
minerals defined, 231
NGSS performance expectations, 237–44
plate tectonics/tectonic plates and, 227, 228, 230, 231–32, 238, 239
role of water in surface processes, 228–29
science and engineering practices, 236
seismic waves and, 132–33, 137
what child should already understand, 227
Earthquakes, 132–33, 137, 251. *See also* Plate tectonics/tectonic plates
Earthworms, 166, 178
Eclipses, 212, 214, 219, 220, 221
Ecosystems, 162–79. *See also* Carbon dioxide
about: overview of, 162; review checklist, 178–79
abiotic factors, 166, 167–68
adaptations in, 166, 176
assessing design solutions for biodiversity services and, 176–77
biomes, 168, 177–78
carbon cycle and, 171. *See also* Consumers; Decomposers; Producers
carnivores and, 165, 166
changes affecting population, 175–76

cycles of matter and energy transfer, 164–65
cycling of matter in, 174–75
defined, 166, 167–68
disciplinary core ideas, 163–65
discovering effects of resources on, 173–74
dynamics, functioning, and resilience, 165
energy flowing through, 169–70
energy pyramids, 169
experiment, 177–78
food chains and, 166, 170, 171
food webs and, 164–65, 166, 170, 172, 175
habitats, 167, 168, 173, 248, 249
herbivores and, 165, 166
interdependent relationships, 163–64
key concepts, 167–72
key terms, 166–67
matter moving through (cycling), 169, 174–75
NGSS performance expectations, 172–77
niches, 167, 168
nitrogen cycle and, 170–71
omnivores and, 165, 166
oxygen cycle and, 171–72
photosynthesis and, 117–18, 142, 145, 157–58, 166, 169, 235
predicting interaction patterns, 174
science and engineering practices, 172
social interactions and group behavior, 165
symbiosis in, 171
what child should already understand, 163
what organisms need to survive, 167
Electrical energy, 114, 116, 117, 133, 262
Electromagnetic spectrum, 128, 129
Electromagnetism
description of, 95–96
determining electric and magnetic forces, 104–6
energy forms, 233

light/radiant energy and, 116, 128, 129
objects exerting force without touching, 107–8, 136
waves and, 130–31
Electrons
charge of, 78
cloud model, 85
defined, 75, 78
mass of, 78
Elements
atoms, compounds, molecules, mixtures and, 84
defined, 75, 79
table of. *See* Periodic table
types of, determining factors, 79
Endocytosis, defined, 144
Endoplasmic reticulum, 144, 148, 149
Energy, 111–25. *See also* Kinetic energy; Potential energy
about: overview of, 111; review checklist, 124–25
chemical, 89, 114, 116, 117, 262
conservation and transfer of, 113
defined, 144
definitions of, 113, 114, 115, 129
disciplinary core ideas, 113–14
of Earth, 233, 237–38
electrical, 114, 116, 117, 133, 262
experiment, 123–24
experiment with thermal transfer, 121
explaining amplitude relative to, 134–35
flowing through ecosystems, 169–70
forms of, 114, 115–16
investigating transfer of, 122
key concepts, 115–18
key terms, 114–15
law of conservation of, 113, 114, 116, 119
light. *See* Light
matter and, flows/cycles/ conservation, 65–66, 75, 79
mechanical, 115, 116
NGSS performance expectations, 119–23
photosynthesis and, 117–18

relationship between forces and, 114

role in chemical reactions, 84

science and engineering practices, 118–19

showing how food converts to, 158–59

sound. *See* Sound

thermal, affecting matter, 75

thermal, testing, 89–90

transfer, 113, 114, 121–23

transfer cycles of matter and, in ecosystems, 164–65

transformation, 114, 116–17

what child should already understand, 112–13

Energy pyramids, 169

Energy resources

fossil fuels, 117, 248, 249, 252, 253, 259–60

natural resources, 117, 233

natural resources and, 117, 247

nonrenewable, 117, 233, 249

renewable, 117, 233, 250

solar energy, 117, 214, 233, 250

wind energy, 116, 117, 233, 250

Engineering design, 263–77

about: overview of, 263; review checklist, 276–77

analyzing data to create solution, 274

defining, delimiting problems, 265

developing a model, 274–75

developing possible solutions, 265

disciplinary core ideas, 264–66

evaluating design solutions, 272–74

experiment, 275–76

key concepts, 267–71

key terms, 266–67

NGSS performance expectations, 271–75

optimizing design solutions, 265–66

science and engineering practices, 271

solving design problem, 271–72

what child should already understand, 264

Engineering practices. *See* Science and engineering practices

Engineering process, 266, 269–70

English language arts standards. *See* Common Core English language arts standards

Enzymes, 144, 148, 166, 175

Equator, 173, 214, 220, 239

Erosion, 228, 230, 233, 237, 249, 252, 260

Eukaryotic cells, 144, 147–48, 150, 152

Evaporation, change of states and, 71, 73, 74, 82, 88

Evaporation, water cycle and, 228, 229, 230, 234–35, 237, 240, 241, 243

Evidence, citing textual, 50–51

Evidence, defined, 266

Evolution. *See* Biological evolution

Exocytosis, 144

Experiments. *See also* Science fair projects

about: how they are designed, 268; hypotheses, 266, 268; review checklist, 208–9; variables, 266, 267, 269

biological evolution, 207–8

Earth and human activity, 260–61

Earth's place in universe, 224–25

Earth's systems, 244–45

ecosystem, 177–78

energy, 121, 123–24

engineering design, 275–76

force and motion, 108–9

heredity, 192–93

matter, 90–91

organism, 160–61

soil, 224–25

standards for measurements, technical tasks and, 51–52

waves, 138

Explanatory writing, 40–42

Extinction, 196, 198, 201, 202, 203, 248

Facilitated transport, 144

Feet to centimeters, 36

Fertilization, defined, 144, 183

Fission, defined, 144

Fitness, of species, 198

Food chains, 166, 170, 171

Food webs, 164–65, 166, 170, 172, 175

Force and motion, 93–110

about: overview of, 93; review checklist, 109–10

balanced forces and objects, 100–101

calculating force, 99

describing motion, 97

determining electric and magnetic forces, 104–6. *See also* Electromagnetism

disciplinary core ideas, 94–96

energy and, 114. *See also* Energy

experiment, 108–9

force defined, 96, 99, 114

force opposite motion. *See* Friction

key concepts, 97–101

key terms, 96–97

motion defined, 96

net force, 100

NGSS performance expectations, 102–8

problem of colliding objects, 102–3

proving force affects motion, 103–4

proving gravity depends on mass, 106–7

proving objects exert force without touching, 107–8

science and engineering practices, 101–2

tools for measuring, 101

types of interactions, 95–96

unbalanced forces and objects, 101

what child should already understand, 94

Fossil fuels, 117, 248, 249, 252, 253, 259–60

Fossils

defined, 198

exploring for patterns, 202–3

giving evidence of common ancestry and diversity, 196–97

history of Earth and, 213, 216–17, 224, 228, 239, 240

index, 217

Fossils—*continued*
  plate movement and, 232, 239, 240
  records, defined, 198
  researching evolutionary
    relationships using, 203–4
  trace, 203
  types of, 203
Frequency, of waves, 129, 131, 132
Friction, 96, 99, 101, 102, 104, 110, 125
Function, structure and, 66
Fusion, nuclear, 213

Galaxy. *See also* Milky Way
  defined, 217
  using models to show patterns in,
    219–21
Gallons to liters, 36
Gamete cells, defined, 183
Genes. *See also* Heredity
  defined, 183, 186, 198
  showing how changes affect
    proteins, 190–91
Genetic adaptation, 187, 198
Genetic code, 144, 187, 206
Genetic engineering, defined, 183
Genetics, defined, 183. *See also* DNA
  (deoxyribonucleic acid); Heredity
Genome, defined, 183
Genotypes, 183, 185, 189
Geologic timescale, 213, 218, 224
Geoscience investigation, 238–39
Geosphere, defined, 230
Gibbous moon phase, 214, 235
Global climate change/warming, 184,
  248, 249, 252–54, 259–60
Golgi complex (apparatus), 144, 148,
  149
Grade levels, disciplinary core ideas,
  23–24, 67
Grams, measuring with, 37
Gravity/gravitational force
  attractive nature of, 96
  defined, 71, 96, 99, 214
  Earth origin and, 216
  energy, wave amplitude and, 135
  exploring/demonstrating, 221–22
  as potential energy, 116, 120, 125
  proving dependence on mass,
    106–7
  solar system and, 212–13, 221–22

summary of principles, 110
tides, water cycle and, 215, 228,
  235–36, 240
weight and, 72–73, 94, 95, 97, 99
what child should already
  understand, 94
Greenhouse effect/gases, 248, 249,
  252–53, 259–60, 273
Group, defined, 75
Guanine, 184, 185

Habitats, 167, 168, 173, 248, 249
Hazards, natural, 247, 249, 250, 251,
  256–57
Hectograms, 37
Hectoliters, 37
Hectometers, 37
Helping child. *See* Parent, helping
  child
Hemispheres, 211, 214, 215, 235
Herbivores, 165, 166
Heredity, 180–94. *See also* DNA
  (deoxyribonucleic acid); Genes
  about: overview of, 180; review
    checklist, 193–94
  characteristics defined, 183
  defined, 183, 184
  differences in reproduction
    types, 191–92. *See also*
    Asexual reproduction; Sexual
    reproduction
  disciplinary core ideas, 181–83
  experiment, 192–93
  genetic code and, 184, 187, 206
  genotypes and, 183, 185, 189
  Gregor Mendel and, 187
  inheritance of traits, 182, 198
  key concepts, 184–89
  key terms, 183–84
  law of segregation and, 187
  NGSS performance expectations,
    190–92
  phenotypes and, 189
  predicting offspring, Punnett
    square for, 188
  science and engineering
    practices, 189–90
  showing how genetics influences
    growth, 157
  traits defined, 184, 185

variation of traits, 182–83, 184. *See
  also* Mutations
what child should already
  understand, 181
Heterogeneous and homogeneous
  mixtures, 81–82
Heterozygous genotypes, 183, 185
Homeostasis, 144, 151
Homogeneous and heterogeneous
  mixtures, 81–82
Homozygous genotypes, 183, 185
Humidity, 230, 234, 242
Hydrosphere, 230, 234, 238
Hypertonic, defined, 144
Hypotheses, 266, 268, 280
Hypotonic, defined, 144

Identify, defined, 266
Inches to centimeters, 36
Independent variable, defined,
  266
Inertia, 96, 100, 104, 110
Infer, defined, 266
Inheriting traits. *See* Heredity
Intensive properties, 74. *See also*
  Density
Interactive science notebook. *See*
  Notebook, interactive science
Interpret, defined, 266
Investigations, defined, 266
Investigations, planning and
  carrying out, 59. *See also*
  Research; Science fair projects
Ions, defined, 80
Isotonic, defined, 144

Key terms. *See* Terms, key
Kilograms, measuring with, 37
Kiloliters, 37
Kilometers, measuring with, 35–36,
  37
Kinetic energy
  characteristics of, 112
  defined, 113, 114, 115
  energy transfer and, 122
  equation for, 112
  forms of, 116
  investigating changes in, 123
  objects gaining, 118
  potential energy vs., 113, 115

showing relationship to mass and speed, 119–20

Kingdoms, 158, 166

Latitude, 211, 229, 230, 244
Length, measuring, 35–36, 37
Lenses, concave and convex, 129
Light
    Coriolis effect, 235, 244
    defined, 114, 129
    energy, defined, 114
    interacting with matter, 125
    opaque materials and, 129
    properties of, 132
    rarefaction of, 129, 132
    reflection of, 127, 128, 129, 131, 132, 133, 235
    refraction of, 131, 132, 133
    translucent material and, 129
    transparent material and, 128, 129
Light years, 216, 217, 223
Literacy standards. See Common Core English language arts standards
Liters, measuring with, 36–37
Litter, defined, 166
Longitudinal waves, 129, 131, 132
Lysosomes, 144, 148, 149

Magnets and magnetic forces, 94, 101, 104–6. See also Electromagnetism
Maps, helping understand Earth, 218, 228
Mass
    atomic, 75, 78
    atomic number and, 78
    colliding objects and, 102–3
    defined, 71, 96
    density and, 73
    energy transfer and, 122
    force and, 99, 104–5
    gravity and, 71, 106–7, 221–22. See also Gravity/gravitational force
    inertia and, 104
    kinetic energy and, 112, 113, 114, 115, 118, 119–20
    law of conservation of, 80, 82, 89
    matter/objects and, 72–73, 99
    measuring, 36–37, 72–73

portraying conservation of, 89
    potential energy and, 120–21
    of protons, neutrons, electrons, 78
    proving gravity dependence on, 106–7
    weight vs., 72–73, 94, 95, 99
Mass number, defined, 75
Mathematics
    scale, proportion, and quantity, 64–65
    using computational thinking and, 60
Mathematics standards. See Common Core mathematics standards
Matter (and its interactions), 68–92. See also Atoms; Chemical reactions
    about: overview of, 68; review checklist, 91
    cycles of, 164–65, 230
    defined, 71, 72
    disciplinary core ideas, 69–70
    energy and, flows/cycles/conservation, 65–66, 75, 79
    experiment, 90–91
    key concepts, 72–75
    key matter terms/definitions, 71–72
    living and non-living, 75
    measuring, 72–73
    moving through ecosystem, 169, 174–75
    NGSS performance expectations, 86–90
    physical processes, 74–75
    physical properties of, 74
    properties of, 74
    science and engineering practices, 85
    states of, defined, 72
    states of, Q&A, 73–75
    structure and properties of matter, 70
    thermal energy affecting, 75, 89–90
    transfer cycles of energy and, in ecosystems, 164–65
    what child should already understand, 69

Measuring
    force and motion, 101
    length/distance, 37
    length/distance (meters), 35–36
    mass (grams), 36–37
    matter, 72–73
    metric system and, 35
    standards for experiments, technical tasks and, 51–52
    understanding measurement, 35
    volume, 37
    volume (liters), 36
Mechanical energy, 115, 116
Mechanical waves, 128, 130, 136
Medium, defined, 129
Meiosis, defined, 183
Membrane, cell, 143, 147, 148, 149, 150–51
Membrane, plasma, 145, 148, 150
Memories, formation of, 159–60
Mendel, Gregor, 187
Metamorphosis, defined, 145
Meters, measuring with, 35–36, 37
Metric system. See Measuring
Migrate, defined, 198
Miles to kilometers, 36
Milky Way, 211, 212, 216, 217, 219–21, 222, 223
Milligrams, measuring with, 37
Milliliters, measuring with, 36–37
Millimeters, measuring with, 36
Minerals, defined, 231
Mitochondria, 145, 148, 149
Mitosis, 143, 152, 183, 187
Mixtures, chemical
    atoms, elements, compounds, molecules and, 84
    colloids and solutions, 81, 82
    defined, 80, 81
    heterogeneous and homogeneous, 81–82
    results of, 81
    separating, 82
    solutes, solvents and, 82
Models, science
    defined, 266
    describing atoms, 86
    developing and using, 34–35, 58–59, 274–75
    evaluating research using, 58–59

Models—*continued*
examining universe, 222–23
explaining seasons, 212–13, 219, 220–21
showing galactic patterns, 219–21
of solar system, 212–13, 222–23
systems and system models, 65
uses of, 34–35
Molecules, defined, 79, 80
Molecules, evidence of evolution and common ancestry, 201
Molecules to organisms, 140–61. *See also* Cells; Ecosystems
about: overview of, 140; review checklist, 161
adaptation and, 143, 157
asexual reproduction, 141, 142, 143, 144, 191–92
carrier proteins and, 143
disciplinary core ideas, 141–42
experiment, 160–61
growth/development of organisms, 142
how behaviors affect reproduction, 156–57
investigating photosynthesis, 157–58
key concepts, 146–52
key terms, 143–46
multicellular organisms, 141–42, 145, 154–55, 204
NGSS performance expectations, 153–60
organisms defined, 145
organization for matter/energy flow, 142
organization levels, 147
photosynthesis and, 117–18, 142, 145, 157–58, 166, 169, 235
proving that brain reacts to stimuli to form memories, 159–60
science and engineering practices, 152–53
showing how food converts to energy, 158–59
structure and functions, 141–42, 147
unicellular organisms, 141, 143, 146, 147, 154, 203

what child should already understand, 141
what makes up all living things, 146–47
Moon
crescent, 214
eclipse of, 212, 214, 215, 219, 220
first quarter, 214, 235
formation of, 216
full, 214, 235
gibbous, 214, 235
phases of, 214, 235
third quarter, 215
tides and, 214, 215, 219, 221, 235–36
waxing and waning, 215, 235
Mutations
adapting to environment, 157, 204–5
affecting proteins, 190–91
asexual reproduction and, 191–92
branching off of species and, 203
causes of, 189, 201
changing traits, 183
chromosomal, 189, 190–91
defined, 145, 188–89, 198, 201
investigating how some lead to survival, 204–5
range of effects, 183

Narrative writing, 46
Natural hazards, 247, 249, 250, 251, 256–57
Natural resources, 117, 247, 250, 255–56. *See also* Energy resources
Natural selection, 197, 198, 199, 200, 202, 206–7
Net force, 100
Neutrons, characteristics of, 76, 77, 78
Newton, Sir Isaac, 100, 133
Newtons, measurement, 73, 100
Newton's laws
defined, 96, 100
first law, 100, 110, 123
second law, 100, 102, 110
third law, 95, 100, 102, 103, 110
Next Generation Science Standards (NGSS), 20–25. *See also* Science and engineering practices

about: overview of, 10, 20
Achieve reform group and, 19, 21
alignment with other standards, 25
coherence and, 22
college, career and, 25
connection between classroom and real world, 24–25
crosscutting concepts, 23, 63–67
dimensions of, 23–24
disciplinary core ideas, 23–24, 67
focus on performance, not curriculum documents, 24–25
foundations and, 22
key shifts in, 24–25
origins of, 21
performance and, 22
previous science benchmark standards and, 21–22
reasons for, 21
Next Generation Science Standards (NGSS) performance expectations
biological evolution, 202–7
Earth and human activity, 255–60
Earth's place in universe, 219–24
Earth's systems, 237–44
ecosystem, 172–77
energy, 119–23
engineering design, 271–75
force and motion, 102–8
heredity, 190–92
matter and its interactions, 86–90
molecules to organisms, 153–60
waves, 134–37
Niches, 167, 168
Nitrogen cycle, 170–71
Nonrenewable resources, 117, 233, 249
Northern hemisphere, 214, 235
North pole, 105, 215, 220
Notebook, interactive science, 29–32
about: overview of, 29–30
benefits of, 30
ensuring success with, 32
how to make, 30–31
sections of, 30–32
setting up, 31–32
video for additional information, 31

Notes
    concept maps and, 32–33
    fill-in-the-blank, 34
    illustrations and models, 34–35
    poems as, 33
    question notes, 33
    question response strategies and,
        33–34
    strategies for taking, 32–33
    taking, 29. *See also* Notebook,
        interactive science
    Venn diagrams and, 33
Nuclear forces/energy, 95, 116, 124,
    233
Nuclear fusion, 213
Nucleolus, 145, 150
Nucleotides, 144, 184, 185, 187, 188,
    192
Nucleus, atomic, contents of, 76–78
Nucleus, cellular
    cell types with and without, 156
    contents of, 143, 144, 145, 147–48,
        150, 185
    defined, 145, 150, 184
    division of, 152, 183
Nutrients, defined, 145

Observations, 266–67, 270–71
Ocean currents, 74, 229, 230
Offspring, defined, 198. *See also*
    Heredity
Omnivores, 165, 166
Opaque materials, defined, 129
Orbit, electron, 75, 78, 86
Orbit, planetary, 106–7, 211, 212–13,
    214, 215–16, 219–20, 221, 222, 235
Order of importance text, 53
Organ, defined, 145
Organisms. *See* Cells; Ecosystems;
    Molecules to organisms
Organizing writing, 42
Osmosis, 145
Ounces to grams. *See* Mass
Ounces to milliliters, 36
Ova, defined, 184
Oxygen cycle, 171–72
Ozone layer, 248, 249, 252, 260

Parent, helping child, 26–37. *See also*
    Notebook, interactive science;

Notes; Science fair projects;
    specific topics
    about: overview of, 26
    developing good study habits,
        27–29
    with measurements. *See*
        Measuring
    question response strategies,
        33–34
    understanding science, 27
Particles, predicting changes in,
    88–89. *See also specific particles*
Passive transport, 145, 151
Patterns, on periodic table, 79
Patterns, recognizing and using, 63
Periodic table, 76, 79
Periods, defined, 76
Phenotypes, 189
Photosynthesis, 117–18, 142, 145,
    157–58, 166, 169, 235
Physical change, defined, 71
Physical processes, 74–75
Physical property, defined, 71, 74
Pints to liters, 36
Plasma membrane, 145, 148, 150
Plate boundaries, 230, 232, 251
Plate tectonics/tectonic plates, 227,
    228, 230, 231–32, 238, 239–40. *See
    also* Earthquakes
Plate tectonic theory, 232
Poems, as notes, 33
Pollution, 176, 206–7, 249, 252, 256,
    259, 273, 283
Population, defined, 198. *See also*
    Biological evolution; Heredity
Potential energy
    defined, 113, 115
    energy transfer and, 122
    forms of, 116
    kinetic energy vs., 113, 115
    objects at rest and, 123
    researching, 120–21
    of waves, 135
Pounds to grams. *See* Mass
Precipitates, 87, 89, 120, 122
Precipitation, 196, 228, 229, 230, 234,
    237, 241, 242, 255–56
Predators, 164, 166
Prey, 166
Problem and solution text, 53

Problems, defining/asking questions,
    57–58
Producers, 164, 165, 166, 169, 170
Products, defined, 80
Prokaryotic cells, 147–48, 158
Proportion, scale, and quantity,
    64–65
Proteins
    active transport/passive
        transport and, 151
    amino acids and, 183, 186, 201
    carrier, 143
    chromosomes encasing, 150. *See
        also* Chromosomes
    defined, 145, 186
    DNA and production of, 185, 186
    enzymes and, 144, 148, 166, 175
    facilitated transport and, 144
    formation of, ribosomes and, 145,
        148, 150, 184, 186
    functions of, 155, 186
    genes and, 186, 190–91
    mutations of, 188–89, 190–91
    synthesis. *See* formation of,
        ribosomes and
    traits, heredity and, 182, 183
    what child should already
        understand, 141
    why organisms build, 186
Protists, 158, 167
Protons, characteristics of, 76, 77, 78
Punnett square (Reginald C.
    Punnett), 188
Pure substance, defined, 76

Qualitative observation, defined,
    266
Quantitative observation, defined,
    267
Quantity, scale, proportion and,
    64–65
Quarts to liters, 36
Question notes, 33
Questions, asking and defining
    problems, 57–58
Questions, strategies for responding
    to, 33–34

Rarefaction, 129, 132
Reactants, defined, 80

Reading, 47–55
    about: overview of, 47
    cause and effect text, 53
    chronological text, 53
    citing textual evidence, 50–51
    compare and contrast text, 53
    comparing and contrasting
        information, 55
    craft and structure standards,
        52–54
    determining author's purpose,
        53–54
    determining relevant terms, 52
    distinguishing facts, 54–55
    drawing conclusions from text, 51
    explaining text visually, 54
    indexes and, 28
    integrating knowledge and ideas,
        54–55
    key ideas and details, 50–52
    love of, developing, 48
    order of importance text, 53
    problem and solution text, 53
    rereading passages, 49
    science textbooks, 28–29, 48–50
    sequence text, 53
    spatial text, 53
    tables of contents and, 28–29
    text structure, organization and,
        52--53
    text types and purposes, 39–43
    tips for child, 48–50
    tips for parents, 28–29
Recessive allele, 184, 207–8
Reflection, of light/waves, 127, 128,
    129, 131, 132, 133, 235
Refraction, of light, 131, 132, 133
Relative age, 218
Renewable resources, 117, 233, 250
Replication, DNA,187, 184
Reproduction, how behaviors affect,
    156–57
Research, 43–46
    analyzing and interpreting data,
        59–60
    models for evaluating, 34–35,
        58–59
    planning, carrying out
        investigations, 59
    projects, performing, 44

    sources, gathering/using/
        presenting, 44–45
    using evidence from texts, 45–46
Resonance, 131–32
Resources, additional, 289–90
Resources, natural, 117, 247, 250,
    255–56. See also Energy resources
Respiration, cellular, 118
Revising writing, 42–43
Revolving, planets, 214, 215, 216
Ribosomes, 145, 148, 149, 150, 186
Rock(s)
    cycle, 230
    geoscience investigation, 238–39
    movement within Earth. See Plate
        tectonics/tectonic plates
    types of, 230
    weathering of, 228, 230, 233, 237,
        239
Rotation, of Earth, 211, 215–16, 220,
    221, 235, 243–44

Scalar quantity, 100
Scale, proportion, and quantity,
    64–65
Scavengers, 167, 206
Science
    Common Core State Standards
        and, 10
    standards. See Next Generation
        Science Standards (NGSS)
    understanding, 27
Science, skills and practices
    analyzing and interpreting data,
        59–60
    asking questions and defining
        problems, 57–58
    cause and effect, mechanism and
        explanation, 63–64
    developing and using models,
        58–59
    energy and matter, flows/cycles/
        conservation, 65–66
    obtaining, evaluating,
        communicating information, 62
    pattern identification/use, 63
    planning, carrying out
        investigations, 59
    scale, proportion, and quantity,
        64–65

    stability and change, 66–67
    structure and function, 66
    systems and system models, 65
    using mathematics,
        computational thinking, 60
Science, three dimensions of, 56–67.
    See also Science and engineering
    practices
    about: overview of, 56
    crosscutting concepts, 23, 63–67
    disciplinary core ideas, 23–24, 67
Science and engineering practices
    about: overview of, 23
    analyzing and interpreting data,
        59–60
    asking questions and defining
        problems, 57–58
    biological evolution, 201–2
    constructing explanations,
        designing solutions, 61
    defined, 57–62
    developing and using models,
        58–59. See also Models, science
    Earth's place in universe, 218–19
    Earth's systems, 236
    ecosystem, 172
    energy, 118–19
    engaging in argument from
        evidence, 61–62
    engineering design, 271
    force and motion, 101–2
    heredity, 189–90
    matter and its interactions, 85
    molecules to organisms, 152–53
    obtaining, evaluating,
        communicating information, 62
    planning, carrying out
        investigations, 59
    science and engineering
        practices, 85
    using mathematics,
        computational thinking, 60
    waves, 133–34
Science fair projects, 278–88
    about: overview of, 278
    designing experiments, recording
        results, 280–83
    drawing conclusions, 282–83
    forming hypothesis, 280
    helping child choose, 279–80

oral presentations, 287–88
projects that make a difference, 283
reports, 286–88
safety tips, 285–86
sharing results, 283
stages of, 284–85
Science notebook. *See* Notebook, interactive science
Scientific law, defined, 267
Scientific method, 267
Scientific theory, defined, 267
Seasons
    availability of plant nutrients and, 173
    cause of, 213, 216
    defined, 214
    identifying, 211
    models for explaining, 212–13, 219, 220–21
Segregation, law of, 187
Seismic waves, 132–33, 137
Sequence text, 53
Sexual reproduction, 141–42, 146, 182, 191–92, 204
Shifts in standards
    English language arts, 16–18
    mathematics, 18–19
    science, 24–25
Solar eclipse, 212, 214, 219, 220, 221
Solar energy, 117, 214, 233, 250
Solar system
    atomic structure and, 86
    Earth in relationship to, 212–13, 216, 223
    gravity and, 212–13, 221–22
    Milky Way and, 211, 212, 216, 217, 219–21
    models of, 212–13, 222–23
    objects in, 211, 213
    relationship of movements of objects in, 215–16
    seasons explained by, 212–13, 215
Solubility, defined, 80, 82
Solutes, defined, 82, 146
Solutions (engineering), 267, 270–71
Solutions (liquid), defined, 80
Solvents, defined, 82, 146
Sound
    defined, 114, 129

digitized signals and, 127, 128, 133, 136–37
energy, defined, 114
exploring how transmitted, 135–36
properties of, 132
Southern hemisphere, 215, 235
South pole, 105, 215, 220
Spatial text, 53
Species, defined, 167, 198
Species, vast number of, 200
Speed
    acceleration and. *See* Acceleration
    calculating, 97–98
    defined, 96, 115
    kinetic energy and, 112, 114, 118, 119–20, 123
    of light, 128
    potential energy and, 122
    velocity and, 97–98, 115
    of waves, 131, 132
    what child should already understand, 94
Sperm, defined, 184
Stability and change, 66–67
Stars, formation/development of, 217
State, change of, 71, 73
Stimulus/stimuli, 146, 159–60
Stratosphere, 250
Structure and function, 66
Studying
    best place for, 27
    best time for, 28
    developing good habits, 27–29
    note taking and. *See* Notebook, interactive science; Notes
    question response strategies, 33–34
    reading textbooks and, 28–29
    time limit for, 28
Sun
    as Earth's energy source, 233
    eclipse of, 212, 214, 219, 220, 221
    planets revolving around, 215–16
Superposition, law of, 218
Symbiosis, 171
Systems and system models, 65

Technical tasks, standards for experiments, measurements and, 51–52
Technology
    digitized signals and, 127, 128, 133, 136–37
    presenting ideas with, 43
    role in evolution, 205–6
Tectonic plates. *See* Plate tectonics/tectonic plates
Temperature
    changes in particles and, 88, 89
    chemical reactions and, 87
    defined, 230
    energy/energy transfer and, 113, 114, 121, 122
    experiment investigating, 260–61
    global climate change/warming and, 247, 249, 252–54, 259–60
    seasons and, 173
    states of matter and, 86
    of sun, 213
    water cycle and, 228, 240–41
    weather, climate and, 234, 242, 243
    what child should already understand, 69, 112
Terms, key
    atomic terms, 75–76
    biological evolution, 198
    Earth's place in universe, 214–15
    Earth's systems, 229–30
    ecosystem, 166–67
    energy, 114–15
    engineering design, 266–67
    force and motion, 96–97
    heredity, 183–84
    matter, 71–72
    molecules to organisms, 143–46
    waves, 129
Textbooks. *See also* Reading
    citing evidence from, 51
    drawing conclusions from, 51
    features of, 29
    reading, guidelines, 28–29, 48–50
    standards for experiments, measurements, technical tasks, 51–52
    studying and, 28–29
    understanding layout of, 28–29

Thymine, 184, 185
Tidal bulge, 215
Tides, 214, 215, 219, 221, 235–36
Timescale, geologic, 213, 218, 224
Tissues
    cells and, 153–54, 155–56
    defined, 146
    organs from, 155–56
    structure and functions of
        organisms and, 141–42, 147
    what child should already
        understand, 141
Tons to kilograms. *See* Mass
Tornadoes, 252
Traits. *See* Heredity
Translucent material, 129
Transparent material, 128, 129
Transpiration, 228, 230, 235, 241
Transverse waves, 116, 127, 129, 130–31

Unicellular organisms, 141, 143, 146,
    147, 154, 203
Universe, 211–12, 215

Vacuoles, 146, 148, 149
Variables, about, 266, 267, 269
Variation, defined, 198. *See also*
    Biological evolution
Vectors/vector quantity, 96, 100
Velocity, 97–98, 100, 115, 123, 135
Venn diagrams, 33
Vestigial structures, 200
Vibration
    defined, 129
    kinetic energy and, 116
    light and sound as, 114, 132
    resonance and, 131–32
    seismic waves and, 132–33
    waves as, 115, 127, 130–31, 135–36
Volcanoes, 132–33, 228, 238–39, 251,
    256–57, 279
Volume, defined, 72
Volume, measuring, 36, 37, 72

Waste/waste disposal, 117, 141, 146,
    174, 176, 260, 283
Water cycle, 228–29, 230, 234–35,
    237, 240–42
Water vapor, 121, 230, 233, 234, 235,
    241

Waves, 126–39. *See also* Light
    about: overview of, 126; review
        checklist, 138–39
    amplitude, 129, 130, 131, 134–35
    changing direction, 132
    compression, 129, 132, 133, 136
    concave lenses and, 129
    convex lenses and, 129
    crests of, 129, 130, 131, 135
    defined, 115, 130
    digitized signals, 127, 128, 133,
        136–37
    disciplinary core ideas, 127–28
    electromagnetic spectrum and,
        128, 129
    experiment, 138
    explaining amplitude relative to
        energy, 134–35
    exploring how transmitted, 135–36
    frequency of, 129, 131, 132
    information technologies,
        instrumentation and, 129
    interacting with other waves or
        objects, 131–32
    key concepts, 130–33
    key terms, 129
    longitudinal, 129, 131, 132
    NGSS performance expectations,
        134–37
    properties of, 127–28, 131
    rarefaction of, 129, 132
    reflection of, 127, 128, 129, 131,
        132, 133, 235
    refraction of, 131, 132, 133
    resonance of, 131–32
    science and engineering
        practices, 133–34
    seismic, 132–33, 137
    transferring information and
        energy, 126
    transverse, 116, 127, 129, 130–31
    troughs, 129, 131, 135
    types of, 130–31
    vibration, defined, 129
    as vibrations, 115, 127, 130–31,
        135–36
    wavelength of, 127–28, 129, 131,
        132, 134–35
    what child should already
        understand, 127

Weather and climate
    defined, 229, 230, 234, 249
    Earth rotation inducing wild
        weather, 243–44
    exploring weather, 242
    global climate change/warming
        and, 248, 249, 252–54, 259–60
    greenhouse effect/gases and, 248,
        249, 252–53, 259–60, 273
    humidity and, 230, 234, 242
    NGSS performance expectations,
        240–44
    precipitation and, 196, 228, 229,
        230, 234, 237, 241, 242, 255–56
    relationship of, 229
    tornadoes and, 252
    water cycle and, 228–29, 230, 234–
        35, 237, 240–42
    winds and, 242, 243, 252
Weathering, 228, 230, 233, 237, 238
Weight. *See also* Mass
    calculating, 73
    colliding objects and, 103
    defined, 72, 97
    gravity and, 72–73, 94, 95, 97, 99
    mass vs., 37, 65, 72–73, 95
    what child should already
        understand, 69
Wind energy, 116, 117, 233, 250
Winds, 242, 243, 252
Work, defined, 115
Writing, 38–46
    arguments, 39–40
    explanatory, 40–42
    importance of, 38
    narrative, 46
    organizing, 42
    range of, 46
    research projects, 43–46
    revision process, 42–43
    science fair project reports,
        286–87
    skills, encouraging, 39
    text types, purposes and, 39–43
    using technology to present ideas,
        43

Yards to meters, 36

Zygotes, 146